Communications in Computer and Information Science   2797

Series Editors

Gang Li, *School of Information Technology, Deakin University, Burwood, VIC, Australia*
Joaquim Filipe, *Polytechnic Institute of Setúbal, Setúbal, Portugal*
Zhiwei Xu, *Chinese Academy of Sciences, Beijing, China*

Rationale

The CCIS series is devoted to the publication of proceedings of computer science conferences. Its aim is to efficiently disseminate original research results in informatics in printed and electronic form. While the focus is on publication of peer-reviewed full papers presenting mature work, inclusion of reviewed short papers reporting on work in progress is welcome, too. Besides globally relevant meetings with internationally representative program committees guaranteeing a strict peer-reviewing and paper selection process, conferences run by societies or of high regional or national relevance are also considered for publication.

Topics

The topical scope of CCIS spans the entire spectrum of informatics ranging from foundational topics in the theory of computing to information and communications science and technology and a broad variety of interdisciplinary application fields.

Information for Volume Editors and Authors

Publication in CCIS is free of charge. No royalties are paid, however, we offer registered conference participants temporary free access to the online version of the conference proceedings on SpringerLink (http://link.springer.com) by means of an http referrer from the conference website and/or a number of complimentary printed copies, as specified in the official acceptance email of the event.

CCIS proceedings can be published in time for distribution at conferences or as post-proceedings, and delivered in the form of printed books and/or electronically as USBs and/or e-content licenses for accessing proceedings at SpringerLink. Furthermore, CCIS proceedings are included in the CCIS electronic book series hosted in the SpringerLink digital library at http://link.springer.com/bookseries/7899. Conferences publishing in CCIS are allowed to use Online Conference Service (OCS) for managing the whole proceedings lifecycle (from submission and reviewing to preparing for publication) free of charge.

Publication process

The language of publication is exclusively English. Authors publishing in CCIS have to sign the Springer CCIS copyright transfer form, however, they are free to use their material published in CCIS for substantially changed, more elaborate subsequent publications elsewhere. For the preparation of the camera-ready papers/files, authors have to strictly adhere to the Springer CCIS Authors' Instructions and are strongly encouraged to use the CCIS LaTeX style files or templates.

Abstracting/Indexing

CCIS is abstracted/indexed in DBLP, Google Scholar, EI-Compendex, Mathematical Reviews, SCImago, Scopus. CCIS volumes are also submitted for the inclusion in ISI Proceedings.

How to start

To start the evaluation of your proposal for inclusion in the CCIS series, please send an e-mail to ccis@springer.com.

José Abdelnour-Nocera · Torkil Clemmensen ·
Marta Kristín Lárusdóttir · Teresa Macchia ·
Marta Rey Babbarro · Nurha Yingta
Editors

Academic Research and Professional Practice in Interaction Design

First International Conference, ARPPID 2025
London, UK, July 10–11, 2025
Proceedings

 Springer

Editors
José Abdelnour-Nocera [iD]
University of West London
London, UK

Torkil Clemmensen [iD]
Copenhagen Business School
Frederiksberg, Denmark

Marta Kristín Lárusdóttir [iD]
Reykjavik University
Reykjavík, Iceland

Teresa Macchia [iD]
Rolls-Royce
London, UK

Marta Rey Babbarro
Zillow
Seattle, WA, USA

Nurha Yingta [iD]
University of West London
London, UK

ISSN 1865-0929   ISSN 1865-0937 (electronic)
Communications in Computer and Information Science
ISBN 978-3-032-15515-3   ISBN 978-3-032-15516-0 (eBook)
https://doi.org/10.1007/978-3-032-15516-0

This Springer imprint is published by the registered company Springer Nature Switzerland AG
The registered company address is: Gewerbestrasse 11, 6330 Cham, Switzerland

If disposing of this product, please recycle the paper.

Preface

This volume presents a collection of revised and extended papers originating from workshops held as part of the Academic Research and Professional Practice in Interaction Design (ARPPID 2025) conference, hosted at the University of West London, London, UK, on 10–11 July 2025 in hybrid format. The ARPPID conference was established as a forum for dialogue between scholars, design professionals, and industry practitioners, fostering a culture of collaboration between academic research and professional practice in the evolving field of interaction design. The overarching theme of the 2025 conference highlighted the need for cooperation, challenges, needs, and best practices across academia and industry. The conference emphasised the importance of integrating academic insights with real-world applications, highlighting how rigorous research can meaningfully inform and enhance industry innovation. By bringing together voices from both academia and industry, ARPPID 2025 aimed to address the shared challenge of designing technologies that are not only usable and efficient but also ethically responsible, inclusive, and sustainable.

The conference welcomed submissions on a wide range of topics related to interaction design, user experience, and human-computer interaction, with a particular focus on bridging the gap between academic research and industry practice. Three thematic strands guided this year's discussions and workshops. The first, Collaboration Methods, examined long-term and short-term academic-industry partnerships, highlighting case studies of successful collaborations and the role of research centres and joint initiatives in fostering sustained cooperation. Contributors explored strategies for building robust networks, maintaining partnerships, and ensuring mutual respect and value creation between academia and industry. The second strand, Knowledge Transfer and Communication, focused on the challenges of translating academic research into industrial practice. Participants discussed innovative approaches to knowledge dissemination, effective communication of research findings for industrial audiences, and methods for ensuring that academic insights are meaningfully integrated into real-world design and production contexts. The third strand, Methodologies, Practices, and Techniques, emphasised the importance of developing and applying research methods that balance academic rigor with industrial relevance.

Discussions explored best practices for commissioning, recognising, and applying high-quality HCI research in industry settings, as well as approaches for integrating research outcomes with company strategies, product development, and innovation roadmaps. Each paper underwent a rigorous review process by the ARPPID Program Committee for originality, relevance, and contribution to advancing interaction design practice. Reviews were double blind, and submissions received three reviews each on average. Authors of accepted papers were invited to extend their contributions for inclusion in this post-conference volume, which was further peer reviewed by an international committee to ensure scholarly quality and coherence. From the original 28 submissions, 17 were selected and developed into the chapters contained in this volume.

We would like to extend our deepest gratitude to the University of West London for hosting this hybrid event and supporting an environment where global collaboration could thrive. We also thank all the program committee, session chairs, and participants for their dedication, expertise, and enthusiasm, which made this conference and volume possible. It is our hope that this compendium of papers emerging from ARPPID 2025 will serve as a valuable resource for practitioners and researchers in academia and industry, inspiring new approaches to collaboration, knowledge transfer, and practice-based innovation. The ARPPID 2025 working conference reaffirmed the importance of bridging academia and industry, reminding us that the most impactful interaction design arises when research and practice meet to shape a more human, ethical, and sustainable digital future.

José Abdelnour-Nocera
Torkil Clemmensen
Marta Larusdottir
Teresa Macchia
Marta Rey Babbarro
Nurha Yingta

Organization

Organizing Committee

Conference Chairs

Academic Chair
José Abdelnour Nocera   University of West London, UK

Technical Chair
Marta Rey Babarro   Zillow, USA

Program Chair
Teresa Macchia   Rolls-Royce, UK

Full Papers Chairs

Marta Kristín Lárusdóttir   Reykjavík University, Iceland
Ali Gheitasy   University of West London, UK

Case Studies Chairs

Lene Nielsen   IT University of Copenhagen, Denmark
Robin Gissing   Chart Industries (Howden), UK

Posters Chairs

Karin van den Driesche   Kaden Design, The Netherlands
Parisa Saadati   University of West London, UK

Proceedings Chair

Nurha Yingta   University of West London, UK

Sustainability Chair

Torkil Clemmensen   Copenhagen Business School, Denmark

Local Organization and Student Volunteer Chair

Nurha Yingta   University of West London, UK

Program Committee

Alan Dix   Swansea University, UK
Åsa Cajander   Uppsala University, Sweden
Christina Li   Infinite Interactive, UK
Elisa del Galdo   del Galdo Consulting, UK
Elizabeth Buie   Nexer Digital, UK
Gavin Sim   University of Central Lancashire, UK
Helen Petrie   University of York, UK
Helen Sharp   Open University, UK
Karin van den Driesche   Kaden Design, The Netherlands
Lene Nielsen   IT University of Copenhagen, Denmark
Marta Kristín Lárusdóttir   Reykjavík University, Iceland
Parisa Saadati   University of West London, UK
Paula Kotze   University of Pretoria, South Africa
Pedro Campos   WOW Systems and ITI/Larsys, Portugal
Ria Sheppard   Wood Mackenzie, UK
Robin Gissing   Chart Industries (Howden), UK
Susan Dray   Dray & Associates, USA
Souleymane Camara   BP, UK
Tony Russell-Rose   UX Labs and City St. George's, University of
                                     London, UK
Torkil Clemmensen   Copenhagen Business School, Denmark
Victor M. González   Sperientia, Mexico

Sponsors and Partners

Contents

Perspectives on Personas in Practice – An Analysis of LinkedIn Discussions Among UX Professionals

Lene Nielsen[1]([⊠]) [iD] and Sabine Madsen[2] [iD]

[1] IT University Copenhagen, 2300 Copenhagen S, Denmark
lene@itu.dk
[2] Copenhagen Business School, 2000 Frederiksberg, Denmark
sama.digi@cbs.dk

Abstract. It is a challenge to gain insight into the development and application of personas across multiple companies. Moving beyond single case studies to understand the industry perspective, this study employs analyses of social media data on persona practice to capture and conceptualize practitioner experiences. The paper reports on an analysis of three LinkedIn discussions among 75 UX practitioners on their real-world experiences and attitudes towards the persona method, examining both the perceived benefits and obstacles. Positively, personas support user-centered design and decision-making during the UX design process. Criticism concerns poor data quality, misconceptions about the method, and a negative discourse, which hinder effective method adoption and persona creation during the persona design process. This aligns with previous research. However, the study's demonstration that negative perspectives often stem from the flawed application of the method is novel. Furthermore, the study presents a new way to obtain knowledge from practical experiences.

Keywords: Personas · Practice · Theory · Social Media · LinkedIn Discussions

1 Introduction

Earlier studies have divided the persona practices literature into three different categories: case studies where the researchers have been part of the UX design process either as facilitators or researchers (e.g., [32]), in situ studies where the researchers observed the use of the method in practice (e.g., [4, 10]), and empirical studies where researchers capture, analyze, and report practitioners' perceived understandings of the method, using qualitative or quantitative methods (e.g., [20]). Lately, a fourth category, literature studies, that analyze literature on persona use (e.g., [13]) has appeared. The current study provides a fifth category for understanding practice through the analysis of social media discussions, which to the best of our knowledge is new in the domain of persona research.

To obtain knowledge on industrial practices is not simple and to look across multiple sites is even more challenging. To move beyond single case studies to understand

J. Abdelnour-Nocera et al. (Eds.): ARPPID 2025, CCIS 2797, pp. 1–16, 2026.
https://doi.org/10.1007/978-3-032-15516-0_1

the industry perspective, this study employs analyses of social media data in the form of LinkedIn discussions on persona practice to capture and conceptualize practitioner experiences.

Personas are fictitious user types [8] representing the diverse needs, wants, and contexts [27] of real user groups during design processes. UX designers, software developers, marketers, and other stakeholders use personas to make user-centric decisions [31]. Prior research has shown that personas are widely applied in both research and industry practices [36]. Despite the growing interest over the past two decades in human-computer interaction (HCI) and similar fields, few studies are based on real-world experiences of how personas are applied in practice. Most studies of practice apply surveys [33], case studies, or interviews [37], where researcher interests drive the data collection, and in the case of interviews and case studies, focus on a limited data set.

In this paper, we report based on insights into persona practice through unmonitored and unstimulated discussions and opinions arising from problems and questions, which practitioners have shared in LinkedIn discussions. To extract findings from these discussions, we explore data that differs significantly from traditional quantitative and qualitative data, focusing on the dialogues, and practical references provided by the practitioners who partook in the discussions.

2   Related Literature

The literature on personas covers various topics and domains, including software development, healthcare, robotics, dialogue systems, games, privacy and security, recommendation systems, marketing, and architecture [28]. It is recommended to create personas at the beginning of the design process [20] as they can facilitate customer segmentation, help prioritize segments and features and address the most crucial audiences [26]. The literature on personas primarily emphasizes the use of personas in the design process of digital systems and services, secondarily for software development, such as for requirement elicitation [38] and product design e.g. within health [34]. Personas are often integrated with or supported by other methods such as scenarios [18] and participatory design practices [19]. Personas are primarily created using qualitative data such as interviews, quantitative data such as surveys or online data, or a mix hereof [15, 16]. Each method has its strength and weaknesses, as will be presented below.

In the following, we present literature on the positive and negative perspectives concerning the method as an understanding hereof forms the backdrop for this study, particularly for how we frame our findings and draw conclusions.

2.1   Positive Perspectives on Personas

Research shows that researchers and practitioners consistently display interest in creating and using personas toward user-centric design goals [12, 27, 33, 40]. In the following we will focus on research on persona practice. The research has found that the UX designers who understand the persona method have multiple ways of applying and using it [6]. The benefits are related to data, ideation, problem understanding, vision creation, marketing

[25], evaluation, and implementing design [1, 20], thus covering both the design process, the implementation of the design, and the sales and marketing processes.

In the UX design process, personas are beneficial as they make data about users explicit [26]. During ideation, personas help in understanding users' needs and context. They also align user understanding and improve communication among stakeholders and design team members [14, 24]. For the implementation process, it can support the creation of implementation and adaptation strategies (see e.g. [21]). In sales and marketing personas provide knowledge of the relevant target groups of buyers, that might differ from the users and provide understanding of these (see e.g. [5]).

The literature emphasizes well-implemented personas processes with the necessary prerequisites. Thus, there are specific circumstances related to a positive experience and attitude toward personas, particularly formal training in the method, extensive knowledge from working with personas in practice [24], and general expertise in qualitative methods [1]. Two smaller studies found that [2, 3] personas are more successful when designers and developers work closely together. In this case, they help to ensure that developers understand the intended users. Additionally, personas are more successful if scenarios and user stories are used in combination with personas to capture behaviors and behavioral change [14].

2.2   Negative Perspectives of Persona Use

Within the literature on personas the critique of the method falls into two strands. Firstly, research-based critique problematizes the research and assumptions that go into creating the persona descriptions, the applicability of personas, and the difficulty of demonstrating the value of applying the persona method [7, 10, 15, 23, 27, 33]. Secondly, practice-based critique has found that designers rarely use personas in meetings and decision-making [10], skepticism towards personas persists as they are considered too abstract and potentially misleading [24], internal agendas and politics challenge the use of personas [32], and organizations lack the maturity to adopt personas [36]. Finally, specific prerequisites need to be in place for personas to be successful [2, 20]. Thus, the criticism from studies with practitioners can be categorized into persona creation, evaluation, implementation, and organizational factors [35].

Most of the criticism refers to the persona design process, covering data collection about users, data analysis, and development of persona descriptions [27]. The persona design process is often time-consuming, especially when using qualitative data [15], and persona projects aimed at developing persona descriptions frequently suffer from a lack of resources, time, and sufficient funding [2, 3]. Personas are rarely based on a continuous data collection process, and in some cases, persona creators use no external data but instead use internal knowledge and experiences to create ad-hoc personas [30] that are validated in later research. Since the information used is not always displayed and often comes from qualitative methods, there can be distrust in the underlying data [24].

It is considered challenging to create useful persona descriptions with enough and proper information for making design decisions [20, 39]. The personas method is perceived as risky as the personas may portray a wrong user group [2, 3]. Finally, some designers prefer to meet real users as opposed to user representations [39].

The personas are not integrated with development [2, 3] or poorly implemented in the organization [32]. Likewise, research points to a connection between poor implementation and low organizational UX maturity [2, 20, 39]. Inadequate training leads to improper method utilization and a lack of understanding of the role the method can play during the UX design process [2, 3, 39]. Moreover, even if there is a before and after effect when using the method, it is difficult to quantitatively evaluate the impact of personas [39].

The major challenges identified in persona research relate to lack of training, lack of resources, lack of standardized instructions for persona creation, and seeing persona creation predominantly as a technical exercise [37]. Floyd et al. [9] nicely sums it up: *"It is both a strength and a weakness of PBD [persona-based design] that the idea seems so appealing that many people choose to adopt it and knowingly or inadvertently modify it in both positive and negative directions."* [9] p. 14. More than ten years later, there is still limited understanding of practitioners' perceptions of the benefits and obstacles of using personas, including integration with other methods. This study aims to explore what practitioners perceive as beneficial and which obstacles arise when and where (e.g., during the persona design process, the UX design process, or during implementation and method integration).

3   Method

Based on extensive personal LinkedIn connections (+2000) it was apparent that there still is a need for discussions of personas and the persona method. We analyzed three discussions on that appeared between 2021 and 2022: (A) a request to share real-world persona success stories from 2021 with 41 comments, the latest from the same year, (B) a request to share examples of personas in behavioral design or behavior change, and also potential critiques of personas from 2022 with 112 comments, the latest from the same year, and finally, (C) an invitation to share how product teams, designers, researchers or stakeholders reference personas from 2022 with 71 comments, the latest from March 2023. In total, we analyzed 224 comments from 75 professionals (see Table 1).

These social media data differ significantly from traditional qualitative data, such as interview data. While interview data typically involves longer transcribed texts collected from a limited number of participants engaged in synchronous dialogue, social media data consists of dialogue threads with several shorter posts exchanged asynchronously among numerous participants. In the following, we present our process.

3.1   Data Collection

The data was collected from three practitioner discussions on LinkedIn. The first discussion from 2021 was prompted by a question from a UX designer: *"Looking for real-world persona success stories. As a designer working in tech for more than 10 years, I've rarely seen personas used well. Often, they're made and then forgotten about, or they become too bloated, too specific etc. to be useful. I teach students about personas and archetypes and want to give them stories about when they actually work. So, I'm curious—does your team actually use personas day-to-day? How and when do you use them? Or if not, why not?"*. The second discussion was prompted by a similar question. A behavioral science consultant asked in 2022: *"I'm looking for examples of personas in behavioral design or behavior change, and also potential critiques of personas (as they have traditionally been created) from a BeSci [behavioral science] perspective."* This spurred a discussion about positive and negative experiences with personas and recommendations for alternatives.

Similarly, in 2022, a UX lead designer created a poll and asked: *"I would love to know how your product teams, designers, researchers or stakeholders reference personas. If you have been on a team that references them often, I want to talk to YOU! I am seeking people who have had success with personas on their projects. Please tell me in the comments."*

Together the three posts got 224 comments from 75 unique participants. The networks of practitioners were diverse, without overlaps between the participants in the three discussions. Despite all three initiatives being US-based, participants were also located in India, Australia, Romania, Holland, Finland, Sweden, and Denmark.

Table 1. Overview of participants

LinkedIn discussion	Number of comments	Number of participants	Examples of job titles
A	41	33	Designers: (Innovation & Service Design Leader, Service Designer, Design Lead) Executive Coach Behavioral Science Expert The Brand Scientist
B	112	15	Managers: (Design and Product Executive, VP-Product, Co-Founder & Principal Experience Strategist) Designers: (Design leader, EX Consulting, Product designer, Principal Product designer) Research: (Design Research Lead, strategist/researcher)

(continued)

Table 1. (*continued*)

LinkedIn discussion	Number of comments	Number of participants	Examples of job titles
C	71	27	Managers: (Design Director, Senior Manager, Global Head of Design) Designers: (Senior Product designer, UX designer, UX lead designer) Product development Design Research UX architect Social Anthropologist

3.2 Data Analysis

Each of the three discussion threads was unfolded, copied, and saved. Next, the data analysis was performed using a three-stage procedure [11], with first-order codes, second-order themes, and third-order concepts, as the framework for inductive thematic analysis.

In the first stage, each discussion thread was analyzed separately to identify first-order codes. Taking inspiration from our literature study, we prompted Chat-GPT3 to identify positive and negative perspectives on personas and to find alternative methods. The following prompts were run: (1) analyze the text for positive perspectives on personas, (2) analyze the text for negative perspectives on personas, (3) analyze for alternative approaches to personas.

From the first order coding, a manual study of the codes found 22 positive second order themes, 35 negative themes, and two themes related to other preferred methods. These themes were reviewed and validated against the data to ensure accuracy.

These themes were finally manually clustered into five high level concepts related to positive aspects comprising creating user understanding supporting a user-centered design process, communication, organization, and validation. The negative aspects fall into seven high level concepts comprising persona data, persona descriptions, long-term persona use, personas and behavioural change, poorly constructed personas, missing the broader picture, and persona implementation. Most themes fall within poorly constructed persona descriptions.

All examples mentioned in the findings section are derived from the first order analysis. We have anonymized the participants. However, by accessing these links, the original quotes can be found:

A: https://www.linkedin.com/feed/update/urn:li:activity:6765035612849496065/
B: https://www.linkedin.com/feed/update/urn:li:activity:6997856412378746880/
C: https://www.linkedin.com/feed/update/urn:li:activity:7013909515859374081/

In the second stage, we shifted to manual coding as prompts for clustering did not provide meaningful results. Thus, in this stage, all codes across the three threads were manually interpreted and collapsed into themes (e.g., codes as such Visualization and Content, Diversity, Empathy and Design, and were summarized into a theme labelled Creating User Understanding). The coding process resulted in 13 themes.

Following this, in the third stage, we analyzed the themes to identify high-level concepts. Manually clustering the themes, we derived five concepts related to the perceived benefits of personas, seven concepts related to the perceived obstacles of personas, and one concept associated with other preferred methods. These concepts represent the core findings of our analysis.

4 Findings

The findings presented in this section cover both the UX design process, the persona design process, and integration with or preferences for other methods. In the following, we will divide the reported findings accordingly.

4.1 The Perceived Positive Perspectives on Personas

The persona method is perceived as a multifaceted approach to enhancing user understanding, facilitating communication, supporting organizational goals, and ensuring validation throughout design decisions. These positive themes concern the use of personas during *the UX design process.*

The LinkedIn conversations reveal a broad spectrum of persona applications, ranging from high-level strategic decision-making to agile short-term project development. This range highlights the adaptability of personas in addressing various stakeholder requirements and contexts. Furthermore, the widespread use of personas across multiple industries and professional domains, including technology, academia, and design, demonstrates their cross-sectoral relevance. The engagement of professionals from diverse backgrounds indicates a shared recognition of the method's value.

The professionals emphasize that personas enhance user understanding, which is strengthened by both the layout and content of persona descriptions. By referencing their research, industry experiences, and case studies, they advocate for the effectiveness of personas in shaping user-centered design strategies. This indicates a commitment to continuously improving how personas are created, communicated, and utilized to support the UX design process.

During the UX design process, the persona descriptions create user understanding and empathy, which facilitate the design of more meaningful and relevant user experiences. Designers gain confidence in their decision-making, knowing that their insights are grounded in data-driven user understanding. This empowerment extends beyond individual designers to entire organizations and design teams, reinforcing the collective pursuit of user-centric innovation.

The visual composition of persona descriptions plays a vital role in making user segments more relatable to design teams. Through compelling layouts and clear representations, the cast of personas help designers visualize the diversity of their target audience. Moreover, the specific details embedded within personas—such as behavioral insights, goals, and motivations—offer designers a deeper understanding of the factors influencing user decisions. As a result, personas not only validate design assumptions but also guide solution development, helping teams avoid costly design errors and ensuring a more informed, user-focused approach to product and experience creation.

Example from the first-order analysis: *"A participant share personas were effective in drawing out user flows and making new website proposals compelling to senior users."*

Furthermore, personas provide shared understanding and serve as a communication tool between different teams and stakeholders. This is both effective and foster collaboration.

Examples from the first-order analysis: *"A participant mentions Nerdwallet as a company that used personas effectively across product teams." "A participant emphasizes the importance of using personas throughout the design process, rather than treating them as a one-time exercise."*

Finally, some participants mention that it is beneficial to supplement personas with user journey maps to better visualize user behaviors, and identify pain points, opportunities, and touchpoints throughout the user journey.

In summary, the positive aspects of personas are the fostering of empathy, the ability to facilitate discussions and decision-making throughout the design process, and the creation of shared understanding among team members and stakeholders. Thus, personas are an embodiment of user-centered design principles, and the participants emphasize that personas play a crucial role in supporting the UX design process (Table 2).

Table 2. The themes concerning the UX design process

User-centered design approach	They keep the focus on users throughout the design process, ensuring that design decisions align with user behaviors and preferences Personas help define and solve problems from a user-centric perspective Personas help prioritize design features and improvements based on the needs and preferences of the most important user segments, leading to more impactful design decisions
Informed decision-making	By having a clear understanding of user archetypes and their needs, teams can make decisions that align with user expectations and preferences

(continued)

Table 2. (continued)

Iterative design approach and long-term planning	The use of personas promotes an iterative design approach. As personas are continuously updated with new insights, the design process evolves to better address user behaviors and preferences Personas offer a foundation for long-term design strategies, as they can evolve over time to reflect changing user needs and market trends
Reduced subjectivity	Personas provide an objective framework for decision-making, reducing the influence of individual biases and assumptions in the design process
Design-contextualization	The contextual information guides the design process. Personas provide context to user behaviors by highlighting the specific situations, environments, and circumstances that influence decision-making
Guidance for innovation	Personas inspire innovation by encouraging designers to think creatively about how to solve user problems and fulfil their needs

4.2   The Perceived Negative Perspectives on Personas

The negative aspects associated with personas encompass seven key themes: persona data, persona descriptions, long-term persona use, personas and behavioral change, poorly constructed personas, missing the broader picture, and persona implementation. A predominant concern is the creation of poorly constructed persona descriptions during *the persona design process.*

One of the major critiques concerns persona data. Many participants doubt the validity of the data used to create personas, questioning whether they accurately represent users and whether the voices and perspectives incorporated truly reflect the diversity of user segments. This mistrust extends to concerns over the authenticity of user descriptions and whether personas are grounded in meaningful research or merely speculative assumptions, e.g., "*A participant shares a concern about introducing bias early in projects while creating personas.*"

The most significant criticisms focus on the persona descriptions themselves. Methodological issues include the risk of oversimplification, the incorporation of fictitious elements, and flawed execution in their development. Some participants argue that personas often rely on generalized stereotypes rather than nuanced user insights, which can lead to misleading representations that fail to encompass the full spectrum of user segments. These shortcomings not only limit the effectiveness of personas in guiding design decisions but also undermine their credibility during UX design, raising broader concerns about their practical application and impact. These challenges are further compounded by perceived difficulties in updating personas when user behaviors evolve, the struggle to effectively apply them in dynamic, fast-paced environments such as agile development, and the tension between prioritizing user needs over broader business objectives.

Several concerns about the implementation of persona descriptions during the UX design process is mentioned. Firstly, some participants highlight that personas may not fully capture user behavior or account for behavioral changes over time. Secondly, the insights derived from personas tend to remain at a high level, lacking the actionable guidance needed for designers, such as specific recommendations for behavioral change interventions. Additionally, personas often fail to consider the broader contextual factors that influence user behavior, limiting their effectiveness in shaping comprehensive design strategies. Moreover, inaccuracies in persona descriptions, whether due to incorrect data or poor presentation, can lead to design decisions based on flawed assumptions or incomplete information. This can, in turn, result in solutions that may be ineffective or misaligned with actual user needs. These concerns underscore the need for a more rigorous and adaptive approach to persona development, ensuring that they provide designers with accurate, actionable insights while minimizing the risk of misrepresentation and bias (Table 3).

Bias is a recurring issue in the discussions, as illustrated in these examples from the first-order analysis: *"Two participants caution that personas can be misused, sometimes reflecting internal biases and hindering inclusive design.", "A participant expresses skepticism about the effective application of personas, stating that each team applies them differently and often with unintended biases"*.

Table 3. Themes for concept of Implementation

Misalignment with agile methods	In fast-paced agile development environments, personas might not be practical due to their static nature and the need for quick iterations
Disconnection from business goals	Personas might focus solely on user needs and overlook the alignment with broader business goals, potentially leading to design solutions that don't drive business value
Limited effective use	Some participants express dissatisfaction with the way personas are often used in practice. They mention that personas are frequently created but then forgotten or become too complex to be practical
Differing perspectives on usage	Some participants mention that personas might not be as universally applicable as initially assumed

In summary, the negative perceptions of personas are primarily related to the persona design process due to poor data, bias, and the static nature of personas. This has consequences for the UX design process where a vague dataset feeds into the design process and design decisions by not incorporating user needs in the desired way, thereby leading to unsuitable designs (Table 4).

Table 4. The themes for poorly constructed persona descriptions

Stereotyping and oversimplification	Critiques point out that personas can lead to oversimplification and stereotyping of users. They may not capture the complexity and diversity of real users, reducing individuals to predefined categories
Lack of realism	Some view personas as overly idealized representations of users, lacking the flaws, contradictions, and complexities that real individuals possess
Complexity of users	Critics stress that users are complex and multi-dimensional, and personas might not capture the entirety of their behaviors, motivations, and needs
Lack of emotional depth	Some participants argue that personas often lack the emotional depth required to understand the underlying motivations and feelings that drive behavior
Oversimplification	Personas can oversimplify complex user behaviors and motivations, potentially leading to shallow or inaccurate representations of real users
Generic stereotyping	Personas might rely on stereotypes and assumptions, contributing to biased and homogenized portrayals of user groups that do not accurately represent their diversity
Limited scope	Personas might not capture all relevant user segments, leading to the neglect of less prominent but equally important user groups
Loss of individuality	Personas aggregate user characteristics, potentially overlooking individual differences and unique preferences
Bias and over-specification	There's a concern raised about bias and over-specification in traditional demographic-based personas. Mention is made of arguments that using attributes like race, photos, and age can lead to bias
Complexity and lack of usefulness	Some participants mention that personas can become too bloated or too specific, diminishing their usefulness
Fictitious elements	There is a mention of end users' complex background stories being woven from seemingly simple statements in personas Another participant mentions that some individuals might struggle with the perceived fiction-writing aspect of personas, indicating that there might be challenges in getting team members to fully embrace and utilize personas

4.3 Other Preferred Methods

Due to a negative discourse about the persona method and in some cases negative experiences, some participants have come to prefer other tools and approaches. Among these 'Jobs To Be Done' is the most mentioned alternative. Other alternatives include Attitudinal Profiling to understand the mental models, attitudes, and motivations that drive behavior. Behavioral frameworks, such as Diffusion of Innovation, Stages of Change, and COM-B (Capability, Opportunity, Motivation, Behavior), and Need-based profiles that focus on understanding the needs, biases, beliefs, and expectations of individuals. An example from the first order analysis: *"A participant suggests using audience segmentation through polling to understand and cluster different groups' attitudes and behaviors. This method provides a more data-driven way to segment users based on their behaviors."*

In summary, many other methods are mentioned, primarily in relation to the negative discourse that surround the persona method (Table 5).

Table 5. Themes for concept of other methods preferred.

Alternative approaches	The conversation introduces alternative approaches such as Jobs To Be Done and Value Proposition Canvases, methods that might be perceived as more focused and actionable than traditional personas
Potential overlooking of alternatives	There is a perception that personas might overshadow other potentially effective methodologies

5 Discussion

In the following section, we will discuss our findings.

As stated in the Related Literature section the benefits of using the persona method relates to the design process, the implementation of the design, and the sales and marketing processes [1, 20, 25]. While the negative aspects relate to persona creation, evaluation, implementation, and organizational factors [35].

Our findings on the positive perceptions and the critique of the persona method align with existing literature. But contrary to much of the research our contribution is built upon many practitioners who have used the method, which refutes the research that designers do not use the method [10].

In contrast to existing literature, we identify and conceptualize the positive aspects as mainly related to supporting the UX design process, while most negative comments pertain to the persona design process. Additionally, the negative discourse itself hinders the effective use and adoption of the method.

Positively, the method facilitates a user-centered design approach, fostering an understanding of users and creating empathy. It also acts as a communication tool that aligns project teams and can validate both design assumptions and projects. Among satisfied users, there are ongoing efforts to enhance the value of personas and from an organizational perspective, we found that personas empower UX designers. This aligns with existing literature [5, 14, 21, 24, 26, 40].

Negatively, some practitioners perceive the method as static, with irrelevant or sparse information, poor descriptions, and a lack of context. The criticisms include three main aspects: 1) the method strictly limits the type of information included in descriptions, 2) poor implementation, often due to inadequate data collection and poor descriptions, and 3) a lack of actionable insights for design. A main finding is that these issues stem from a flawed persona design process and a misunderstanding of how to include information in the descriptions, which has not been reported in earlier literature.

Concerning the misconception, participants noted that the method cannot incorporate information on user behavior. This seems to stem from a misunderstanding of the method as being too restrictive to include necessary information. Interestingly, it was mentioned that when the method is integrated with user journey maps, it can provide adequate insights into behaviors.

Participants often view poor data quality as an inherent flaw of the method, rather than a consequence of insufficient data collection practices. Our analysis reveals that this creates a negative perception of the method as having numerous shortcomings, including stereotypes and oversimplification, which is a result of poor implementation.

Concerning the lack of actionable insights for design, the data collectors for persona descriptions appear unaware of the different information needs among persona users, e.g. UX designers require specific types of information to design, such as user motivations and goals for use, while business stakeholders need different data to make informed decisions, such as buying habits and preferences of diverse user segments.

The above points offer unique insights into the struggles participants face. However, familiarity with the extensive, well-established literature on the method or adequate training could mitigate many of the challenges and negative experiences, see [2, 3, 39]. Thus, a key finding from this research is that there is a gap in practitioners' understanding of the method, as the purpose of personas is precisely to overcome simplification and stereotyping through thorough data collection on users and their diverse needs.

Moreover, the lack of understanding of the method and insights from research does not seem to reach practitioners. This is evident in discussions about the method's inability to align with agile development, despite scientific literature reporting the possibility of integrating personas in agile development (see e.g., [17, 22, 29]).

In general, our analysis shows that misconceptions about the method prevail among practitioners and that these misconceptions lead to a negative perception that might hinder further adoption and much-needed training. However, the willingness to engage in LinkedIn discussions also indicates an interest in the method.

Finally, our contribution to persona research is two-fold. Firstly, while there is a well-established literature-based and empirical research stream about the use of the persona method in practice, we demonstrate that novel insights can be obtained by focusing on LinkedIn data. This data has the advantage of covering numerous practitioners' positive and negative experiences from different roles. Moreover, the discussions are initiated and maintained without researcher intervention. Thus, complementing case studies, in situ studies, empirical studies, and literature studies, the current study provides a fifth category of capturing practice by analyzing LinkedIn discussions, which to the best of our knowledge, is new.

6 Conclusion

This study has two contributions. Firstly, it contributes to the sparse literature on persona practice by examining discussions on LinkedIn among 75 UX professionals, highlighting the perceived benefits and obstacles associated with the method. Our findings indicate that personas facilitate user-centered decision-making during the UX design process. However, issues related to data quality and a negative discourse impede broader adoption and the effective creation of persona descriptions with adequate information during the persona design process. This underscores the necessity of more formal training for persona creators and calls for further research into the varied information needs of diverse persona users (i.e., UX designers, software developers, marketers, and sales personnel). This is furthermore underlined with the notion that insights from research does not seem to reach practitioners.

Secondly, it contributes with a new data source to understand practice, in this case analysis of existing LinkedIn discussions that cast light on practitioners' use and perceptions of the persona method.

References

1. Bashir, E., Attfield, S.: An international survey of practitioners' views on personas: benefits, resource demands and pitfalls. Int. J. Adv. Softw. **11**(3–4), 299–310 (2018)
2. Billestrup, J., Stage, J., Bruun, A., Nielsen, L.: Creating and using personas in software development: experiences from practice. In: International Conference on Human-Centered Software Engineering. Springer, Berlin (2014). https://doi.org/10.1007/978-3-662-44811-3_16
3. Billestrup, J., Stage, J., Nielsen, L., Hansen, K.S.: Persona usage in software development: advantages and obstacles. In: Conference on Advanced Computer-Human Interactions (2014)
4. Blomquist, Å., Arvola, M.: Personas in action: ethnography in an interaction design team. In: Proceedings of the Second Nordic Conference on Human-Computer Interaction, pp. 197–200. ACM (2002)
5. Brangier, E., Bornet, C.: Persona: A Method to Produce Representations Focused on Consumers' Needs. CRC Press (2011)
6. Chang, Y.-N., Lim, Y.-K., Stolterman, E.: Personas: from theory to practices. In: NordiCHI 2008 Proceedings of the 5th Nordic Conference on Human-Computer Interaction: Building Bridges, pp. 439–442 (2008). https://doi.org/10.1145/1463160.1463214
7. Chapman, C.N., Milham, R.: The personas' new clothes. In: Human Factors and Ergonomics Society (HFES), San Francisco, CA (2006)
8. Cherinka, R., Prezzama, J.: The Role of Generative Artificial Intelligence as Research Assistant: Opportunities and Challenges, pp. 89–94. Orlando, Florida, United States (2023). https://doi.org/10.54808/WMSCI2023.01.89
9. Cooper, A.: The Inmates Are Running the Asylum. SAMS, Indianapolis (1999)

10. Friess, E.: Personas and decision making in the design process: an ethnographic case study. In: Proceedings of SIGCHI Conference on Human Factors in Computing Systems, pp. 1209–1218 (2012). https://doi.org/10.1145/2207676.2208572

11. Gioia, D.A., Corley, K.G., Hamilton, A.L.: Seeking qualitative rigor in inductive research: notes on the Gioia methodology. Org. Res. Methods **16**(1), 15–31 (2013). https://doi.org/10.1177/1094428112452151

12. Goh, C.H., Kulathuramaiyer, N., Zaman, T.: Riding waves of change: a review of personas research landscape based on the three waves of HCI. In: IFIP Advances in Information and Communication Technology (2017). https://doi.org/10.1007/978-3-319-59111-7_49

13. Guan, K.W., Salminen, J.O., Nielsen, L., Jung, S.-G., Jansen, B.J.: Information design for personas in four professional domains of user experience design, healthcare, market research, and social media strategy. In: Proceedings of the 54th Hawaii International Conference on System Sciences, pp. 4446–4455 (2021)

14. Gudjonsdottir, R., Lindquist, S.: Personas and scenarios: design tool or a communication device? In: 8th International Conference on the Design of Cooperative Systems, pp. 165–176 (2008)

15. Jansen, B.J., Guan, K.W., Salminen, J.: Strengths and weaknesses of persona creation methods: guidelines and opportunities for digital innovations. In: Proceedings of the 54th Hawaii International Conference on System Sciences, pp. 4971–4980 (2021)

16. Kjøller, J.E.: Personas in Agile Development. MA Thesis, IT University, Copenhagen (2018)

17. Larner, J., HighWire, D.T.C.: Using personas and scenarios in co-creating stakeholder involvement in organisational governance (2016). https://www.researchgate.net/profile/Justin-Larner/publication/338411582_Using_personas_and_scenarios_in_co-creating_stakeholder_involvement_in_organisational_governance/links/5e13739da6fdcc28375a2b61/Using-personas-and-scenarios-in-co-creating-stakeholder-involvement-in-organisational-governance.pdf

18. Nielsen, L.: Acting as Someone Like Me: Personas in Participatory Innovation. Melbourne Australia (2012)

19. LeRouge, C., Ma, J., Sneha, S., Tolle, K.: User profiles and personas in the design and development of consumer health technologies. Int. J. Med. Inf. **82**, 11 (2013). https://doi.org/10.1016/j.ijmedinf.2011.03.006

20. Losana, P., Castro, J.W., Ferre, X., Villalba-Mora, E., Acuña, S.T.: A systematic mapping study on integration proposals of the personas technique in agile methodologies. Sensors **21**(18), 6298 (2021). https://doi.org/10.3390/s21186298

21. Marsden, N., Pröbster, M.: Personas and identity: looking at multiple identities to inform the construction of personas. In: Proceedings of the 2019 CHI Conference on Human Factors in Computing Systems, pp. 1–14 (2019). https://doi.org/10.1145/3290605.3300565

22. Matthews, T., Judge, T., Whittaker, S.: How do designers and user experience professionals actually perceive and use personas? In: Proceedings of the 2012 ACM annual conference on Human Factors in Computing Systems – CHI 2012, p. 1219 (2012). https://doi.org/10.1145/2207676.2208573

23. Miaskiewicz, T., Kozar, K.A.: Personas and user-centered design: How can personas benefit product design processes? Des. Stud. **32**(5), 417–430 (2011)

24. Morgan, D.L.: Exploring the use of artificial intelligence for qualitative data analysis: the case of ChatGPT. Int. J. Qual. Methods 22, 16094069231211248 (2023). https://doi.org/10.1177/16094069231211248

25. Nielsen, L., Hansen, K.S.: Personas is applicable: a study on the use of personas in Denmark. In: Proceedings of the 32nd Annual ACM Conference on Human Factors in Computing Systems (2014). https://doi.org/10.1145/2556288.2557080

26. Nielsen, L.: Personas – User Focused Design, 2nd ed. Springer, New York, NY (2019)

27. Nielsen, L.: Personas, scenarios, journey maps, and storyboards. In: User Experience Methods and Tools in Human-Computer Interaction, 1st ed., pp.71–98. CRC Press, Boca Raton (2024). https://doi.org/10.1201/9781003495161-4
28. Nielsen, L., Larusdottir, M., Larsen, L.B.: Understanding users through three types of personas. In: Human-Computer Interaction – INTERACT 2021, 2021, pp. 330–348. Springer International Publishing, Cham (2021)
29. Norman, D.: Ad-Hoc Personas & Empathetic Focus. Jnd.Org (2004)
30. Pruitt, J., Grudin, J.: Personas: Practice and Theory (2003). http://research.microsoft.com/en-us/um/people/jgrudin/publications/personas/pruitt-grudin.pdf
31. Rönkkö, K., Hellman, M., Kilander, B.: Personas is not applicable: local remedies interpreted in a wider context. Proc. Eighth 112–120 (2004).https://doi.org/10.1145/1011870.1011884
32. Salminen, J., Guan, K., Jung, S.-G., Chowdhury, S.A., Jansen, B.J.: A literature review of quantitative persona creation. In: CHI 2020: Proceedings of the 2020 CHI Conference on Human Factors in Computing Systems, pp. 1–14. ACM, Honolulu, Hawaii, USA (2020). https://doi.org/10.1145/3313831.3376502
33. Salminen, J., Guan, K., Jung, S.-G., Jansen, B.J.: A survey of 15 years of data-driven persona development. Int. J. Hum. Comput. Interact. 37(18), 1685–1708 (2021). https://doi.org/10.1080/10447318.2021.1908670
34. Salminen, J., et al.: Persona preparedness: a survey instrument for measuring the organizational readiness for deploying personas. Inf. Technol. Manag. (2022). https://doi.org/10.1007/s10799-022-00373-9
35. Salminen, J., Nielsen, L., Jung, S.-G., Jansen, B.: Towards a measurement scale of organizational readiness for personas. In: Extended Abstracts of the 2021 CHI Conference on Human Factors in Computing Systems, pp. 1–7. ACM, Yokohama Japan (2021). https://doi.org/10.1145/3411763.3451763
36. Salminen, J., Guan, K.W., Jung, S.-G., Jansen, B.: Use cases for design personas: a systematic review and new frontiers. In: CHI Conference on Human Factors in Computing Systems, pp. 1–21. ACM, New Orleans, LA, USA (2022). https://doi.org/10.1145/3491102.3517589
37. Schneidewind, L., Horold, S., Mayas, C., Kromker, H., Falke, S., Pucklitsch, T.: How personas support requirements engineering. In: 2012 1st International Workshop on Usability and Accessibility Focused Requirements Engineering, UsARE 2012 – Proceedings, pp. 1–5 (2012)
38. Seidelin, C., Jonsson, A., Høgild, M., Rømer, J., Diekmann, P.: Implementing personas for international markets: a question of UX maturity. In: Sider 2014. Royal Institute of Technology, KTH, Stockholm, Sweden (2014). http://sider2014.csc.kth.se/wp-content/uploads/sites/8/2014/04/sider14_submission_9.pdf
39. Törnberg, P.: How to use LLMs for Text Analysis (2023). https://doi.org/10.48550/ARXIV.2307.13106
40. Viana, G., Robert, J.-M.: The Practitioners' Points of View on the Creation and Use of Personas for User Interface Design, pp. 233–244 (2016). https://doi.org/10.1007/978-3-319-39510-4_22

From Deception to Convenience: An Analysis of Design Strategies for Online Shopping

Büşra Gökçe Kurt[(✉)] [iD], Lara Piccolo [iD], and Florian Grote [iD]

CODE University of Applied Sciences, Berlin, Germany
{bursa.kurt,lara.piccolo,florian.grote}@code.berlin

Abstract. Manipulative strategies designed to target shoppers while benefiting online businesses are becoming increasingly common. This exploratory study investigates how varying degrees of deceptive design in an online shopping interface influence online shoppers' perceptions, decisionmaking, and overall satisfaction. As a major online shopping platform worldwide, Amazon's mobile user interface is the reference for this case study. While Amazon is lauded for its convenience, it has been criticised for incorporating manipulative tactics that can steer users toward decisions misaligned with their original intentions. Although seasoned users might overlook these tactics due to their established trust and convenience, new digital shopping platforms may face different challenges if they simply follow arguable industry standards. In this study, the interaction with two high-fidelity redesigns of Amazon's mobile user interface—one that suppressed and one that intensified deceptive elements—were compared against the original app. Based on the perception and feedback of users, we then propose four key recommendations aimed at guiding new designers in creating online shopping experiences that prioritise an ethical approach to design. These recommendations focus on transforming potentially deceptive elements into features that improve users' satisfaction. By addressing the delicate balance between manipulation and convenience in industry practices, this study aims to assist designers in fostering a more ethical digital shopping environment.

Keyword: Deceptive design · Ethical design · Online shopping

1 Introduction

Online businesses increasingly adopt deceptive patterns in interaction design, exploiting cognitive biases to influence decisions that may not align with users' best interests, such as overspending, unintended subscriptions, or excessive data sharing [6, 15]. These practices raise ethical concerns by prioritising short-term gains for the business, or "convenience" for online shoppers over building a longer-term trust.

For example, the "Buy Now" button used by Amazon facilitates rapid purchases. As it eliminates a multi-step checkout, it encourages impulsive decisions [17]. Well-known for applying deceptive patterns as a business strategy, Amazon already faced legal scrutiny for employing deceptive patterns to promote Prime memberships, such

© The Author(s), under exclusive license to Springer Nature Switzerland AG 2026
J. Abdelnour-Nocera et al. (Eds.): ARPPID 2025, CCIS 2797, pp. 17–27, 2026.
https://doi.org/10.1007/978-3-032-15516-0_2

as complicating the cancellation process after a free trial to boost subscriptions and maintain user engagement [13]. Yet, Amazon is a leading force in the e-commerce sector. As of 2025, it is expected to have 310 million active customer accounts global [18] and commands nearly 40% of the US e-commerce market, solidifying its dominance in online retail [22]. This vast influence allows Amazon to set industry standards and shape global consumer behaviour despite ethical concerns. The company is often referenced for its combination of business practices with customer experience design patterns. Amazon's "flywheel" model directly links customer experience gains with increased user engagement, which in turn leads to more competition among sellers, prompting them to reduce prices, which benefits the customer experience [10]. Reduced friction in this cycle drives Amazon's revenue growth.

This paper analyses the controversial business strategy of employing deceptive patterns in online shopping interfaces, with a specific focus on Amazon, from the perspective of online shoppers. It addresses the following research question: How do varying degrees of deceptive design in an online shopping interface influence online shoppers' perceptions, decision-making, and overall satisfaction? Through a primarily qualitative approach, we examine users' awareness and tolerance of these deceptive patterns, exploring how such perceptions influence their satisfaction with the interaction.

This exploratory study contributes to the literature by recommending design strategies for online shopping platforms. These recommendations are grounded on practices by a leader that sets standards in shopping experience online. With an ethical perspective, we suggest shifting from manipulation to enhancing convenience. The study underscores the importance of conducting research on established industry practices with a critical lens.

As follows, a conceptual background on user behaviour and deceptive design is presented, followed by the methodology description. Results on awareness and the deception-convenience trade-off are then reported, concluding with actionable design recommendations.

2 Conceptual Background and Related Works

Transparency, consent, and autonomy are crucial for ethical online shopping. Users should clearly understand pricing, terms of service, and available options. Obscuring this information, complicating service termination, and hiding costs violate these ethical principles [5]. Although features like pre-selected payment and delivery options or subscriptions can reduce purchasing friction and cognitive load, they may also prompt impulsive decisions misaligned with users' original intentions [7]. This presents designers with a dilemma: balancing a simplified user experience with ensuring well-informed, deliberate decisions. Moreover, not all users are actual buyers, but deceptive patterns often aim to convert browsing users into buyers by artificially boosting urgency or incentives to directly influence their decision-making process [23].

Fogg's Behaviour Model (Fig. 1) explains behaviour in such contexts [14], identifying three key variables: Motivation, Ability, and Prompts (MAP). Deceptive patterns exploit these by creating urgency (boosting motivation), simplifying actions (enhancing ability), and timing prompts to align with moments of high emotional engagement or

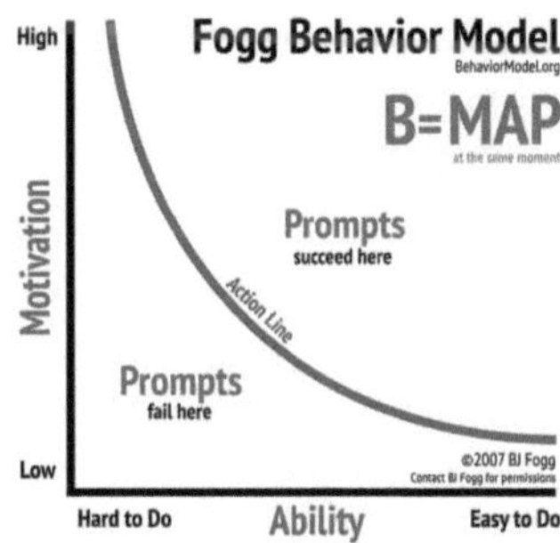

Fig. 1. Fogg Behaviour Model in https://behaviormodel.org

low attention. Conversely, motivation and ability can be reduced when actions, such as cancelling a purchase, lack prompts. This restricts user autonomy and complicates informed decision-making, raising significant ethical concerns [15].

For Cialdini [9], there is a distinction between *ethical persuasion* and *manipulation*, which lies in the user's agency. While persuasion transparently leverages psychological triggers, manipulation covertly exploits users' biases against their best interests. Manipulation of purchase decisions without consumers' full awareness has been documented as early as the 1950s [20]. However, online shopping has expanded opportunities for such strategies, sometimes in subtle ways.

For instance, *visual interference* through vibrant banners or distracting animations promotes certain actions while concealing others [15]. Other examples include strategies like *subscription traps*, *roach motels*, or *forced continuity*, which simplify sign-up processes but make cancellation deliberately difficult [12, 21]. Additionally, *urgency* and *scarcity*, though distinct, both pressure users into acting quickly, often causing emotional stress and reducing satisfaction with the shopping experience [1, 3].

A related concept, *nudging*, from behavioural economics, subtly influences decisions without limiting choice [24]. In online shopping, nudges often appear as pre-selected options, default settings, or prominent "Buy Now" buttons [14]. These tactics exploit cognitive biases, leveraging perceived convenience to shape shopper behaviour in ways that benefit businesses [2]. Such elements are part of the broader concept of *choice architecture*, encompassing all design tactics that influence how choices are presented and made [16]. Many usual deceptive design patterns refer back to psychologically manipulative strategies used in advertisement [1]. Yet, a more recently standardised taxonomy for categorising deceptive patterns remains absent.

3   Methodology

For a comparative analysis of deception awareness and tolerance, Amazon's mobile user interface was first catalogued with deceptive strategies and partially redesigned into two high-fidelity interactive prototypes: a non-deceptive version and a deceptive enhanced version. The versions are illustrated in Fig. 2, where the non-deceptive version of the home screen is on the left side, next to the original (in the centre), while the deceptive-enhanced is on the right. Although Amazon's actual app does not incorporate some of the more extreme deceptive elements featured in the redesign, these elements were included in the enhanced prototype to create a deliberately deceptive shopping experience, enabling the evaluation of users' reactions when facing a deceptive interface.

a) **Non-deceptive version.** In this redesign, the user interface structure remains, but urgency cues, promotional language and pre-selected options were omitted. As an illustration, on the home screen, more subtle colours were chosen to lose the feeling of pressure and shop by categories were favoured rather than deals (as in Fig. 2 left side). Along the checkout process, users could review their choices at each stage, with delivery options presented neutrally, without pre-selected defaults. Extra information to inform decisions about delivery and subscription were added.

b) **Deceptive enhanced version.** This hypothetical prototype based on the original Amazon app portrays highly manipulative experiences. Vivid colours, patterns of urgency (countdown timers), scarcity (e.g., "Only 2 left in stock!"), and nudging (e.g., pre-selected subscription option) were further amplified, as illustrated in the home screen (Fig. 2, left side). Enhanced strategies added to the checkout page are listed and illustrated in Fig. 3.

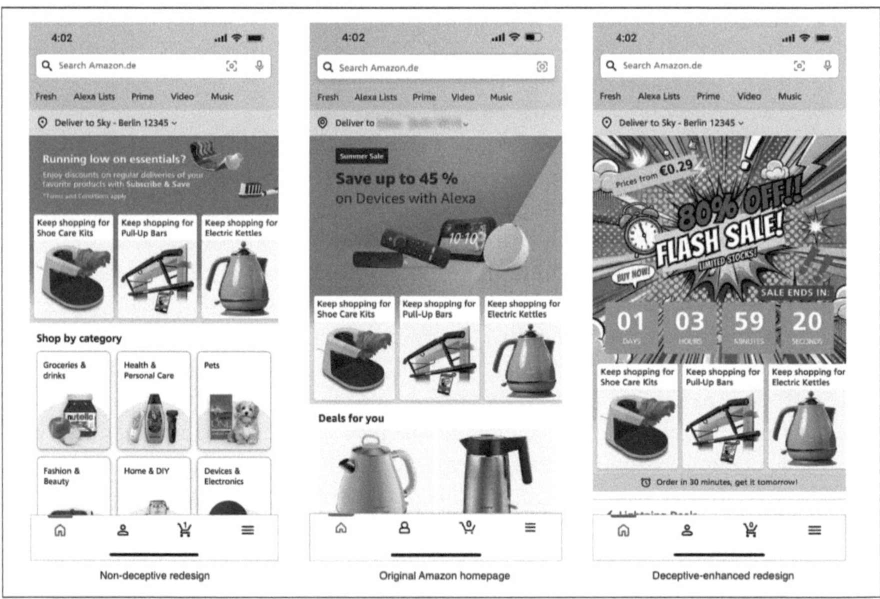

Fig. 2. Illustrations of the redesigned versions (left and right) and the original Amazon app home screen

User Tests: The user tests covered the complete journey from the home screen to checkout, where upselling and obscure navigation could potentially trigger unintended purchases [8]. Participants searched for a product, added it to the basket, and checked out first in the live Amazon app, then repeated the task in one redesigned prototype.

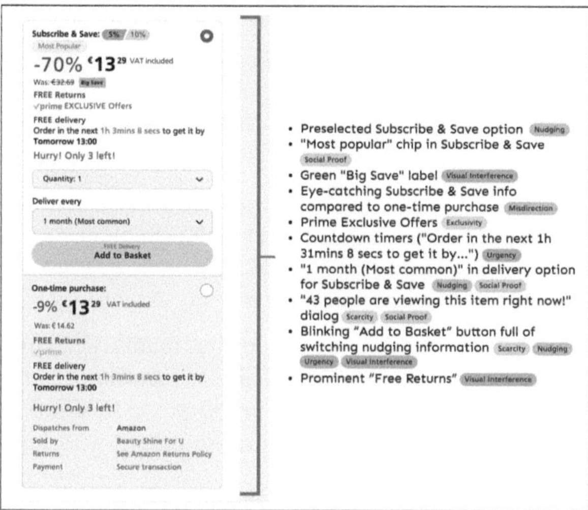

Fig. 3. Checkout page redesign with enhanced deceptive strategies listed

The think-aloud protocol [11] encouraged participants to share their perceptions of usability and clarity, with no mention of deceptive patterns beforehand to avoid bias.

A semi-structured interview followed, focusing on standout elements of the home and product pages, clarity of product information, and features like search, add to cart, and checkout (e.g., "How smooth was the checkout process?" and "Did you feel well-informed about the costs and options available?"). It also explored overall satisfaction, engagement, and distractions. Finally, participants rated their satisfaction with the prototype and the original Amazon app on a scale from 0 to 10 for comparison.

Sessions were recorded and transcribed, and thematic analysis [4] was conducted to identify patterns in the verbalisations and interview data.

4   Results

A total of 10 participants from 25 to 48 years old already familiar with Amazon shopping participated in the study. The sessions were conducted individually, online, and lasted from 30–50 min each. The participants were randomly divided into two groups of 5 each. Both groups interacted with the original Amazon app first, then Group A used the non-deceptive version, while Group B the deceptive enhanced one.

4.1   Qualitative Analysis

While familiarising with the data, the researcher coded text snippets with reactions, mainly to deceptive design patterns. Then, cross-referenced the codes with the prototype version they interacted with. Initial codes identified include "feeling pressured", "feeling in control", "anxiety due to manipulative tactics." Thereafter, these codes were grouped into clusters with similar participants' perspectives, pain points or needs, leading to the following list of themes:

Perceived Pressure: Used when participants felt rushed or manipulated due to urgency, scarcity, Fear Of Missing Out (FOMO), etc. Perceived mainly in the deceptive prototype referring to countdown timers, social proof, and scarcity language. Examples of quotes include *"I don't need this information, but it's making me hurry."* and *"Those notifications make me feel rushed, which is uncomfortable."*

Trust and Transparency: Focuses on users' appreciation for clear communication. In the non-deceptive version, it commonly referred to the simple layout or the clear design language. *"I don't really prefer to use Amazon any more because of these reasons... Everything has the same tag, trying to just get you to buy the thing as quickly as possible."*

Confusion and Frustration: Refers to participants' inability to comprehend terms or expenses associated due to obfuscation, such as hidden fees or unclear options. Example: *"It's like negative feedback right away, you're trying to do something, and you get this immediate effect of having to pay full price, while others who invite a friend get a discount."*

Visual Overload: When participants' reported lost due to the visual distractions, such as *"There was so much going on, I almost forgot what I was shopping for. It was a bit chaotic."*

Manipulation Awareness: Used when participants realised they were being deceived or manipulated, such as the perception of hidden tactics or misdirection. *"It's tricky because it wasn't clear I was adding four. That feels manipulative."*

Convenience vs Ethics: Participants' conflict between choosing convenience despite being aware of unethical design. E.g. *"I actually appreciated not having all the extra product they show (recs). But part of me also kind of missed them? I think I'm used to them helping me finding other stuff."*

Lack of Excitement: The absence of deals or visual stimulation made the shopping experience feel less engaging. *"This version is great for when I want to get something quickly, but it feels less exciting."*

4.2 Prototype Versions Perception

Non-deceptive: Group A reported feeling more in control of their decisions. Transparency and no hidden information were welcomed. Confusion was rarely mentioned and the theme of **trust and transparency** was frequently touched upon, with users commenting on the absence of excessive promoting, the simple layout, in particular the product page, or the clear design language. A few participants noted that the platform's lack of visual clutter allowed them to concentrate more on the pricing details, therefore evaluating the prices more critically and intently.

However, two of five participants thought that the absence of prominent deals and constant product recommendations lowered visual stimulation, which made the shopping experience feel less engaging, even if trust was improved. *"Honestly, it's a bit more boring. It's clean and simple, but it lacks the dynamic, personalized features Amazon offers. Sometimes I like the recommendations, even though they're annoying. It's clean and simple, but it lacks the dynamic, personalised features Amazon offers."*

Deceptive Enhanced: Consistently with remarks of **visual overload** and **confusion and frustration** mainly due to urgency strategies and disguised information, feelings of anxiety and **manipulation awareness** with the deceptive enhanced version were frequent. *"It gives me anxiety to the point that I'm starting to think how I'm gonna be trolled into perhaps spending more money."* Group B participants reported feeling confused when making decisions, as focusing on their very first purchasing goal due was hard to the continual bombardment of discounts, recommendations, and messages.

However, a some participants admitted that they still found the convenience it provided to be appealing. The interviewees' responses, such as *"I felt rushed, but at least it was fast,"* demonstrates the **convenience vs ethics** conflict. *"I know it's pushing me to buy fast, but it's also really convenient when I'm in a hurry."*

Interestingly, some participants could not differentiate enhanced deceptive patterns in the redesigned prototype from the original Amazon app. *"I know it's trying to push me to buy, but I'm so used to it that I just ignore most of it."* Aside from bold components like vividly coloured banners or wordings that evoke a sense of urgency or scarcity; minor tweaks like concealed fees, inflated social proof elements like "x people viewing this item right now!" or the added "popular searches" section in the search page were mostly ignored. *"I think it's quite informative. It's what I'd expect from any Amazon product page I guess."*

4.3 Satisfaction Ratings

Participants rated their overall satisfaction with the interactive experience from 1 to 10 as an indicator across versions, as described in Table 1.

The original Amazon App received an average score of 6.7/10 ($\sigma = 1.57$). When justifying the score, participants often pointed out their familiarity with the interface: *"It's still the easiest way to shop. Even with the countdowns and prompts, I just go with it because it's what I know."* Nonetheless, they also admitted some dissatisfaction over the deceptive patterns inherent in it: *"A little overwhelming, to be honest."*

The non-deceptive prototype, received a slightly higher average rating of 8/10 ($\sigma = 0.71$). This suggests that the majority of participants valued its simplicity and clarity and consistently viewed it to be transparent and user-friendly. The deceptive enhanced was rated an average of 2.8/10 ($\sigma = 1.52$), suggesting a much inferior level of satisfaction when compared to the other versions. This indicates a generally negative experience, justified by expressed annoyance at deceptive elements and lack of transparency.

Table 1. Participants' satisfaction rating assigned to each prototype version and average

	Group A					Group B					Average
	P1	P2	P3	P4	P5	P6	P7	P8	P9	P10	
Original	9	6	5	7	7	5	8	9	5	6	7
Non-deceptive	8	8	8	7	9						8
Deceptive enhanced						2	5	1	3	3	2.8

5   Discussions

5.1   Awareness of deceptive patterns

The notably lower satisfaction rating for the deceptive enhanced prototype aligns with the thematic analysis results, which highlighted users' dissatisfaction with strategies like forced continuity and urgency. However, many of the enhanced deceptive strategies were not mentioned by some participants during interaction. This supports the argument by Bongard-Blanch et al. [3] that deceptive patterns often go undetected unless users are made explicitly aware of them. In this study, participants were not made aware of these patterns before providing satisfaction ratings, suggesting that the difference between the original app and the deceptive version may be attributed to the exaggerated manipulative elements in the latter. This underscores the potential risks posed by large platforms with an established user base, where incremental increases in deceptive tactics could go unnoticed, exploiting user trust without significant backlash.

Although participants declared they were not entirely okay with the deceptive design patterns used in the original application, the difference in the ratings of the original and non-deceptive version was remarkably small. This could be interpreted as that eliminating deceptive patterns alone may not be the best solution to significantly improve user perceptions and to influence user behaviour positively. Other factors such as familiarity, popularity, affordability, etc., play crucial roles. Such findings emphasise the complexity of people's behaviour, wherein convenience can sometimes overshadow concerns about manipulation, leading users to tolerate or overlook deceptive patterns in exchange for a more seamless experience.

5.2   Deception or Convenience

As expected, participants reported not been satisfied with hidden costs and preselected options in the deceptive enhanced version. In line with the arguments in [12], clear pricing, combined with easy-to-understand options for delivery and payment, fosters trust and enhances the overall user experience. Consistently, individuals who interacted with the non-deceptive prototype declared feeling less manipulated and more in charge of their choices compared to the original version. However, it is possible that this transparency could decrease user excitement and engagement. In earlier research [7, 17], the authors argue that ethical design may reduce short-term engagement by removing the psychological triggers that lead to impulsive purchases, even as it increases user trust and long-term loyalty.

Participants reported appreciation for elements that lessened the cognitive burden needed to complete an order, such as personalised product recommendations and preselected shipping alternatives. These same features were acknowledged as manipulative, though, as they were intended to influence users to take particular actions which might not be aligned with their actual preferences.

Convenience remains a powerful motivator even when users spot deception. Per Fogg's Behaviour Model [14] in Fig. 1, prompts like personalised recommendations or a one-tap "Buy Now" increases ability at the moment of choice, boosting motivation. It is important to harness this convenience without slipping into manipulation.

Familiarity is another factor of influence in increasing ability according to Fogg's Behaviour Model (Fig. 1) [14]. Even though participants reported to be more satisfied with the non-deceptive version, some reported feeling more comfortable using the original app, even though they were aware of the deceptive strategies incorporated into the design, suggesting that familiarity can override negative feelings from deception [19]. The tendency to stay loyal to a platform in spite of ethical hesitations highlights the apathy that many users experience in the presence of familiar interfaces. Supporting quotes for familiarity include *"I know it's trying to push me to buy, but I'm so used to it that I just ignore most of it."* and *"It's still the easiest way to shop. Even with the countdowns and prompts, I just go with it because it's what I know."*

While familiarity plays a crucial role in shopping on platforms like Amazon, new online shopping designs lack this advantage, requiring them to build trust from scratch. Users often overlook ethical dilemmas when interacting with familiar interfaces, highlighting a significant challenge for emerging platforms. These new entrants face an uneven playing field, competing against established giants like Amazon that may employ deceptive tactics to retain users. To address these dynamics, it is essential to promote transparent and balanced user experiences across the industry and raise awareness of deceptive practices.

6 Design Recommendations

Aiming at informing design choices while guiding strategic discussion about ethical standards, this set of actionable recommendations is directed to product/service designers or stakeholders who establish design policies and success metrics for the wider organisation.

1. **Balance between engagement and transparency.** Online shopping platforms should aim for a balance between engaging sales strategies and transparency. While visual communication about deals or free delivery, for instance, are still useful, they should never be used to overwhelm or trick users into subscription traps or unwanted extra purchase.
2. **Nudging mechanisms for convenience, not manipulation.** Nudging strategies lead to convenience, but they should not compromise freedom of choice, as opposed to pushing users into decisions. This can entail giving users simple methods to change their selections or access to more thorough information regarding their decisions, such as an info icon and/or no default selections.
3. **Avoid visual manipulation.** Bright colours, large letters, and countdown timers to improve the sense of scarcity or urgency should be avoided. While visual indicators can improve user engagement, their overuse can damage trust. In line with [17], designers should strive to produce a visually balanced hierarchy that captures the users' attention without being overbearing.
4. **Opt-in choices over defaults.** Designers should prioritise offering opt-in choices instead of incorporating pre-selected options. As an example, the preselected "subscribe to the newsletter" option often seen to promote products via email. Pre-selected options are one of the most "effective" yet manipulative strategies, as they subtly pressure users into unintentional commitments. These features should be replaced with

clearly stated, optional choices that empower users to make decisions, without feeling pressured.

7 Conclusion

Our study found that calm, non-manipulative visual communication, as applied in the non-deceptive prototype, was perceived by participants as a satisfactory experience. While this aligns with ethical online shopping design, it may conflict with short-term business goals. Additionally, users still expect some level of "excitement" and strategies that simplify decisions, likely due to familiarity with popular profit-driven platforms like Amazon, where deceptive patterns are tolerated for convenience.

New online shopping platforms cannot rely on such familiarity and must balance deception and convenience. Any new online shopping experience will likely have to compete directly with the Amazon experience, utilising the patterns outlined here to retain its users and keep them engaged in their shopping behaviour. Based on our findings, we offer recommendations for designers to shift from deception toward ethically providing convenience.

This study compared user interactions with original, deceptive enhanced, and non-deceptive prototypes, offering insights into awareness and tolerance of deceptive strategies. The analysis focuses on users' perceptions of the interactive experience, excluding factors like customer service and delivery reliability. A limited sample size may also affect the generalisability of results. Future research should involve larger, more diverse groups to explore the long-term effects of deceptive versus ethical design on user behaviour and business, contributing to more sustainable and ethical digital practices.

Declaration.   There have been no changes to this case study since ARPPID25 Conference.

References

1. Andrews, M., van Leeuwen, M., van Baaren, R.: Hidden persuasion: 33 psychological influence techniques in advertising. BIS Publishers (2013)
2. Benartzi, S., et al.: Should governments invest more in nudging? Psychol. Sci. **28**(8), 1041–1055 (2017)
3. Bongard-Blanchy, K., Rossi, A., Rivas, S., Doublet, S., Koenig, V., Lenzini, G.: I am definitely manipulated, even when i am aware of it. It's ridiculous!" dark patterns from the end-user perspective. In: Proceedings of the 2021 ACM Designing Interactive Systems Conference, pp. 763–776 (2021)
4. Braun, V., Clarke, V.: Using thematic analysis in psychology. Qual. Res. Psychol. **3**(2), 77–101 (2006)
5. Brenncke, M.: Regulating dark patterns. Notre Dame J. Int. Comparat. Law **14**, 39 (2024)
6. Brignull, H.: Dark patterns: deception vs. honesty in UI design. Interact. Des. Usabil. **338**, 2–4 (2011)
7. Brignull, H.: Deceptive patterns: exposing the tricks tech companies use to control you. Testimonium (2023)
8. Business Case Studies: Revealing the dark patterns in online sales (2024),https://businessc asestudies.co.uk/revealing-the-dark-patterns-in-online-sales/. Accessed 20 Jan 2025

9. Cialdini, R.B.: Influence: the psychology of persuasion, vol. 55. Collins New York (2007)
10. Cuofano, Gennaro: Amazon flywheel: amazon virtuous cycle in a nutshell (2024). https://fourweekmba.com/amazon-flywheel/. Accessed 31 Jan 2025
11. Eccles, D.W., Arsal, G.: The think aloud method: what is it and how do i use it? Qual. Res. Sport Exercise Health 9(4), 514–531 (2017)
12. Federal Trade Comission: FTC report shows rise in sophisticated dark patterns designed to trick and trap consumers (2022). https://www.ftc.gov/news-events/news/press-releases/2022/09/ftc-report-shows-rise-sophisticated-dark-patterns-designed-trick/-trap-consumers. Accessed 20 Jan 2025
13. Federal Trade Commission: FTC Sues Amazon for Illegally Maintaining Monopoly Power (2023). https://www.ftc.gov/news-events/news/press-releases/2023/09/ftc-sues-amazon-illegally-maintaining-monopoly-power. Accessed 20 Jan 2025
14. Fogg, B.J.: A behavior model for persuasive design. In: Proceedings of the 4th International Conference on Persuasive Technology, pp. 1–7 (2009)
15. Gray, C.M., Kou, Y., Battles, B., Hoggatt, J., Toombs, A.L.: The dark (patterns) side of ux design. In: Proceedings of the 2018 CHI Conference on Human Factors in Computing Systems, pp. 1–14 (2018)
16. Johnson, E.J.: The elements of choice: why the way we decide matters. Riverhead Books, New York, NY (2021)
17. Mathur, A., et al.: Dark patterns at scale: Findings from a crawl of 11k shopping websites. Proc. ACM Hum.-Comput. Interact. 3(Issue CSCW), 1–32 (2019)
18. Mosby, A.: Amazon statistics 2025 users, customers & revenue (2023), https://www.yaguara.co/amazon-statisticss/. Accessed 20 Jan 2025
19. Nielsen, J.: Usability engineering. Morgan Kaufmann, San Francisco, CA (1993)
20. Packard, V.: The hidden persuaders. Longmans, Green and Co., New York, NY, USA (1957), first edition
21. Sheil, A., Acar, G., Schraffenberger, H., Gellert, R., Malone, D.: Staying at the roach motel: Cross-country analysis of manipulative subscription and cancellation flows. In: Proceedings of the CHI Conference on Human Factors in Computing Systems, pp. 1–24 (2024)
22. Stadista: Number of Amazon Prime users in the United States from 2017 to 2022 with a forecast for 2023 and 2024 (2023). https://www.statista.com/statistics/504687/number-of-amazon-prime-subscription-households-usa/. Accessed 20 Jan 2025
23. Stewart, E.: The psychological traps of online shopping, explained (2022).https://www.vox.com/the-goods/23505330/online-shopping-ecomerce-tricks-dark-patterns-deceptive-design. Accessed 21 April 2024
24. Thaler, R.H., Sunstein, C.R.: Nudge: improving decisions about health, wealth, and happiness. Yale University Press, New Haven, CT (2008)

Biomimicry: A Transdisciplinary Approach for Human Computer Interaction

Catharina van den Driesche[1](✉) [iD], Åsa Cajander[2] [iD], and Shweta Premanandan[2] [iD]

[1] University of Amsterdam, Amsterdam, Netherlands
`c.j.h.m.vandendriesche@uva.nl`
[2] Department of Information Technology, Uppsala University, Uppsala, Sweden

Abstract. Biomimicry, the method of emulating nature's functions, strategies, and systems, offers a transformative perspective for designing intuitive, sustainable, and regenerative Human-Computer Interaction (HCI) systems. The complexity of human-computer interactions, particularly within domains such as augmented reality (AR), virtual reality (VR), and wearable technology, demands interfaces and interactions that are not only intuitive but also transparently integrated into users' environments. Beyond this, when HCI is situated within the context of global challenges, like climate change and biodiversity loss, design approaches need to engage understanding of nonhuman needs and perspectives to ensure that solutions are not only human-centered but also aligned with ecological sustainability. Biomimicry, as a transdisciplinary methodology, offers an approach for knowledge transfer by blending human and nonhuman perspectives. The mimicry of functions, strategies, and systems found in nature enables to integrate theoretical knowledge with practical, actionable applications for interaction design. Furthermore, by co-developing theoretical perspectives on design methodologies with industry partners, it becomes possible to align the biomimicry process with design strategies and company roadmaps, leading to the creation of responsible designs that mitigate unintended consequences on ecosystems. This paper synthesizes insights from two workshops held at Uppsala University in 2023 and 2024, which explored biomimicry's potential to address emerging challenges in HCI by examining the shift from screen-based to immersive scene-based interaction, integrating human and nonhuman perspectives to inspire new collaborative approaches and partnerships for more-than-human participatory design.

Keywords: Biomimicry · More-Than-Human Design · Transdisciplinary Approach · Human-Computer Interaction · Collaborative Design · Analogical Thinking

1 Introduction

Biomimicry, or biometrics, is the imitation of functions, strategies, and systems, found in nature for solving complex problems [3, 21]. The problem-driven approach in biomimetic development focuses on addressing a specific practical human problem, using the identified issue as the starting point for the design process [16]. It involves finding biological

© The Author(s), under exclusive license to Springer Nature Switzerland AG 2026
J. Abdelnour-Nocera et al. (Eds.): ARPPID 2025, CCIS 2797, pp. 28–47, 2026.
https://doi.org/10.1007/978-3-032-15516-0_3

models that perform a particular function or strategy, extracting their underlying principles, and applying them to technological solutions [16, 21]. This approach aligns closely with the iterative design process, which consists of the stages: discover, explore, ideate, develop, and evaluate. In this context, it is useful to briefly distinguish between related design approaches: biomimicry, which draws analogies from nature's strategies; bio-design, which works directly with living organisms; sustainable design, which seeks to reduce harm; and regenerative design, which aims to restore systems and create net-positive impact. Together, these perspectives offer complementary entry points for aligning technological innovation with ecological principles.

While biomimicry seeks to emulate the life principles of the natural world [14] to create more intuitive, regenerative, and sustainable technologies, interaction design focuses on the ways people engage with and make sense of technology. By extending this focus to include how living systems interact with their environments, designers can draw inspiration from nature's adaptive strategies to create experiences that feel natural (i.e., short learning curve) and intuitive (i.e., learned or familiar behavior). For instance, biomimetic principles can inform systems that are not only responsive to user needs but also capable of evolving in response to changing contexts, much like the dynamic systems found in nature.

To explore how biomimicry can inform interaction design, it is essential to understand the concept of 'scene design', designing experiences with multiple technologies in the user environment. Scene design refers to the many ways that people interact with their environment, offering an alternative to screen-based interactions [11]. In this context, users would be able to engage with their environment more naturally and intuitively, rather than relying on screen interfaces. For instance, instead of providing feedback through visual displays, designers might utilize tactile feedback, such as vibrations to create a more immersive user experience. As interaction designers seek to create engaging and intuitive experiences, biomimicry offers an approach for developing interactions that are seamlessly integrated into the environment, capable of supporting complex data engagement without reinforcing reliance on screens.

This paper discusses two workshops conducted in 2023 and 2024 at Uppsala University, which explored a problem-driven biomimicry approach to align natural principles with the challenges of contemporary human computer interaction design. The workshops addressed practical design process challenges by identifying underlying biological principles, such as 'shape change', and abstracting them into potential technological solutions [13]. Participants were independent designers and researchers at the Department of Information Technology at Uppsala University that explore different themes related to humans and technology, e.g., robotics, artificial intelligence, digitalization, gender, work engagement, and educational development. The workshops adopted a Design Exploration approach, positioned as Research for Design, with a focus on the design methods that are currently used, as well as those that could be developed [6]. This approach enabled hands-on experimentation with alternatives to existing methodologies, aimed at expanding them to include both human and natural nonhuman perspectives [20]. Incorporating the nonhuman perspective considering the role of animals, biotic and abiotic ecosystems, encouraged participants to explore how design might respond to ecological needs as well as human ones, shifting the human-centric paradigm to a more eco-centric or systemic viewpoint [20].

The overall goal of the workshops was an initiatory step towards collaborative activities that promote the co-production of a framework that considers the integration of transdisciplinary knowledge (i.e., human knowledge and other knowledge) across science, industries and nature at large [15]. Building on this goal, the central research question for this paper is: *How can biomimicry as a transdisciplinary methodology inform the development of scene-based interactions in Human-Computer Interaction, integrating both human and nonhuman perspectives into design processes?* In pursuing this question, the paper reflects a unique collaboration between industry practitioners and academic researchers, leveraging their combined expertise to explore biomimicry as a transformative approach for interaction design. By bridging academic theory and practical application, this work demonstrates the potential of interdisciplinary efforts to address emerging challenges in the field.

2 Background

2.1 Biomimicry and Technology

As technology evolves, so do the ways people interact with it. From wearable devices and voice-based interactions to virtual reality (VR), and augmented reality (AR), human-computer interactions have undergone a transformation towards immersive experiences for users. Designers create immersive experiences that transport users into "digital worlds" combining multi-sensory technologies. These imaginative scenes provide realistic, interactive environments that allow users to explore virtual spaces as if they were physically present. These developments have expanded the boundaries of HCI, demanding the integration of diverse interaction conditions to accommodate the complexities of scene-based technological systems.

The ongoing development of AR and VR is particularly noteworthy, as these technologies enable the exploration of new interaction methods beyond traditional screen-based models. They allow users to engage with data, technology, and environments more intuitively and immersed. However, this shift also presents challenges, such as the need to design interfaces and interaction that support users to make sense of large datasets and make informed decisions efficiently through cues in the environment, like colour changes, smells, vibrations and through touch. Simultaneously, global challenges like climate change and biodiversity loss necessitate sustainable approaches to interaction design. In this context, biomimicry offers an innovative and creative methodology, drawing inspiration from nature's strategies and systems to inform sustainable and regenerative solutions [21].

Biomimicry has inspired a wide range of technological innovations by emulating strategies and structures found in nature. Notable examples include the stable wing of early aircraft derived from the gliding seeds of 'Alsomitra macrocarpa', Velcro inspired by burdock seeds, and self-cleaning surfaces modelled on lotus leaves. Other applications range from low-drag designs inspired by penguins and shark skin to advanced adhesives mimicking gecko feet, robotic control systems based on insect neural circuits, and architectural structures referencing spider webs, demonstrating how nature's principles can inform sustainable, efficient, and regenerative design solutions. By observing how natural systems optimize energy use, promote resilience, and create balance within their ecosystems, biomimicry allows HCI designers to develop user experiences while actively contributing to environmental restoration. For example, interaction designs inspired by regenerative principles [9] can integrate adaptive feedback loops, resource efficiency, and waste-minimizing processes, mimicking how ecosystems regenerate and sustain themselves over time [21].

Biomimicry has been applied across diverse fields, such as engineering, aviation, urban design, product design, architecture, and art. In the context of HCI, it offers a pathway to designs that not only accommodate the complexities of scene-based interactions but also promote balance between human centered technology and the natural world.

2.2 Biomimicry as a Problem Driven Approach

Biomimicry, unlike human-centered design approaches, reframes nature as a model for mimicking biological principles to inform solutions. Following Fayemi's model (see Fig. 1), once a relevant biological model is identified, the designer abstracts the principle (e.g., distributed regulation of activity to avoid overload) and begins translating it into potential design solutions.

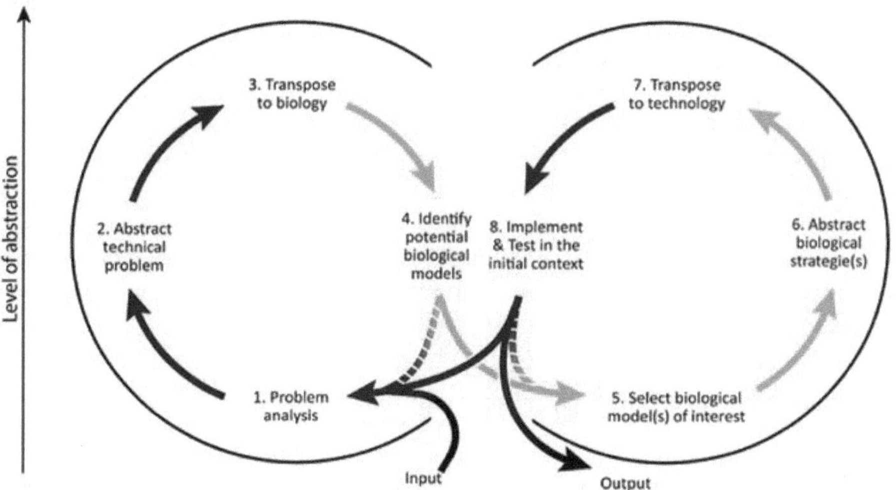

Fig. 1. The unified problem driven biomimetic process from Fayemi [7]

Biological models can be identified through literature reviews, online searches, database exploration, field observations and collaboration with biologists, ecologists, and experience experts [7]. This biomimetic process, rooted in analogical thinking, identifies and applies biological principles to develop sustainable and regenerative solutions [12, 17, 19] by creating multiple scenarios, each leading to distinct, relevant ideas, concepts, and prototypes. For instance, the Eastgate Centre in Harare, Zimbabwe, maintains stable temperatures by mimicking the self-regulating airflow found in termite mounds [18].

Take, for instance, a design challenge on how we might design a remote work interface that helps users manage cognitive load throughout the workday? While a human-centered approach might focus on user feedback, interface simplicity, or productivity metrics, the biomimetic process encourages us to explore how nature regulates energy flows under high-pressure or fluctuating environments. From there, the search for biological analogues might include how certain tree species manage energy, or how octopuses distribute control across semi-autonomous limbs, reducing central processing demands, strategies that might inspire decentralized interface features, or gentle environmental feedback mechanisms that support flow.

Throughout the biomimicry process, analogical thinking plays a central role in translating principles from nature into human-centered solutions. It requires not only understanding and extracting key concepts from biological systems but also adapting them to align with technological and cultural constraints and possibilities. Given the interconnected and simultaneous functioning of natural systems, an analogical way of thinking is essential to enable exploration of natural phenomena and events [1, 19].

Analogical reasoning entails the process of accessing elements from prior knowledge to design new solutions or "the ability to notice and draw similarities across contexts" [19]. Analogical reasoning involves several steps, including focusing on relevant knowledge identifying relationships within and across items, and mapping these relationships across domains to generate insights or uncover shared principles [10]. General biomimetic design phases support this identification to facilitate transitions between broader knowledge domains by exploring potential scenarios guided by specific strategies found in nature [2]. The goal is to transcend apparent differences between a strategy found in nature and to identify the shared relational structures that link diverse knowledge domains. The core of this process lies in recognizing structural relationships between domains, beyond superficial similarities [8]. Encouraging analogical thinking can help designers avoid misinterpreting or oversimplifying biological models [1]. Another important element of using biomimicry is understanding how interaction designs can affect the environment (i.e., the environmental impact of interaction designs) by mimicking interconnectedness between ecosystems.

2.3 Biomimicry as a Transdisciplinary Approach

Collaborative and participatory design processes generally focus on the needs of humans and human-made technological systems, without the integration of the natural nonhuman world as a stakeholder, either indirectly or in design time [20]. By studying how different species interact with one another and their environment, provides valuable insights into balancing the needs of humans, technology, and nature. These interactions reveal complex ecosystems where mutual dependence and synergy that support adaptability. Moving beyond the concept of 'survival of the fittest,' and instead embracing a philosophy of collaboration and interdependence within a diversity of perspectives.

The challenges of making nature a partner in the domain of interface and interaction design, for both academia and industries, aligns with the principles of regenerative design, which advocate for shaping human activities in harmony with nature. Regenerative design seeks to address the disconnection between humans and nature by supporting a co-creative partnership, treating natural nonhumans as partners in a shared design process [5].

The possibility of incorporating natural strategies and systems into the domain of human interaction development provides an abundance of resources. However, this abundance poses a challenge, as finding an example in nature that can solve design, or technological problems can be difficult. Moreover, the connections between biology and human computer interactions are often non-obvious. Identifying these connections requires a systems-thinking approach of exploration across multiple system levels. This approach relies on analogical thinking, which involves identifying similarities and differences between objects or recognizing patterns within groups of objects or the "shared relational structure between domains" [19].

In the next section insights from two workshops held at Uppsala University in 2023 and 2024 which explored the potential of biomimicry to address emerging challenges in HCI are presented. These workshops focused on transitioning from screen-based to immersive scene-based interaction paradigms, aiming to offer alternative perspectives on interaction design.

3   Method of Research-Based Workshops

Central to both workshops in 2023 and 2024 was underscoring the importance of analogical thinking in transferring knowledge across contexts. In total, 14 participants, including researchers, assistant professors, PhD students, and lecturers, from the Department of Information Technology at Uppsala University and one designer from both industry and academia, identified connections between biological and technological systems (see Fig. 2). Two participants took part in both workshops. The workshops facilitated the exploration of multiple scenarios, allowing participants to pinpoint examples and transition between broader domains through structured phases guided by the biomimetic process [7].

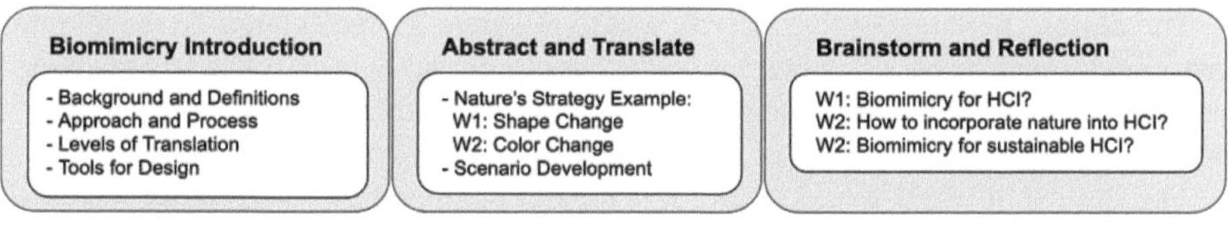

Fig. 2. Global overview for each of the two workshops

3.1   Workshop 1: Brainstorming Interactions Using Nature's Shape Changes

On January 26th, 2023, the first of two workshops was held at Uppsala University on the possibilities of the method biomimicry for Human Computer Interaction. The growing complexity of human interactions dealing with large amounts of data and the shift away from screen-based interactions is pushing the boundaries of Human Computer Interaction. By indirectly embedding knowledge of how nature operates into design processes, the workshops explored how biomimetic principles can reshape individual and collective perspectives, avoid unsustainable systems, and embed adaptive and intuitive nature-inspired solutions into HCI design.

3.1.1 Outline and Activities of Workshop 1

Through a series of reflective activities, the participants explored how biomimicry can be applied to the design of interactive products, services, and environments. Nine participants from the department of Information Technology engaged in a reflection process that consisted of three interactive activities. The activities began with an individual part and then transitioned into a reflective part in pairs or trio, followed by discussions.

The overall setup consisted of:

1. An introduction to the method of biomimicry.
2. Activity 1: 'Researcher Identity Memo' about biomimicry.
3. Activity 2: Biomimicry brainstorming using shape changes in nature.
4. Activity 3: Brainwriting on options and ideas for 'Biomimicry and HCI'.
5. Wrap-up and follow-up.

Activity 1: Researcher Identity Memo' about biomimicry.

After being introduced to biomimicry, the participants created a Researcher Identity Memo in the form of a mind map (see Fig. 3). This mind map helps to identify questions, biases, assumptions, and other elements of their thinking. It also allows them to visualize any changes in their thinking over time. Creating a Researcher Identity Memo was a useful tool to help the participants better understand their own thoughts on biomimicry.

Activity 2: Biomimicry brainstorming using shape changes in nature.

During the next activity, participants experienced biomimicry by 'thinking like nature operates' when designing a new interactive experience, discussing alternative possibilities for existing screen interactions (e.g., instructing, conversing, manipulating, and exploring) and translating systems found in nature into new ways of interaction in public space.

The design challenge of this activity was to integrate 'shape change' to create future scenarios for new ways of interacting as if having a conversation. The shape changes in nature are Elastomers, Auxetics, Rollable, Foldable, Inflatable, Anisotropic, Multistable, and Shape memory [13].

The context of a real-world setting was the environment of a train station where the person waiting for the train to arrive has a conversation explaining that they are late to someone who is not present at the station. Every participant could choose the shape change they wanted to integrate into the design of an intuitive and natural conversation using any kind of (imagined) technology (see Fig. 4).

The first step in this activity was an individual brainstorm using the technique of the 'Crazy Four' for 4 ideas in 4 min (see Fig. 5). While the standard 'Crazy Eight' encourages fast-paced ideation with eight ideas in eight minutes, this activity was reduced to four ideas to ensure participants had enough time for reflection and discussion to choose an idea for the creation of a 'Future Scenario'.

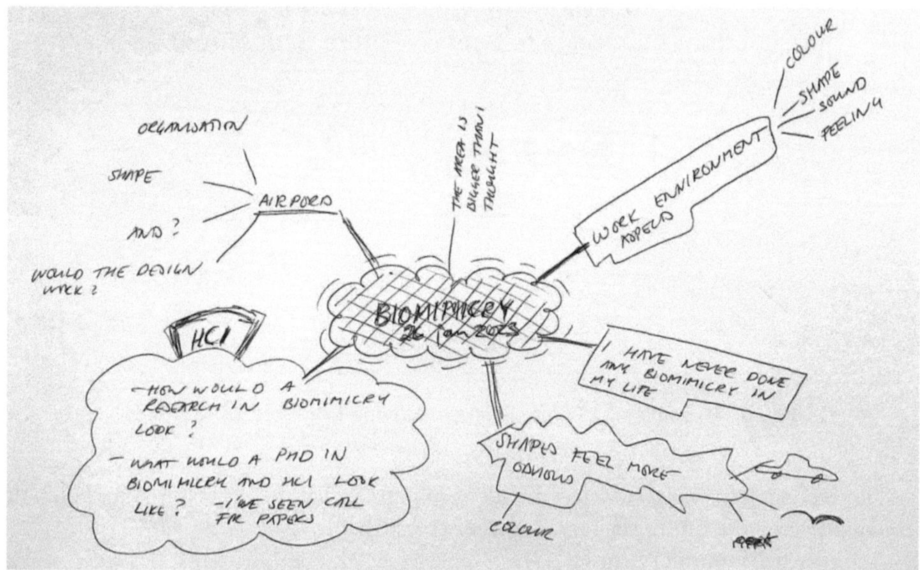

Fig. 3. Example of a Research Identity Memo: mind map on current thoughts and ideas about biomimicry.

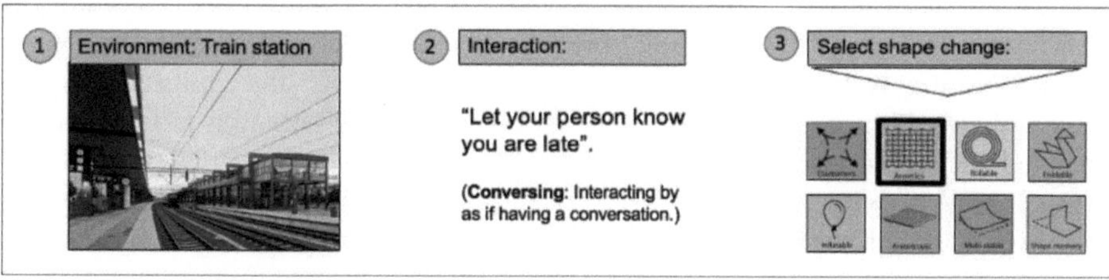

Fig. 4. The design challenge using shape change [13]

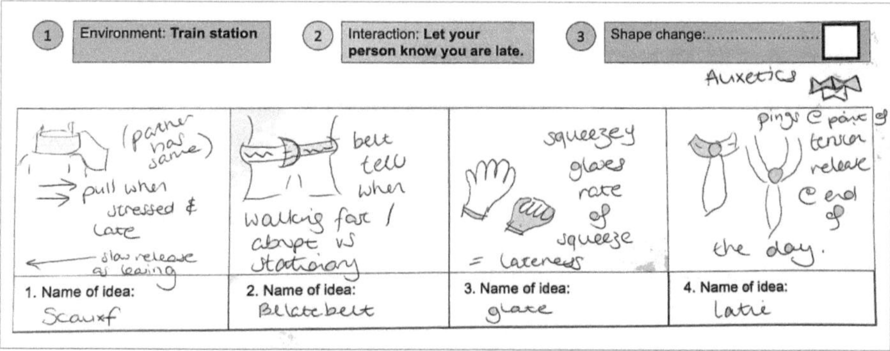

Fig. 5. Example of the 'Crazy Four' brainstorm

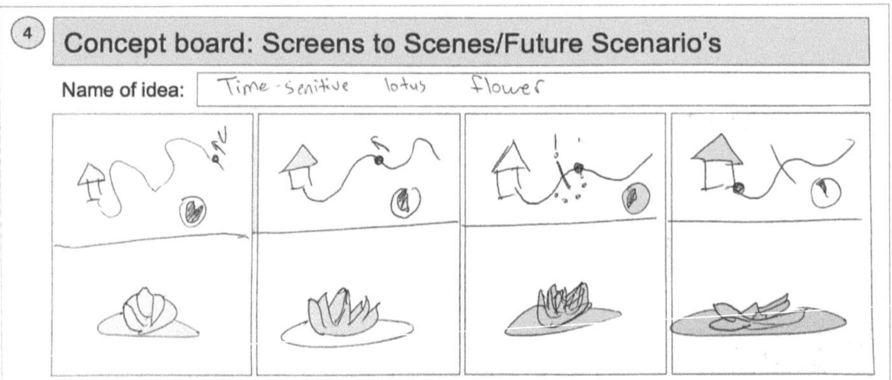

Fig. 6. Example of a Future Scenario moving from screens to scenes

The second step was to discuss the ideas in pairs or trio to get inspired and pick the best idea to create a future scenario together (see Fig. 6).

Activity 3: Biomimicry for HCI?

The last activity consisted of a brainstorm session and a discussion on what components of HCI could benefit from the method of biomimicry. The brainstorm technique consisted of two parts: individual creation of three How Might We' s, followed by the Round Robin or Brainwriting technique. Round Robin or Brainwriting is a brainstorming technique that encourages people to reflect on each other's ideas and generate new ideas collaboratively. By discussing various components of HCI and exploring the potential for utilizing biomimicry, the participants could identify potential pitfalls and risks associated with a proposed HMW.

The HMW activity was supported by two options for integrating the biomimicry method for HCI; 'preparing human interaction for biomimicry' and 'what components of human interaction would be an interesting start for using the biomimicry method'? During the Round Robin or Brainwriting activity participants reflected on possible ethical implications.

3.2 Workshop 2: An Interface like a Beetle

On October 24th, 2024, the second of two workshops was held at Uppsala University on the possibilities of the method biomimicry for Human Computer Interaction. This workshop aimed to:

- Explore the convergence of biomimicry and HCI by brainstorming and designing organic, "living" interfaces.
- Conceptualize interfaces beyond traditional screen-based designs, inspired by nature's methods of sensing and disseminating information.
- Develop a deeper understanding of information dissemination and design new, intuitive human-information interfaces that reflect natural processes and functions.

The decision to focus on a beetle-inspired interface emerged from the beetle's unique physical adaptations of layering fluids to inform its environment of its emotional state and therefore its potential for rich metaphorical and functional translation into interface and interaction design.

3.2.1 Outline and Activities of Workshop 2

The overall setup consisted of:

1. An introduction to the method of biomimicry
2. Introduction to Processing Information as Nature's 'Interface'.

The workshop provided an in-depth look into how natural systems process information as interfaces, offering insights into potential applications in HCI. Nature's strategies for navigating, sending, processing, and sensing signals were presented as an alternative perspective on interface and interaction design.

3. Activity 1: Designing a Beetle-Inspired Interface
4. Activity 2: How might we: incorporate nature into HCI
5. Wrap-up and follow-up.

Activity 1: Designing a Beetle-Inspired Interface

Participants explored the unique properties of the golden tortoise beetle, focusing on its "chirped" multilayer structure, which enables it to toggle between two distinct colors depending on moisture levels. This beetle's adaptation serves as a model for designing interfaces that reveal information dynamically through environmental interaction.

The processes of Functional Abstraction and Translation aligned with Phase 6: Abstract Biological Strategies and Phase 7: Transpose to Technology in the Biomimicry Process framework by Fayemi [7]. Worksheets (see Fig. 7) provided for these phases guided participants in abstracting and translating three key functionalities of the beetle's adaptations:

1. **Toggle Between Layers**: Mimicking the beetle's ability to reveal different layers to access varied information, the interface could allow users to switch views or data levels by manipulating the "layers" of the system.
2. **Displacement of Fluid in Grooves**: Similar to the beetle's moisture-displacing grooves, an interface could display new information by user interaction, revealing hidden data in a structured, layered manner.
3. **Porous Patches for Moisture Displacement**: Patches that respond to environmental changes could add an organic element to HCI, revealing new patterns or information based on user engagement.

During these two phases, participants analyzed how the beetle's colour-changing mechanism can be abstracted into functional design principles, such as responsiveness, material efficiency, and environmental adaptability. They then explored ways to translate these principles into interface features, including humidity-sensitive displays and dynamic visual cues that provide context-aware feedback.

Activity 2: How Might We Incorporate Nature into HCI?

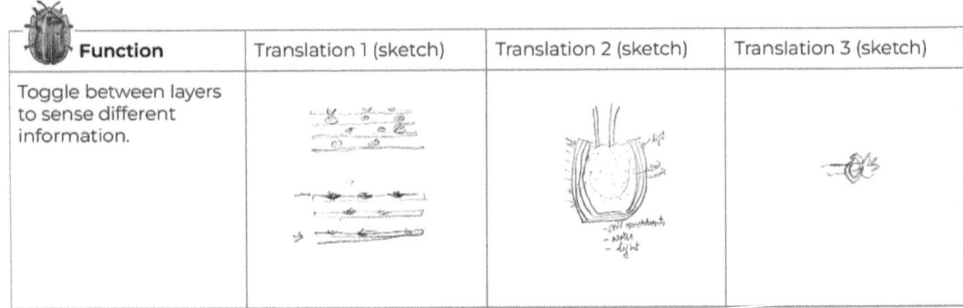

Fig. 7. Example of Function Worksheet: Abstraction and Translations

Participants individually tackled two questions, and the answers were shared and discussed within the group.

1. **How might we incorporate nature into HCI?**
2. Participants brainstormed design solutions for incorporating biomimicry principles, aligning with the biomimicry taxonomy [4] group Process Information consisting of functionalities:

   - Navigate
   - Send Signals
   - Process Signals
   - Sense Signals/Environmental Cues

3. **How might biomimicry support sustainable HCI?**
4. Participants explored how biomimicry could promote sustainable practices in HCI, emphasizing the reuse and adaptation principles observed in natural systems.

The outcomes would serve as a foundation for further exploration, prototyping, for academic research and industries on integrating nature's strategies and sustainable design into the domain of human-computer interaction.

4   Results

The results of Researcher Identity Memo offer a glimpse into how the participants perceive biomimicry in relation to HCI, as well as potential ways of implementing biomimicry for HCI in a practical way. Before presenting the outcomes of the thematic inventory, it is important to note that out of a total of 14 researchers, 13 had no prior experience applying biomimicry in previous projects, highlighting both the novelty of the topic within HCI and the openness of participants to explore unfamiliar territory. Inductive coding was performed on the responses, allowing key themes to emerge in a bottom-up way from the data. This approach helped capture both the diversity of ideas and the underlying conceptual patterns that informed participants' thinking about biomimicry as a speculative, ethical, and interdisciplinary design lens.

4.1 Outcome of Workshop 1, Activity 1: Researcher Identity Memo on Biomimicry

The Researcher Identity Memos provided a diverse range of reflections on biomimicry in the context of Human-Computer Interaction (HCI). Using a deductive approach, these insights were categorized into nine key themes, presented here in alphabetical order:

Applicability: Questions arose about when and how biomimicry is appropriate in design, its practical feasibility, and whether it is taken seriously as a scientific approach rather than a novelty. Participants wondered: "When is biomimicry considered rigorous research versus a hobby?".

Ecosystems: Some participants explored biomimicry beyond individual organisms, asking how entire ecosystems could inform sustainable HCI solutions. "To save our planet, we must become part of it, saving ourselves is not separate from saving the planet."

Evolution: Many emphasized biomimicry's foundation in evolution, noting that nature's designs have been tested over millennia. Some reflected on abstract evolutionary principles, such as "spirals as a fundamental abstraction at higher levels."

Feeling & Inspiration: Participants expressed excitement and curiosity, describing biomimicry as "thought-provoking" and a source of "new inspiration." Others highlighted its aesthetic appeal, asking if beauty itself could be a guiding design principle.

Human and Nature: A recurring theme was the blurred boundary between humans and nature. Some questioned whether humans themselves could be mimicked, while others explored biomimicry as a way to reconnect with natural systems. "Mind = body = environment. The means is the ends."

Specific Ideas from Nature: Participants brainstormed tangible biomimetic concepts, including colour-changing tattoos, hive intelligence, and airport layouts inspired by biological organization.

Sustainability & Conservation: Some responses focused on biomimicry's potential to support ecological balance, while others warned of risks, such as exploitation. "So much potential vs. exploitation—when is it truly beneficial?".

Working with Nature: Many framed biomimicry as a collaboration with nature rather than mere imitation. This included questions about nonhuman agency and interaction: "How does nature communicate, and can this improve human pedagogy?

A key insight was the participants shared lack of prior experience with biomimicry, underscoring the novelty of this approach within the field. Despite this unfamiliarity, the method sparked genuine interest, particularly for its interdisciplinary potential offering an innovation space where biology and interaction design could intersect. At the same time, the enthusiasm was tempered by thoughtful questions around ethics, feasibility, and the risk of superficial or inappropriate applications. These reflections highlight the importance of building frameworks that not only support the creative potential of biomimicry but also ensure its responsible and context-sensitive use.

4.2   Outcome of Workshop 1, Activity 2: Moving from Screens to Scenes Using Biomimicry.

The outcome of this activity was an engaging and analogical-thinking provoking experience within the biomimicry process. After a short time (30 min.) of creative exploration, the participants experienced the potential for applying natural systems to develop new ways of interacting in public space. Using the shape changes in nature as a starting point, participants discussed new possibilities for existing screen interactions, such as smart clothes, time sensitive materials, colour as information, tree and clouds communication, changing of shared objects (e.g., balls), and shape memory. It was inspiring to witness how, through the lens of biomimicry, participants were able to create and discuss alternative possibilities for existing screen interactions. This activity was a success in the sense that participants expanded possibilities for advancing and innovating technologies and the ways people interact with it using nature as inspiration.

4.3   Outcome of Workshop 1, Activity 3: How Biomimicry for HCI?

During the Round Robin/Brainwriting activity, participants generated a wide range of ideas exploring how biomimicry could inform Human-Computer Interaction. The responses revealed imaginative and critical engagements with natural systems as inspiration for new technological solutions. Through inductive analysis, five overarching research themes emerged, in alphabetic order:

Alternative Solutions: Participants envisioned non-conventional HCI designs inspired by natural behaviors or phenomena. Examples included nature-responsive clothing, intuitive classroom feedback systems, and brain-computer interfaces replacing traditional input devices. These concepts aimed to create more seamless, sensory-rich interactions.

Ethical Issues: Several contributions highlighted the ethical complexities of bio-inspired design, such as privacy concerns in health monitoring, the risk of misinformation in assistive technologies (e.g., for people who are blind), and the emotional implications of human-like lifecycle (e.g., birth, youth, old age, death) design in machines. Participants stressed the importance of considering unintended consequences.

Improvement of Existing Solutions: Ideas under this theme sought to refine current systems by learning from nature. This included intuitive information delivery (e.g., beyond email), enhancing human-machine collaboration, or using biomimicry in education to improve programming exercises and in public transport.

Nature as Partner: Proposals involved incorporating natural feedback systems (e.g., trees or ants informing environmental or transport apps), integrating biomimicry in games, and exploring e-health and wellbeing applications. These ideas promoted mutual benefit and sensitivity to ecological rhythms.

Symbioses Between Human and Machine: Participants explored designs where humans and machines work in a mutually supportive relationship, such as devices powered by the human body or interfaces that adapt to environmental conditions. This theme underscored a shift toward more integrated, reciprocal systems.

Although almost none of the participants had prior experience applying biomimicry in HCI, their contributions reveal that they did not treat biomimicry as a ready-made toolkit but as a speculative and exploratory space that invites critical reflection. Their ideas highlighted tensions between innovation and responsibility, the possibilities of alternative futures, and the practical challenges of implementation. The discussion also surfaced the need for new interdisciplinary collaborations, as well as educational strategies to support the integration of biomimicry into HCI research and practice.

4.4   Outcome of Workshop 2, Activity 1: Designing a Beetle Interface

Participants began to rethink static interface elements, shifting toward dynamic, responsive systems that adapt to environmental or user inputs, taking inspiration from the beetle's multilayer structure. The strategy of toggling between data layers, prompted by the workshop task, sparked ideas for interface designs in which users could seamlessly transition between complex data views without losing contextual relevance.

In total, 11 distinct ideas were generated during this activity, each exploring how information could emerge or shift in response to environmental triggers or user actions, such as changes in temperature, humidity, or touch. Many of these concepts were inspired by the beetle's structural coloration and responsive surface properties. Inspired by the beetle's multilayer structure, participants envisioned systems that allow users to "toggle" between data or interface states by manipulating virtual or physical layers. While this activity enabled exploration of a specific biological strategy, it may have limited the diversity of conceptual directions.

4.5   Outcome of Workshop 2, Activity 2: Brainstorm on HCI and Nature

As part of this activity participants were asked to brainstorm and discuss how nature could be integrated into Human-Computer Interaction towards sustainable solutions and approaches. The outcome of this activity generated a wide array of ideas, focusing on the application of natural principles to enhance HCI. These ideas spanned various aspects of design, from learning through forest ecosystems and evolutionary processes to sensory integration and sustainability practices:

- Learning Through Forest Ecosystems: Exploring how trees teach and support young saplings to translate intergenerational knowledge sharing in HCI.
- Evolutionary Processes in Nature: Investigating nature's adaptive evolution to design resilient interfaces.
- HCI Community and User Understanding: Examining how natural principles could enhance user understanding within the HCI community.
- Nature's Approach to Sustainability: Looking at natural cycles as a model for sustainable HCI practices.
- Sensory Integration in Interfaces: Incorporating multi-sensory cues in HCI, inspired by how organisms use all five senses.
- Nature's Warning Signals: Adapting natural warning systems to develop more effective alerts and notifications.
- Enhancing Existing Systems: Leveraging nature's ability to enhance current resources to improve existing HCI systems.

These ideas collectively show how nature's principles can offer valuable insights for designing HCI systems that are more adaptive, sustainable, and nature-centered, reinforcing the importance of biomimicry in future HCI practices. In the next section the synthesized insights from the workshops are presented.

5 Discussion

As a result of the workshops, participants gained a first glance of how biomimicry can be used to explore how nature can be seen as a source of inspiration for interaction design. Additionally, they learned to use biomimicry to transition from screens to scenes approaches to create future scenarios based on nature's principle of shape change. This allows them to further explore the idea of working with nature, directly (i.e., as a partner or design time) or indirectly, to create solutions that could be beneficial to both humans and the nonhuman environment.

Reflection at the end of each workshop revealed that translating nature's principles into human-centered solutions relies heavily on analogical reasoning as a foundational cognitive process. Participants found abstraction and translation challenging but acknowledged that focusing on structural relationships helped bridge biological systems and technological applications. However, applying this approach also ensures the integrity and accuracy of biomimetic design, underlining the importance of analogical thinking in unlocking the full potential of nature-inspired strategies for developing adaptive solutions across knowledge domains.

The findings suggest that biomimicry complements and extends current HCI approaches by offering a structured but flexible method to engage with biological principles. While bio-design, speculative design, and more-than-human perspectives advocate similar values, biomimicry offers a repeatable process for analogical transfer from biology to technology. This discloses pathways for practice-based inquiry, material prototyping, and regenerative interaction design that remain grounded in empirical biological insight.

However, challenges remain. The process of analogical reasoning is cognitively demanding and can be prone to misinterpretation or oversimplification of biological models. In addition, current design workflows are often not structured to accommodate long-term engagement with ecological systems or to involve biological experts in early ideation phases. Overcoming these hurdles will require changes in design education, interdisciplinary collaboration models, and funding structures that recognize the value of nature-inclusive innovation.

Although biomimicry presents promising pathways for reimagining interaction design, participants identified several critical challenges such as:

- Balancing inspiration with practicality.
- Avoiding the idealization of nature's solutions.
- Navigating ethical implications, such as unintended consequences of bio-inspired designs.

To address these complexities, the integration of biomimicry into HCI must go beyond treating nature as a repository of solutions—it must recognize natural nonhuman entities as co-creators in the design process. This shift entails cultivating a mindset that values nonhuman perspectives and ecological systems as equal participants in shaping interaction paradigms. To move toward this paradigm, design processes must involve practices that account for nonhuman needs, roles, and impacts by engaging ecological expertise, long-term observation, and methods for embedding reciprocity. It calls for rethinking fundamental design principles, fostering inter- and transdisciplinary collaboration, and developing new tools and frameworks to move beyond anthropocentric models.

Early engagement with stakeholders, ranging from local communities to policy makers and industry, can help define ethical boundaries, practical constraints, and long-term visions. Designers, engineers, ecologists, philosophers, and ethicists must work alongside one another, with input from all types of knowledge (e.g., experiences, observations, photographs, sketches, stories and songs passed on from generations, raw data, insights) in biomimicry. Such distributed collaboration ensures that both the functional and ecological implications of biomimetic design are taken into account from the outset.

Another challenge in translating nature-inspired concepts into scalable, user-friendly interaction design often involves technical and financial constraints. Researchers and designers must find ways to implement these concepts without sacrificing accessibility or affordability to avoid mismatches in expectations and outcomes. This is particularly important given that nature operates on scales (e.g., time, space, system) that require long-term organizations and commitment.

As such, the decision to adopt biomimicry as a method should be carefully considered within inclusive, cross-sector collaborations between academia, industry, and other relevant actors. The value of biomimicry lies in its potential to inform the broad field of human technology interactions toward solutions that support both functionality and nature's principles, mirroring the interconnectedness of ecosystems. Collaborative efforts between academia and industry can strengthen nature-centered approaches' impact, and vice versa, towards intuitive, sustainable, and regenerative innovations in interaction design.

6 Conclusion

The insights derived from the workshops at Uppsala University demonstrate that biomimicry not only supports the transition from screen-based to immersive scene-based interaction paradigms but also supports an understanding of the parallels between biological and technological systems. The outcome of Activity 2 of the first workshop, "Moving from Screens to Scenes Using Biomimicry", demonstrated the potential of natural systems as a source to envision alternative, nature-inspired interactions that challenge traditional screen-based technologies. The participants were challenged to create ideas beyond predictable and known interfaces and interactions. The diverse ideas generated illustrate that nature inspires for generative solutions for human technology interaction. This activity not only expanded the participants' understanding of biomimicry but also gave insights on how nature can inform the development of more intuitive, responsive technologies in public spaces.

Workshop 2, Activity 1, further emphasized biomimicry's practical value. Participants reimagined interface design through the lens of the beetle's adaptive, multilayered structure. The exploration of dynamic, responsive systems such as environmental sensors and colour-changing interfaces, demonstrated the value of incorporating nature's strategies into HCI. Through scenario-based exploration and structured phases in the biomimicry process, they identified actionable pathways for integrating adaptive and sustainable interfaces for interaction design. Moreover, the iterative and scenario-driven approach supported them to recognize the potential of analogical thinking for knowledge transfer across disciplines. By the end of both workshops, participants also gained practical tools for applying biomimetic strategies to complex challenges.

6.1   Biomimicry as a Transdisciplinary Collaborative Approach

Collaboration between industry and academia is critical in generating innovation [15]) as such partnerships ensure that academic research remains relevant to practical applications. Biomimicry exemplifies this synergy by integrating diverse disciplines—biology, technology, computer science, ecology, and design—to address complex design challenges. The findings from the workshops underscore biomimicry's capacity to bridge theoretical biological knowledge with practical applications, providing a valuable framework for designing solutions that advocates for a shift that aligns human technologies with natural systems.

The workshops also underscored the potential for biomimicry to dissolve traditional disciplinary silos, encouraging inter- and transdisciplinary problem-solving. By engaging nature as a partner, biomimicry enables the development of alternative interactions grounded in the symbiosis between humans, nature, and technology. The outcomes of the workshops emphasize the transdisciplinary nature of biomimicry. The integration of ecological, philosophical and technological dimensions that support shared relational structures between disciplines is essential for effective collaboration between academia and industries.

With the main author's expertise from an industry perspective, the workshops bridged the gap between academic exploration and practical application, illustrating how biomimicry can seamlessly integrate into professional design processes. This collaboration offers actionable insights for industry practitioners, demonstrating how sustainable, nature-inspired methodologies can be applied to innovate within existing design workflows.

Furthermore, the method of biomimicry has demonstrated its potential for broader application in a range of industries, including architecture, product design, systems engineering, and even organizational development. Hence, its emphasis on systems thinking, contextual awareness, and multi-species relationships aligns well with current industry needs for sustainable, regenerative, and adaptive innovation (co-) creating long-term visions.

6.2   Applications and Future Directions

The Researcher Identity Memos have revealed nine key themes Applicability, Ecosystems, Evolution, Feeling, Human and Nature, Idea from nature, Inspiration, Sustainability - Conservation, and Working with Nature, research and industries should focus on deepening the integration of these themes to encapsulate the multifaceted relationship between biomimicry and its application in the domain of HCI. These nine key themes were enhanced by the identification of five core research concepts on biomimicry for HCI: Alternative Solutions, Ethical Issues, Improvement of Existing Solutions, Nature as Partner, and Symbiosis between Human and Machine. These research concepts reflect the diverse ways in which biomimicry can inspire innovative approaches to HCI, from ethical considerations to new design possibilities.

The outcome of Workshop 2, Activity 2, generated a wide array of ideas for incorporating nature into HCI. These ideas spanned various aspects of design, from learning through forest ecosystems and evolutionary processes to sensory integration and sustainability practices. Participants explored how nature's adaptive evolution, intergenerational knowledge sharing, and multi-sensory cues could inspire more resilient, intuitive, and sustainable interfaces. The potential to apply nature's warning systems and enhance existing technologies was also recognized as a key avenue for improving user interactions. These ideas collectively highlight how nature's principles can offer valuable insights for designing HCI systems that are more adaptive, and nature centered. The workshops highlighted several viable and relevant applications of biomimicry in HCI:

- **Caregiving and E-Health**: Nature-inspired interfaces for patient monitoring and wellbeing.
- **Education**: Using biomimicry to design immersive learning environments.
- **Public Spaces**: Shape-changing installations for enhancing community interactions.

Future research could refine biomimicry methodologies for HCI, promote inter- and transdisciplinary collaboration with practical processes for industries, and address ethical considerations for sustainable and regenerative innovations.

Moreover, future collaborations between academia and industry could explore structured frameworks to guide the biomimicry process and expand dialogue across disciplines by bringing together HCI researchers, design theorists, biologists, ecologists, and industry practitioners. While the content of the workshops was primarily inspired by natural forms and processes, they did not demonstrate ecological responsibility. This raises the important question: how can we assess whether a system is truly ecologically responsible, within the biomimetic approach? Ecological responsibility requires criteria such as lifecycle impact, resource use, long-term effects on ecosystems, and engagement with sustainability metrics which were not addressed during the workshops. By embedding these considerations into human-technology interaction practices, designers could work toward systems that are not only user-centered but also aligned with ecological systems, setting a grounded precedent for sustainable and regenerative innovation in interaction design.

Acknowledgments. We are most grateful for the invitation to host the two workshops 'Biomimicry for HCI' at the Human Technology Organisations Research Group at Uppsala University in 2023 and 2024. Many thanks to all the participants for an open attitude and the many ideas they shared. Finally, special thanks for the 'Visiting Researchers to promote equal opportunities' funding from the host department of Information Technology initiated by Prof. Åsa Cajander as Visiting Sponsor.

Disclosure of Interests. The authors have no competing interests to declare relevant to this article's content.

References

1. Ahmed-Kristensen, S., Christensen, B.T., Lenau, T., et al.: Naturally original: Stimulating creative design through biological analogies and random images. In: DS 77: Proceedings of the DESIGN 2014 13th International Design Conference, pp. 427–436 (2014)
2. Badarnah, L., Kadri, U.: A methodology for the generation of biomimetic design concepts. Archit. Sci. Rev. **58**(2), 120–133 (2015). https://doi.org/10.1080/00038628.2014.922458
3. Benyus, J.M., et al.: Biomimicry: Innovation inspired by nature (1997)
4. The Biomimicry Global Design Challenge Toolbox Homepage. http://toolbox.biomimicr y.org. Accessed 26 Jan 2025
5. Du Plessis, C.: Towards a regenerative paradigm for the built environment. Build. Res. Inform. **40**(1), 7–22 (2012). https://doi.org/10.1080/09613218.2012.628548
6. Fallman, D.: The interaction design research triangle of design practice, design studies, and design exploration. Des. Issues **24**(3), 4–18 (2008)
7. Fayemi, P.E., Wanieck, K., Zollfrank, C., Maranzana, N., Aoussat, A.: Biomimetics: process, tools and practice. Bioinspir. Biomim. **12**(1), 011002 (2017). https://doi.org/10.1088/1748-3190/12/1/011002
8. Gentner, D.: Bootstrapping the mind: analogical processes and symbol systems. Cogn. Sci. **34**(5), 752–775 (2010). https://doi.org/10.1111/j.1551-6709.2010.01114.x
9. Gibbons, L.V.: Regenerative—the new sustainable? Sustainability **12**(13), 5483 (2020). https://doi.org/10.3390/su12135483
10. Holyoak, K.J.: Analogy and relational reasoning. The Oxford handbook of thinking and reasoning, pp. 234–259 (2012)
11. Huang, M., Zhang, Z.: Research on multi-modal scene design under the development of digital ecological culture industry. Int. J. Educ. Hum. **9**(1), 220–225 (2023)
12. Nagel, J.K., Pidaparti, R.M.: Significance, prevalence and implications for bio-inspired design courses in the undergraduate engineering curriculum. In: International Design Engineering Technical Conferences and Computers and Information in Engineering Conference. vol. 50138, p. V003T04A009. American Society of Mechanical Engineers (2016) https://doi.org/10.1115/DETC2016-59661
13. Qamar, I.P., Stawarz, K., Robinson, S., Goguey, A., Coutrix, C., Roudaut, A.: Morphino: a nature-inspired tool for the design of shape-changing interfaces. In: Proceedings of the 2020 ACM Designing Interactive Systems Conference, pp. 1943–1958 (2020) https://doi.org/10.1145/3357236.339545
14. Rowland, R.: Biomimicry step-by-step. Bioinspired, Biomimetic Nanobiomater. **6**(2), 102–112 (2017). https://doi.org/10.1680/jbibn.16.00019
15. Sjöö, K., Hellström, T.: University–industry collaboration: a literature review and synthesis. Ind. High. Educ. **33**(4), 275–285 (2019). https://doi.org/10.1177/0950422219829
16. Speck, O., Speck, T.: An overview of bioinspired and biomimetic self-repairing materials. Biomimetics **4**(1), 26 (2019). https://doi.org/10.3390/biomimetics4010026
17. Stevens, L., Kopnina, H., Mulder, K., De Vries, M.: Biomimicry design thinking education: a base-line exercise in preconceptions of biological analogies. Int. J. Technol. Des. Educ. **31**, 797–814 (2021). https://doi.org/10.1007/s10798-020-09574-1
18. Turner, J.S., Soar, R.C.: Beyond biomimicry: what termites can tell us about realizing the living building. In: First International Conference on Industrialized, Intelligent Construction at Loughborough University, pp. 1–18 (2008)
19. Vendetti, M.S., Matlen, B.J., Richland, L.E., Bunge, S.A.: Analogical reasoning in the classroom: Insights from cognitive science. Mind Brain Educ. **9**(2), 100–106 (2015). https://doi.org/10.1111/mbe.12080

20. Veselova, E., Gaziulusoy, İ: Bioinclusive collaborative and participatory design: a conceptual framework and a research agenda. Des. Cult. **14**(2), 149–183 (2022). https://doi.org/10.1080/17547075.2021.2019455
21. Vincent, J.F., Bogatyreva, O.A., Bogatyrev, N.R., Bowyer, A., Pahl, A.K.: Biomimetics: its practice and theory. J. R. Soc. Interface **3**(9), 471–482 (2006). https://doi.org/10.1098/rsif.2006.0127

Collaboration in Action: A Multi-grounded Analysis of Academia-Industry Partnerships in Interaction Design

Jonathan Källbäcker[1][(✉)] [iD], Åsa Cajander[1] [iD], and Catharina van den Driesche[2] [iD]

[1] Department of Information Technology, Uppsala University, Uppsala, Sweden
`jonathan.kallbacker@it.uu.se`
[2] University of Amsterdam, Amsterdam, Netherlands

Abstract. Academia-industry collaborations are vital for tackling complex, real-world challenges in Interaction Design. This paper explores the collaborative process of a project focused on integrating digital tools and automation in the aviation industry. Using the Multi-Grounded Action Research (MGAR) framework, we analyse how theoretical, empirical, and practical dimensions informed and shaped the collaboration. Emphasising the process over specific research outcomes, the paper provides insights into stakeholder engagement, iterative decision-making, and integrating diverse knowledge sources. The findings reveal that while socio-technical systems theory and participatory design principles guided the collaboration, practical implementation often required navigating competing priorities and addressing usability issues. Empirical data from aviation workers and managers highlighted the benefits of digital tools, such as reduced cognitive load and ergonomic improvements and their limitations, including increased technostress and operational inefficiencies. The study also explores how the fixed project plan occasionally conflicted with the iterative demands of action research and Interaction Design. The paper concludes with lessons for fostering impactful academia-industry collaborations, emphasising the importance of flexibility, stakeholder alignment, a shared language between collaborators, and actionable research outcomes. These insights contribute to bridging the gap between academic research and industry practice, offering a model for future projects seeking to advance Interaction Design through collaborative methodologies.

Keywords: Interaction Design · Multi-Grounded Action Research · Academia-Industry Collaboration · Human-Centered Design · Socio-Technical Systems

1 Introduction

Interaction Design is at the intersection of technological innovation and human behaviour, making it increasingly vital to address real-world challenges through collaborative efforts between academia and industry. Designing functional, usable, and inclusive systems becomes paramount as automation and digital tools transform workplaces. While these transitions offer opportunities for efficiency and innovation, they

© The Author(s), under exclusive license to Springer Nature Switzerland AG 2026
J. Abdelnour-Nocera et al. (Eds.): ARPPID 2025, CCIS 2797, pp. 48–68, 2026.
https://doi.org/10.1007/978-3-032-15516-0_4

also pose significant challenges, including technostress [1, 2], usability issues, and work environment problems [3].

The TARA project exemplifies this intersection by focusing on the aviation industry's ground personnel. In a sector grappling with economic challenges and operational pressures [4], TARA investigates how new technologies—from autonomous vehicles to digital scanning devices—impact worker health, efficiency, and ergonomics. The project aims to increase knowledge about the implementation and effects of these technologies on workplace conditions and to identify ways to mitigate potential risks, such as technostress and repetitive strain injuries, while supporting sustainable practices in the industry.

This paper delves into the collaborative dynamics of the TARA project, analysing how academia and industry partnered to navigate the complexities of introducing new technologies in the workplace. Using the Multi-Grounded Action Research (MGAR) [5–7] framework as an analytical lens, the paper focuses on the collaborative process rather than the specific outcomes of the research studies. It examines how theoretical, empirical, and practical insights were integrated to ensure the partnership's success. MGAR is well-suited to addressing Interaction Design's iterative and participatory demands in collaborations between academia and industry.

The paper contributes to the ongoing discourse on academia-industry collaboration by:

- Analysing the TARA project's collaborative process through the MGAR framework.
- Highlighting strategies for effective stakeholder involvement, iterative decision-making, and knowledge integration.
- Offering insights and recommendations for structuring future collaborations in Interaction Design.

The paper begins with a background section contextualising Interaction Design and introducing the TARA project. The methodology section outlines the application of MGAR to analyse the collaboration process. This is followed by the results section, which discusses theoretical, empirical, and practical grounding findings. The discussion reflects on lessons learned and their broader implications for academia-industry partnerships, while the conclusion summarises the key insights and suggests directions for future research.

2 Background

2.1 Collaboration in Interaction Design

Interaction Design focuses on designing intuitive and meaningful interactions between people and technology, particularly in contexts where usability and user experience are critical [8]. In recent years, integrating digital tools and automation into complex workplace environments has amplified the need for effective academia-industry collaborations. These partnerships leverage academic expertise in Interaction Design theories and socio-technical systems alongside industry practitioners' practical knowledge, fostering innovative and human-centred solutions.

Collaboration between academia and industry in Interaction Design is increasingly recognised as vital for translating research into innovative products and services. According to Sjöö and Hellström [9], university-industry partnerships are essential for creating and applying new knowledge, relying on trust, shared incentives, and effective knowledge transfer processes. This shift aligns with a broader emphasis on academic entrepreneurship and the university's "third mission" to drive societal and economic progress. Research shows that frequent communication between industry professionals and academics improves knowledge transfer, with personal relationships often more impactful than formal mechanisms such as technology transfer offices [9]. While research excellence is less critical when forming partnerships, it nonetheless impacts the quality of the collaborative outcomes, underlining the importance of aligned goals and robust networks in facilitating impactful collaborations between academia and industry in interaction design [9].

Wohlin et al. [10] highlight the importance of long-term commitment, clearly defined objectives, and equitable power relationships for successful academia-industry collaborations. Their analysis reveals that the industry prioritises the company's management and the researcher's dedication to providing concrete support, while academia emphasises the collaborators, including the key champion within the company. The top two success factors for industry-academia collaboration are company management support and an on-site collaboration champion. These findings suggest that the industry's active commitment is crucial for successful partnerships, with the primary benefit often realised at the organisational level. Conversely, academia tends to focus on individual researchers or students gaining value, and short-term outcomes for universities are less critical. This underscores that industry seeks measurable organisational benefits, whereas academic value is often more personal or project-specific.

However, the success of such collaborations often hinges on overcoming significant challenges. One common difficulty is aligning goals: while academia may prioritise theory-building and long-term research, industry partners are often driven by immediate, practical outcomes. Communication gaps between stakeholders from diverse professional and cultural backgrounds can impede collaboration [11]. For example, researchers, engineers, and end-users may interpret priorities, constraints, and outcomes differently, complicating the design process. Finally, ensuring that theoretical insights translate into practical applicability requires iterative methods incorporating stakeholder feedback and maintaining flexibility as new challenges emerge.

Despite these challenges, collaboration in Interaction Design offers immense potential for effectively addressing real-world needs. By drawing on academic and industry perspectives, these partnerships can lead to functional and usable systems and processes, improving usability, efficiency, and overall user satisfaction. With insights from these types of collaboration, the TARA project aims to improve the work environment of the ground handling staff at airports. The insights from collaborations in interaction design are also central for understanding the management of interdisciplinary integration and the establishment of knowledge commons in collaborative projects, which is a focus of this specific paper.

Furthermore, with a lack of perspectives from ground handling staff as end users when new technology is introduced [12], gaining insights in how to develop the collaboration between academia and industry to integrate interaction design perspectives becomes especially important.

2.2   Extending Collaboration in Interaction Design with Knowledge Commons

In the context of collaboration in interaction design, establishing 'knowledge commons' is essential for leveraging diverse forms of knowledge: practical, theoretical, and experiential [13]. Knowledge commons refers to a shared pool of resources—theoretical frameworks, personal experiences, and collected insights—that participants collaboratively build, maintain, and utilise [14]. By critically analysing and synthesising shared knowledge contributions, participants can achieve a nuanced understanding of the problem domain and harness their collective expertise [15]. Knowledge Commons also offers a mechanism to align the goals of academia, industry, and end-users, ensuring that both immediate and long-term objectives are addressed through co-creation methodologies.

However, achieving an integration of knowledge commons for collaboration in interaction design is inherently challenging. Therefore, not only the design or research methodologies must align with interaction design collaboration, but also the architecture of the research process itself. This architecture should actively support collaborative partnerships for the concept of 'knowledge commons' to emerge within the collaboration process [16].

In conclusion, addressing complex and multi-layered challenges for interaction design collaboration requires an accessible and deliberative approach that actively co-creates the collaborative process. Hence, according to this theory, the collaboration process must be intentionally designed, consistently monitored and co-created to redefine all participants' relationships, roles, and goals.

2.3   The TARA Project

The TARA project exemplifies a collaborative effort between academia and industry, aiming to explore the impact of new technologies on the workplace conditions of aviation ground personnel. The project emerged in response to the aviation industry's critical challenges, including labour shortages, increased automation, and sustainable operational practices [4, 17]. With a focus on roles such as baggage handlers, aircraft technicians, and refuelling staff, TARA investigates how technologies like digital scanning devices and autonomous vehicles influence workers' health, ergonomics, and overall efficiency.

The collaboration involves researchers from Uppsala University and the Transportfackens Yrkes- och Arbetsmiljönämnd (TYA), a Swedish organisation focused on workplace safety and competence development in the transport sector. This partnership leverages the strengths of academia and industry: academic expertise in socio-technical systems and Interaction Design and industry insights into the practical realities and challenges of implementing workplace technologies.

Moreover, the TARA project involved diverse stakeholders to ensure the collaboration was inclusive and addressed multiple perspectives. A reference group comprising representatives from unions, employers, managers, and end-users was established to provide strategic input and ensure the project's relevance to all parties. Additionally, the project team included members from TYA, the union Transportarbetarförbundet, and the organisation Transportarbetaren, alongside senior and junior researchers. This multidisciplinary composition enabled the project to integrate academic insights with practical expertise.

The TARA project aims to address knowledge gaps surrounding technology-induced challenges, such as technostress [1, 2] and repetitive strain injuries, through participatory methods, such as contextual inquiries, interviews, and workshops [18]. The project aligns with interaction design principles by focusing on these issues, emphasising user-centred approaches and the interplay between humans and technology in real-world settings. Ultimately, TARA improves workplace design while providing actionable insights for the aviation industry (Fig. 1).

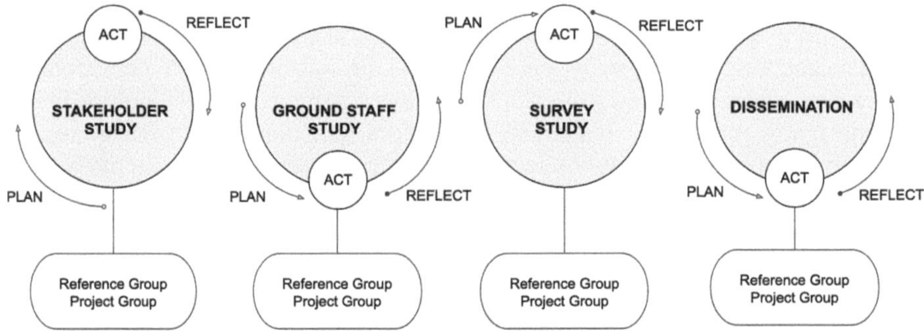

Fig. 1. An Overview of the project's milestones.

2.4 Multi-grounded Theory and Multi-grounded Action Research

Multi-Grounded Theory (MGT) offers a methodological framework for developing theories grounded in empirical data, aligned with existing theoretical constructs, and applicable to practical contexts. Proposed by Goldkuhl and Cronholm [6, 7], MGT expands upon traditional Grounded Theory by incorporating three complementary dimensions of grounding:

- Empirical Grounding: Ensures the theory is supported by data collected from observed phenomena.
- Theoretical Grounding: Aligns the theory with established frameworks and prior research.
- Practical Grounding: Emphasizes the applicability and usefulness of the theory for real-world challenges.

This iterative process involves data collection, analysis, and validation cycles to refine theoretical constructs and enhance their relevance and coherence.

Multi-Grounded Action Research (MGAR) [5] extends the principles of MGT into the action research domain [19]. MGAR combines the structured grounding dimensions of MGT with the iterative and participatory characteristics of action research. It emphasises co-creation with stakeholders to ensure that interventions and outcomes are theoretically informed, empirically validated, and practically relevant. The approach balances theoretical insights, empirical findings, and practical applications, fostering a dynamic and adaptive process for addressing complex, real-world issues.

In a systematic review, Oberschmidt et al. [20] synthesised best practices and lessons learned from 40 AR projects in eHealth design and implementation. These findings underscore AR's versatility and effectiveness, providing insights that extend beyond the eHealth domain. Key practices include fostering stakeholder collaboration through transparent communication, building stakeholder confidence and skills, and embedding flexibility into project processes through ongoing evaluation and adaptation. The review also highlighted the value of employing diverse methods—such as personas and journey mapping—and disseminating findings in accessible formats to maximise impact and applicability.

These practices are transferable to other AR settings, including education, community development, and organisational change. The collaborative and cyclical nature of AR lends itself to addressing complex, multi-stakeholder challenges across diverse contexts. The emphasis on iterative adaptation and stakeholder empowerment ensures relevance and sustainability, regardless of the specific application domain. In the TARA project, the MGAR framework provided a structured approach for analysing and guiding our academia-industry collaboration (Fig. 2).

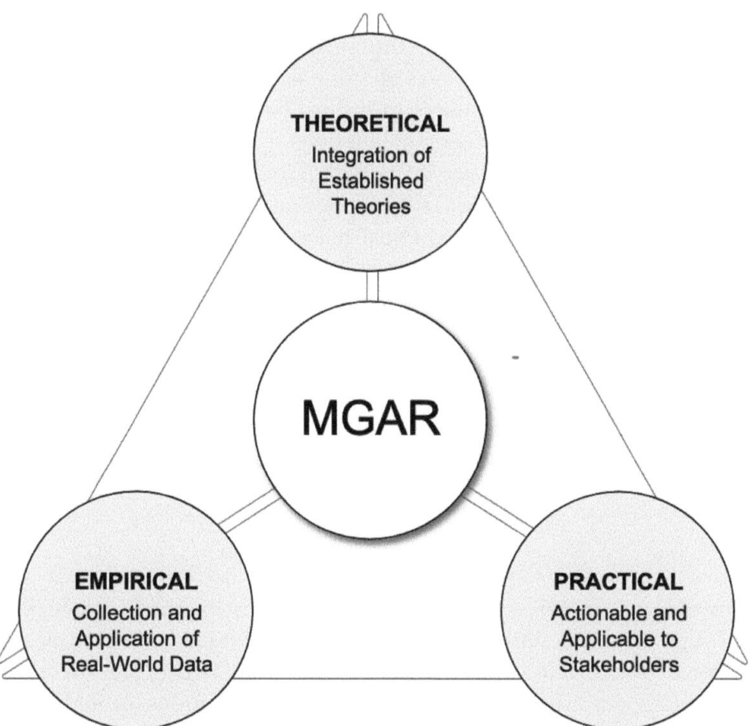

Fig. 2. The Multi-Grounded Action Research (MGAR) framework is adapted from [6, 7].

3 Methodology

This study focuses on analysing the collaborative process of the TARA project using the Multi-Grounded Action Research (MGAR) framework [5–7]. The primary aim is not to evaluate the research results but to understand how the collaboration was structured, iterated, and grounded in three key dimensions: theoretical, empirical, and practical contexts. By examining the interplay of these dimensions, this study seeks to uncover actionable insights into the dynamics of academia-industry partnerships.

The Multi-Grounded Action Research (MGAR) framework offers an iterative approach to studying and refining collaborative processes. Central to MGAR are three interconnected forms of grounding: theoretical, empirical, and practical. This triad ensures that collaboration processes are systematically informed, validated, and adjusted to meet diverse stakeholder needs.

Theoretical Grounding: MGAR integrates established theories—such as sociotechnical systems, participatory design, and Interaction Design principles—into the collaborative process. These theories provide a foundation for understanding and guiding stakeholder interactions, technology integration, and user-centred practices.

Empirical Grounding: The framework emphasises the collection and application of real-world data, such as interviews, field studies, and observations. This data shapes the collaborative process, offering insights into stakeholders' lived experiences and validating the relevance of theoretical assumptions.

Practical Grounding: MGAR ensures the collaboration's outcomes are actionable and applicable to stakeholders. This involves aligning the project's results with the practical needs of industry partners and end-users, ensuring that theoretical and empirical insights translate into meaningful, usable recommendations.

In the TARA project, MGAR served as both a reflective lens and a methodological guide for enhancing the collaboration. It facilitated an iterative process where theoretical constructs, empirical findings, and practical relevance were continuously aligned and refined.

Preliminary findings were presented and discussed with representatives from TYA and participating researchers. This step ensured the accuracy of interpretations and the alignment of results with stakeholder expectations and needs.

Researchers reflected on their roles throughout the process, acknowledging potential biases and documenting their influence on the collaboration. This reflexivity enhanced the credibility of the analysis and ensured that multiple perspectives were considered.

4 Results

Table 1 provides an overview of key project activities mapped to their corresponding MGAR dimensions to illustrate how the multi-grounded action research (MGAR) framework guided the TARA project. This structure highlights the interplay between theoretical insights, empirical findings, and practical applications throughout the project lifecycle (see Fig. 3 for visual representation).

Table 1. An overview of how the Multi-Grounded Action Research (MGAR) framework was applied in the TARA project.

Grounding Dimension	Description	Examples from the TARA Project
Theoretical Grounding	Integration of established theories to inform and guide the collaborative process	Applied socio-technical systems theory to explore human-technology interactions; used participatory design principles to structure stakeholder involvement
Empirical Grounding	Collection and validation of real-world data to shape and adjust the research	Conducted field studies, interviews, and observations to understand challenges like technostress and usability issues in aviation workplaces
Practical Grounding	Alignment of findings with the needs and priorities of stakeholders to ensure actionable outcomes	Engaged with unions and employers to validate insights; planned the development of brochures, training materials, and implementation studies for workplace solutions

4.1 Theoretical Grounding

The TARA project's collaborative process was guided by established theories that provided a foundation for aligning academic and industry perspectives. These theories, including socio-technical systems (STS) [21, 22], participatory design [23], User-Centred Systems Design [24] and Interaction Design principles [8], informed the project's approach to stakeholder involvement, usability considerations, and iterative decision-making. Together, these frameworks ensured the collaboration was theoretically robust and practically relevant. We also had discussions in the project to make these theories a part of knowledge commons.

Theoretical Foundation from Research Expertise. While the TARA project did not include an explicit literature review, it benefited significantly from the project leader's extensive research background in action research and digital work environments [24–27]. This expertise brought a deep understanding of existing theories and frameworks related to workplace design and human-technology interaction. Previous work on improving the digital work environment informed the project's focus on usability, technostress, and the impacts of new technologies.

Socio-Technical Systems Theory. Socio-technical systems theory [21, 22] was central to the TARA project's approach, emphasising the interconnectedness of technical systems and human factors in the workplace. This theory provided a framework for analysing how new technologies—such as hand scanners and autonomous vehicles—affect workers' physical and cognitive environments. By optimising the relationship between humans and technology, STS theory guided discussions on mitigating technostress, reducing repetitive strain injuries, and ensuring that technological interventions improved overall workplace ergonomics.

Participatory Design. Participatory design principles [23] were instrumental in structuring the collaboration, ensuring that diverse stakeholders—from aviation workers to industry representatives—were actively involved in shaping the project's direction. This approach emphasised co-design and inclusivity, enabling stakeholders to contribute their expertise and perspectives throughout the project. The participatory design also guided the design of workshops and feedback loops, creating spaces where stakeholders could reflect on findings, share insights, and refine objectives collaboratively.

Interaction Design Principles. Theories from Interaction Design [8], particularly those focusing on usability and user-centred systems design, informed the project's attention to how technologies are integrated into workers' routines. These principles emphasised the need to design systems that are intuitive, accessible, and aligned with user needs. In the TARA project, this translated into a focus on minimising cognitive load, improving interface usability, and ensuring that technological solutions were adaptable to the diverse contexts of aviation workplaces.

Work Environment. Theories connected to work environment and technology were also a fundamental part of the project [1–3]. These include theories like the technostress and demand resource model, which can identify different stressors and mediators, as well as how technology can be a tool for support or strain in the work environment. These theories were part of how the interview guides were formed to identify the potential issues and advantages associated with the ground handling staff's technology.

4.2 Empirical Grounding

Empirical grounding was critical in the TARA project, ensuring that decisions and strategies were firmly rooted in real-world data. The project gathered extensive insights into aviation ground personnel's experiences, challenges, and needs through field studies, interviews, and surveys.

Stakeholder interviews were conducted to understand the implementation process of new technologies in aviation workplaces. These interviews captured diverse perspectives from ground staff and managers in various positions in airport operations. The interviewed stakeholders included union representatives, airport managers, managers working at technical departments as well as managers responsible for the work environment. The perspectives from these stakeholders provided valuable insights on the integration of technologies such as mobile devices, belt loaders, and vacuum lifters. These studies revealed:

- Diverse Stakeholder Interests: Safety, regulatory compliance, and economic factors emerged as primary drivers in implementing new technologies, often balancing against work environment concerns.
- Role of External Stakeholders: Airlines, regulatory bodies, and suppliers were pivotal in influencing technological choices, often prioritising efficiency and compliance over user-centred design.

- Barriers to Effective Implementation: Misalignment between managerial decisions and ground staff needs underscored challenges in incorporating user perspectives while adopting new systems.

Field observations and interviews were conducted at multiple aviation workplaces to capture the day-to-day interactions between the ground handling workers and new technologies, such as digital scanning devices and autonomous vehicles. These studies examined the existing technologies and the consequences of using them. Technologies included scanner devices, expandable belt loaders for loading and offloading luggage, iPad tablets for planning the loading tasks, and vacuum lifters used during luggage sorting. Physical positives could be identified, such as reducing the need to lift luggage in uncomfortable positions with the belt loaders and supporting lifting with the vacuum lifters. However, with the hand-held scanners, scanning with one hand and lifting the luggage with the other could cause strain. These scanners could also reduce the cognitive load by automatically keeping track of the number of luggage packed, but having multiple devices with separate passwords for planning loading was identified as a negative in terms of cognitive load.

These findings informed the project's focus on usability and worker well-being, prompting adjustments to research priorities and stakeholder engagement strategies. For example, issues related to connectivity were prioritised in discussions with TYA representatives to identify potential technical solutions.

Finally, the reference group played a pivotal role in the empirical grounding of the TARA project and in creating knowledge commons. Comprised of stakeholders from unions, employers, managers, and workers, the group provided critical insights into workplace challenges, validated the relevance of preliminary findings, and contributed to the focus of forthcoming studies. Their contributions ensured that the research remained connected to the realities of aviation workplaces, shaping iterative adjustments to the project's focus and methods.

4.3 Practical Grounding

Practical grounding in the TARA project ensures that the research findings are academically significant, actionable, and relevant to stakeholders. While much of the work has focused on theoretical and empirical grounding, several efforts have been made—and more are planned—to translate the project outcomes into practical benefits. A significant part of the practical grounding is thus to make the most out of the established knowledge commons developed between the stakeholders in the project.

Dissemination. To effectively communicate the project's findings and ensure their practical applicability, a variety of dissemination activities have been undertaken or are in progress:

- Media Engagement: A series of interviews in transportation-focused and work environment magazines has shared the project's key themes with industry professionals, raising awareness about workplace challenges and promoting the practical implications of the research.

- Information Campaigns: A short information campaign has been conducted to communicate early findings to a broader audience, ensuring preliminary results inform ongoing discussions in the aviation sector.
- Stakeholder Presentations: Results have been presented at critical forums such as Transportarbetarförbundet's annual meeting and TYA's industry council ("branschråd"). These presentations have provided opportunities for direct discussions with key stakeholders, enhancing the project's practical relevance.
- Marketing Materials: A concise report and brochure summarising the project's findings and recommendations are being prepared. These materials will be distributed to unions, industry representatives, and aviation workplaces to promote awareness and support implementation efforts.

Collaboration with Industry Partners. The project team works closely with TYA's communications department to design a targeted marketing initiative. This collaboration aims to raise awareness among key stakeholders about workplace challenges such as technostress and repetitive strain injuries, ensuring that actionable insights reach industry decision-makers.

Future Practical Applications. The TARA project has identified several practical goals outlined in its project application. These efforts will further enhance the practical grounding of the research findings:

- Training and Educational Resources: Plans include developing training materials, including micro-lectures, to help workers and managers adapt to new technologies and better address workplace challenges.
- Collaborative Refinement Workshops: Additional workshops with stakeholders will focus on refining and validating recommendations, ensuring that proposed solutions align with the aviation sector's specific needs and constraints.

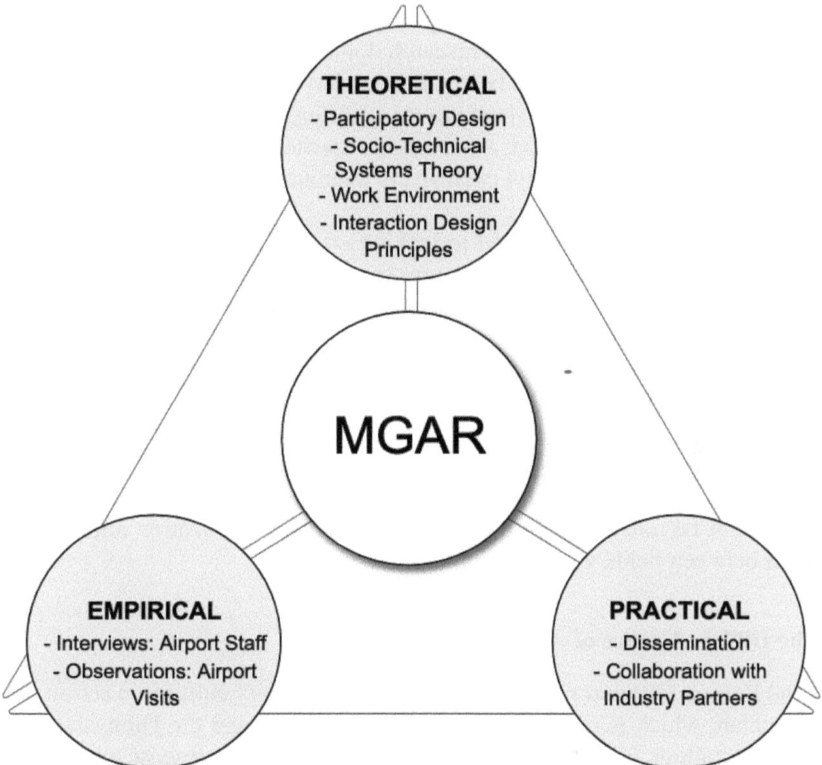

Fig. 3. The MGAR framework adapted to the TARA project.

5 Discussion

5.1 Challenges in Publishing Research Results

A challenge faced in the TARA project was the difficulty in positioning the research findings within a single academic field. The project's interdisciplinary nature—spanning interaction design, workplace ergonomics, and socio-technical systems—meant that the results did not fully align with the established expectations of any specific research domain. While this interdisciplinarity enriched the project's insights, it also created barriers to publishing, as journals in each field often seek highly specialised contributions.

To address this, the findings can be framed for different research communities. The study's focus on technostress and ergonomics contributes to work and occupational health research, while usability and participatory design insights align with human-computer interaction (HCI). Additionally, findings on automation's impact on aviation workers are relevant to aviation and transport research.

However, for a PhD student working within a specific field such as HCI, the broad disciplinary spread of potential publication venues raises strategic questions. While interdisciplinary dissemination increases the research's reach and impact, it may also challenge establishing a clear academic profile and meeting field-specific expectations. This highlights the tension between interdisciplinary relevance and the need for a coherent publication strategy within a defined research domain.

Additional challenges can also be due to boundaries of the field of HCI in relation to the airport context. For example, there are many different types of technologies that can be examined in the airport context. Attempting to write and publish papers that include different relevant technologies, not exclusively computers, can make it more difficult to publish in HCI.

This issue can also be connected to lacking or unfocused research questions. The difficulties in establishing research questions for papers in this project and the project in general may be due to the difficulty of understanding the airport context itself. Because of the vastness of the industry, and the close to unlimited research possibilities of interaction design and work environment, it can be difficult to establish a clear goal. Ultimately this leads to a difficulty of prioritization of the papers' research questions and focus.

The challenges of publishing can also relate to the lack of understanding of other fields, like information systems or work environment studies. This can lead to not knowing what results are interesting in each field, risking generic results for one field, even though it might be interesting in another. Making this prioritization and handling the navigation between fields was also challenging.

5.2   The Diffuse Nature of Action Research

Heron and Reason [19] describe two complementary inquiry cultures in action research: the Apollonian, which is rational, linear, and systematic, and the Dionysian, which is expressive, spiralling, and tacit, with reflection as an improvised sense-making process. The TARA project aligns more with the Dionysian approach due to the complexity of the problems it addressed, evolving through overlapping and iterative data collection cycles, stakeholder engagement, and analysis. However, structured reflections and stakeholder meetings occasionally reflected an Apollonian character, creating a dynamic balance between the two inquiry cultures.

This flexible process was both a strength and a challenge. On the one hand, it allowed the project to remain responsive to emerging issues, such as the ergonomic impacts of handheld scanners, which became a focal point only after initial field studies. On the other hand, the absence of well-defined phases sometimes created confusion on what to do next.

The TARA project demonstrates that action research need not adhere strictly to predefined steps to be effective. Instead, its iterative and adaptive nature can offer significant value in complex, multi-stakeholder contexts, where evolving priorities and unforeseen challenges demand flexibility and ongoing recalibration.

Another challenge encountered during the TARA project was the fixed nature of the project plan, due to funding agency stipulations, which conflicted with the inherently iterative and adaptive approaches of both action research and Interaction Design. The rigid plan limited the team's ability to respond to emergent findings and evolving stakeholder needs, creating tension between the need for flexibility and the predefined objectives and timelines. This highlights the importance of designing project structures that accommodate iterative processes, particularly in collaborative, user-centred research.

An additional challenge was found in the intersection between theoretical and practical knowledge between researchers and practitioners, and how to communicate the study outcomes. An example can be taken from one of the reference group meetings with the airport stakeholders when suggestions for communicating the study results were presented to the stakeholders. The concepts "UX" and "Usability Studies" were used when presenting the take-home messages. The usage of these theoretical concepts, very familiar in a research context, leads to a discussion centred more around the concepts rather than how to work according to their principles. This example shows that not only can there be challenges in publishing results based on this kind of project, but making sure to get the most out of the insights in a practical setting might need some adjustments to the theoretical language most commonly used in academic contexts, pointing at a need for researchers in academia-industry projects to develop competences in this method of research communication.

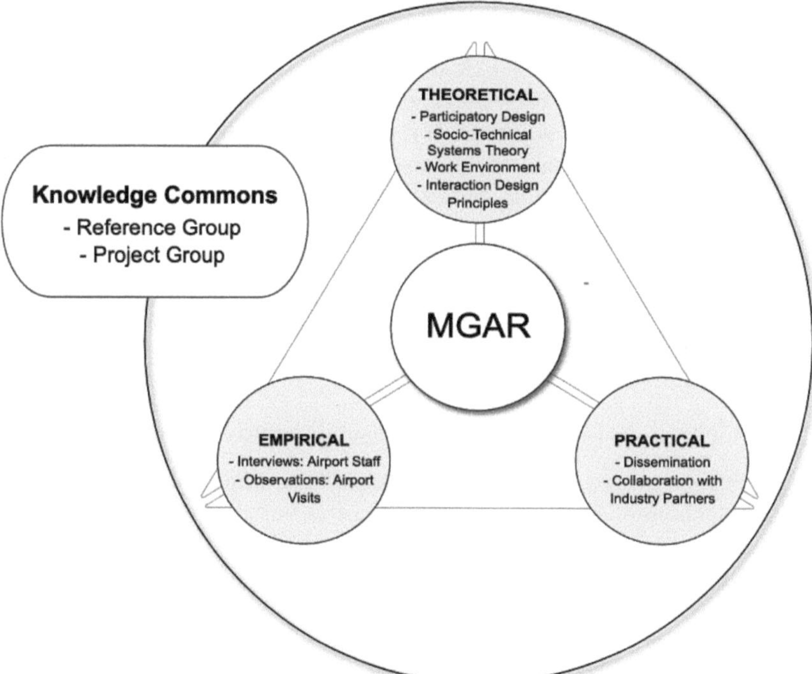

Fig. 4. Knowledge commons related to the TARA-adapted MGAR framework.

The concept of Knowledge Commons, as discussed in Sect. 2, can serve as a practical and critical framework for addressing the recurring challenges in academia-industry partnerships (Fig. 4). By collectively sharing a pool of resources from the outset, stakeholders can more effectively integrate diverse knowledge streams, ensuring that academic and practical outcomes are achieved in various forms and mutually reinforcing each other. Incorporating Knowledge Commons as a guiding framework facilitates cross-disciplinary synthesis and the creation of outputs accessible to both academic and practitioner audiences.

The perspectives of MGAR and Knowledge Commons can be combined in the practical case of TARA. One perspective that can be identified is a lack of Knowledge Commons at the beginning of a project. The researchers have theoretical knowledge, the industry has practical knowledge and access to empirical data, and together, the goal is to generate new theoretical and practical knowledge. In the case of TARA, as illustrated in Fig. 4, this was done via project and reference group meetings. With a basis in MGAR and combining different data collection methods and collaboration with the industry, researchers should aim to build knowledge commons, ensuring that immediate practical and long-term theoretical objectives are met.

5.3   Critical Reflection on Multi-grounded Action Research (MGAR)

While MGAR provided a structured framework for integrating theoretical, empirical, and practical insights, the method also presented challenges in collaboration with industry partners. The iterative nature of MGAR sometimes clashed with the fixed project plans and deadlines expected by industry stakeholders. Additionally, MGAR is a relatively complex approach that requires extensive reflection and theoretical grounding, which made it challenging to communicate effectively to practitioners.

Other possible methodological choices included Design-Based Research (DBR), which emphasises iterative design cycles in applied contexts, and Pragmatic Action Research (PAR), which focuses on direct interventions in practice. However, MGAR was chosen because it allows for an interplay between theoretical constructs and real-world constraints, ensuring that industry-relevant knowledge production is grounded in empirical data and informed by existing theory.

5.4   Post-conference Reflection – Concept Usability and Non-use

The primary insight gained from the conference is regarding the usability and non-use of HCI and interaction design concepts. Non-use in this case meaning that there are concepts available which might not be used in industry due to the concepts complexity, and because of the different incentives between industry and academia.

As we have previously presented in this paper, there is a gap between academia and industry. This gap was discussed during the conference presentations and papers as well, however the conference additions did add some complexity to the division between the two. Similarly, to what we argue in this paper, it was widely agreed among the conference participants that academia focuses on aspects like knowledge and long-term insights, whereas industry focuses on short term value and impact. However, one insight that did add complexity to the binary distinction is that of the various roles within and between the two. For example, a researcher that has been in academia for many years and moves over to industry might have a considerably different perspective on what research, concepts, and methods are available compared to a designer who was educated many years ago, and compared to a practitioner who does not have a design background whatsoever.

The steps between roles and the difference in incentives taps into a central issue that we have presented in this paper, that of having common language between academia and industry. One point brought up during the conference discussions was that research both shapes and is shaped by the lexicon, and that this lexicon might not be the same between academia and industry. This translation can be a problem when people are expected in academia to use the same concepts and terminology to publish in certain journals. This terminology might not be the same as used in industry, making the translation difficult. The issue of wanting to publish in specific journals and using the correct lexicon on the one hand and fruitful collaboration based on a common language on the other is similar to what we have encountered during the TARA project. For example, the scenario presented above when the concept "Usability Studies" was used during a reference group, leading to a discussion about the concept instead of how to use the insights the concept entails, can serve as a powerful anecdote. Adjusting language based on collaborator, which might be distinct from what is used in a final research paper that is published in an academic outlet, is more important in that context rather than strictly sticking to what is agreed upon by fellow academics. Furthermore, an example was also given during the conference where a method was being dismissed by students, but appreciated by the practitioners in the right context, making the judgement of when to use certain methods, concepts, and terminology important. This can be a way of establishing trust between practitioners and academics – because as per one comment, there is a risk that us researchers go into projects with good intentions, without establishing this trust, which can lead to unfruitful collaborations and undesirable outcomes.

There were also articles and presentations talking about the misunderstanding of methods. These presentations prompted a discussion regarding where practitioners in industry get their understanding from. However, given the other insights from the conference and this paper, incorrect use of terminology, methods, concepts are not the most important things in collaborations. There needs to be a trade-off balancing correct understanding, context adaptation, and trust enabling pragmatism on the one hand, and academically correct use of the methods on the other. Using the same terminology for a concept in a project and collaboration is more important than the exact wording that other academics use. Research collaborations form one context of shared understanding, while industry collaborations may require a different, more flexible approach to concepts. Adapting the methods, terminology, and concepts to be understandable and usable for practitioners should be done as a means to achieve a successful academia-industry collaboration.

What can we learn in terms of improving collaboration and avoiding methods not being understood or used? Having the approach to survey collaborators in industry, asking from where they get their understanding, could be of value in projects like TARA in order to establish knowledge commons. This can be done during project group and reference groups meetings for example. This can also be done to understand what the difference between the collaborator's expertise is. Other examples of solutions included adapting methods used in HCI to the context in which the project is carried out, despite not necessarily including computers, to get started with collaborations. By considering the dimensions presented in this section, researchers in academia-industry projects can make use of the plethora of HCI methods and concepts available, as well as increase the positive outcomes of these collaborations.

5.5 Implications for Future Research

The TARA project highlights important lessons for structuring and managing future academia-industry collaborations. These lessons can be summarized in three core recommendations to consider in collaborations such as TARA. The first recommendation is to establish the various MGAR dimensions in one's project. The second recommendation is to based on the MGAR dimensions create a plan on how to translate these dimensions to knowledge commons and a common language between stakeholders in the project. The final recommendation is to have clear goals and expectations at the outset, but be prepared to adapt throughout the project.

Aligning the academic priorities of generating theoretical insights with the industry's demand for actionable and practical outcomes proved challenging during the project. Future collaborations should dedicate time early to co-develop shared objectives, balancing theoretical contributions with stakeholder needs, with a shared language based on knowledge commons. This approach can help mitigate potential mismatches in priorities and ensure that both parties benefit from the partnership. Establishing clear, domain-specific research questions at the outset could help align academic and industry expectations more effectively. Early co-creation of research goals among all stakeholders—including researchers, industry partners, and practitioners—would ensure that the theoretical contributions are sufficiently robust for academic dissemination, while also remaining actionable and relevant for practical application. Such an approach may help mitigate interdisciplinary publishing challenges by clearly articulating the project's academic positioning while retaining the flexibility needed for real-world problem solving.

Interdisciplinary collaborations, like the TARA project, underscore the value of integrating diverse disciplinary perspectives while exposing inherent challenges. The project's findings, which span Interaction Design, workplace ergonomics, and socio-technical systems, did not align perfectly with the publishing norms of any single field. This lack of fit complicates the dissemination of results in traditional academic outlets. Future projects could address this by identifying interdisciplinary publication platforms that accommodate cross-domain findings or creating tailored outputs for academic and practitioner audiences.

Another insight relates to the iterative nature of action research, which emerged as both a strength and a challenge in the TARA project. The flexibility of action research allowed the team to adapt to emerging priorities, such as addressing ergonomic issues identified during field studies. However, this diffuse process also challenges maintaining alignment among stakeholders and managing expectations. Future projects should embrace this iterative nature but structure it with regular reflection and feedback mechanisms to ensure coherence and alignment with project goals.

Although less emphasised in the TARA project, practical grounding remains critical for ensuring research impact. Future efforts should integrate practical applications throughout the project lifecycle rather than treating them as a final step. Stakeholder collaboration in co-developing solutions can help ensure the research effectively translates into actionable outcomes.

Future projects could incorporate the Co-creation of Collaboration as a foundational activity [15]. Such a framework emphasises designing the collaboration process, including participatory goal-setting exercises, iterative process monitoring, and adaptive organisational structures that allow for validated adjustments based on stakeholder feedback throughout the research lifecycle. This collaborative strategy could mitigate misaligned priorities, enhance sustained stakeholder engagement, and ensure the practical relevance of research outcomes. Moreover, it would contribute to advancing the broader discourse on Academia-Industry Collaborations by demonstrating the value of inclusive and adaptive project structures.

Finally, including diverse stakeholder groups, such as unions, managers, and end-users, enriched the project's findings and introduced complexities in balancing competing interests. Future collaborations should develop structured approaches for managing diversity and fostering inclusivity while focusing on shared objectives. The long-term impact could also be enhanced by creating follow-up plans to assess the effectiveness of implemented recommendations and by developing open-access resources that allow others to adapt and apply the findings in different contexts.

The key contributions and insights from this paper is that establishing MGAR dimensions of a project, having plans for creating knowledge commons, and defining clear goals at the outset with an understanding of action research complexities can foster meaningful connections between research and practice. By addressing these challenges and building on the strengths of the TARA project, future academia-industry partnerships can achieve more significant impact and relevance.

5.6 Limitations

While this study provides valuable insights into academia-industry collaborations and the application of the Multi-Grounded Action Research (MGAR) framework, several limitations should be acknowledged to contextualise the findings.

The project plan's fixed nature occasionally conflicted with the iterative and adaptive demands of action research and Interaction Design. This rigidity constrained the team's ability to fully respond to emergent issues or to explore unforeseen opportunities during the collaboration. As a result, certain aspects of the process may not have been as thoroughly examined as they could have been in a more flexible research setup.

Finally, the findings are context-specific, focusing on the aviation sector and its unique technological and organisational challenges. While some insights are likely transferable to other industries, the generalizability of the results may be limited. Future work should explore how similar methodologies and frameworks can be adapted to other contexts, such as logistics or manufacturing, to validate and extend the findings.

6 Conclusion

The TARA project is a valuable case study for exploring the complexities and potential of academia-industry collaborations in Interaction Design. By applying the Multi-Grounded Action Research (MGAR) framework, the project effectively integrated theoretical, empirical, and practical dimensions to address the challenges of implementing new technologies in aviation workplaces. Through iterative and participatory processes, the project highlighted critical issues such as technostress, usability challenges, and ergonomic risks while fostering meaningful engagement with diverse stakeholders, including unions, managers, and workers.

The contribution of this paper therefore centres around the complexities of action research projects, and provides insights how to establish a MGAR foundation for the co-creation of knowledge commons between stakeholders, in order to mitigate the action research complexities and get the most out of projects such as TARA.

The project illuminated the inherent challenges of such collaborations. Aligning academic research outputs with industry partners' immediate, actionable needs was a recurring tension. Furthermore, the interdisciplinary nature of the findings, while enriching, complicated the dissemination of results in traditional academic and industry-focused channels. These challenges underscore the need for flexible methodologies, adaptive communication strategies, and clear expectations and dissemination pathways agreements.

Despite these difficulties, the TARA project demonstrates the potential for academia and industry to collaboratively address complex workplace challenges, creating theoretically and practically relevant solutions. The insights gained from this project offer valuable guidance for structuring future collaborations, particularly in balancing theoretical exploration with stakeholder priorities and ensuring the broad dissemination of results.

Future work will focus on translating the project's findings into tangible workplace interventions, such as educational resources, ergonomic recommendations, and practical tools for mitigating technostress. By continuing to build on the lessons learned, the TARA project exemplifies the transformative potential of academia-industry partnerships in advancing Interaction Design and improving workplace conditions.

Acknowledgments. We would like to express our gratitude to AFA Försäkring for funding this research project. The financial support received from AFA Försäkring, with reference number 220244, has been crucial in carrying out this study. We are also deeply thankful to the Transportfackens Yrkes- och Arbetsmiljönämnd (TYA) for their invaluable collaboration and to all the stakeholders and participants who shared their experiences and insights, enriching our understanding of technological implementation in airport operations.

Disclosure of Interests. The authors have no competing interests to declare relevant to this article's content.

References

1. Nastjuk, I., Trang, S., Grummeck-Braamt, J.V., Adam, M.T.P., Tarafdar, M.: Integrating and synthesising technostress research: a meta-analysis on technostress creators, outcomes, and IS usage contexts. Eur. J. Inf. Syst. **9**, 1–22 (2023)
2. Tarafdar, M., Tu, Q., Ragu-Nathan, T.S., Ragu-Nathan, B.S.: Crossing to the dark side: examining creators, outcomes, and inhibitors of technostress. Commun. ACM **54**(9), 113–120 (2011)
3. Bhutkar, G., et al. User experiences and wellbeing at work. In: IFIP Conference on Human-Computer Interaction, pp. 754–758. Springer (2019)

4. Kovynyov, I., Mikut, R.: Digital technologies in airport ground operations. NETNOMICS Econ. Res. Electron Netw. **20**(1), 1–30 (2019)
5. Goldkuhl, G., Cronholm, S., Lind, M.: Multi-grounded action research. Inf. Syst. E-Bus. Manag. **18**(2), 121–156 (2020)
6. Goldkuhl, G., Cronholm, S.: Adding theoretical grounding to grounded theory: toward multi-grounded theory. Int. J. Qual. Methods **9**(2), 187–205 (2010)
7. Goldkuhl, G., Lind, M.: A multi-grounded design research process. In: Winter, R., Zhao, J.L., Aier, S., (eds.) Global Perspectives on Design Science Research [Internet], pp. 45–60. Springer Berlin Heidelberg, Berlin, Heidelberg (2010) [cited 2024 Nov 25].. (Hutchison D, Kanade T, Kittler J, Kleinberg JM, Mattern F, Mitchell JC, et al., editors. Lecture Notes in Computer Science; vol. 6105). http://link.springer.com/10.1007/978-3-642-13335-0_4
8. Kurniawan, S.: Interaction design: Beyond human?computer interaction by Preece, Sharp and Rogers (2001), ISBN 0471492787. Univers. Access Inf. Soc. **3**(3–4), 289 (2004)
9. Sjöö, K., Hellström, T.: University–industry collaboration: a literature review and synthesis. Ind. High. Educ. **33**(4), 275–285 (2019)
10. Wohlin, C., Aurum, A., Angelis, L., Phillips, L., Dittrich, Y., Gorschek, T., et al.: The success factors powering industry-academia collaboration. IEEE Softw. **29**(2), 67–73 (2011)
11. Wohlin, C.: Empirical software engineering research with industry: top 10 challenges. In: 2013 1st international workshop on conducting empirical studies in industry (CESI) [Internet], pp. 43–46. IEEE (2013) [cited 2024 Dec 19]. https://ieeexplore.ieee.org/abstract/doc ument/6618469/?casa_token=J6vyRIWeyhEAAAAA:EcmNZ2ntGT5EbzKtKcPeY-LQ4 jaHVW1cFrONUht1NbrV0o_OQj6gPysQta9Lbc5P4G_CEGiNMA
12. Wandelt, S., Wang, K.: Towards solving the airport ground workforce dilemma: a literature review on hiring, scheduling, retention, and digitalization in the airport industry. J. Air Transp. Res. Soc. **2**, 100004 (2024)
13. Lafuente, A., Estalella, A.: Ways of science: public, open, and commons (2015) [cited 2024 Dec 19] https://digital.csic.es/handle/10261/359225
14. Vaughn, L.M., Jacquez, F.: Participatory research methods – choice points in the research process. J. Particip. Res. Methods [Internet] **1**(1). (2020). [cited 2024 Dec 20]. https://jprm.scholasticahq.com/article/13244-participatory-research-methods-cho ice-points-in-the-research-process
15. Van Den Driesche, C.: Touching on "Collective collaboration mapping": how can co-creation contribute to the process of equal collaboration for an inclusive citizen science approach? Des. Princ. Pract. Int. J.—Ann. Rev. **17**(1), 23–40 (2023)
16. Senabre Hidalgo, E., Perelló, J., Becker, F., Bonhoure, I., Legris, M., Cigarini, A.: Participation and co-creation in citizen science. Chapter 11 Vohland K Al Eds 2021 Sci. Citiz. Sci. Springer HttpsOrg101007978-3-030-58278-4, pp. 199–218 [Internet] (2021) [cited 2024 Dec19]. https://library.oapen.org/bitstream/handle/20.500.12657/46119/2021_Book_TheSci enceOfCitizenScience.pdf?sequence=1#page=202
17. Kılıç, S., Üçler, Ç., Martin-Domingo, L.: Innovation at airports: a systematic literature review (2000–2019). Aviation [Internet] (2021) [cited 2024 Feb 20]. https://eresearch.ozyegin.edu. tr/handle/10679/7769
18. Holtzblatt, K., Wendell, J.B., Wood, S.: Rapid contextual design: a how-to guide to key techniques for user-centered design, 321 p. Elsevier (2004)
19. Heron, J., Reason, P.: The practice of co-operative inquiry: Research 'with'rather than 'on'people. Handb Action Res Concise Paperb Ed, pp. 144–154 (2006)
20. Oberschmidt, K., Grünloh, C., Nijboer, F., van Velsen, L.: Best practices and lessons learned for action research in eHealth design and implementation: literature review. J. Med. Internet Res. **24**(1), e31795 (2022)
21. Baxter, G., Sommerville, I.: Socio-technical systems: from design methods to systems engineering. Interact. Comput. **23**(1), 4–17 (2011)

22. Fox, W.M.: Sociotechnical system principles and guidelines: past and present. J. Appl. Behav. Sci. **31**(1), 91–105 (1995)
23. Bodker, K., Kensing, F., Simonsen, J.: Participatory IT design: designing for business and workplace realities [Internet]. MIT press (2009) [cited 2024 Mar 29]. https://books.google.com/books?hl=en&lr=&id=Oncc6OEn9rMC&oi=fnd&pg=PR9&dq=Participatory+IT+Design:+Designing+for+Business+and+Workplace+Realitie&ots=ab5vh7Vrkd&sig=QZaEmMRxVGSgTmn1f5XaLeiiv1w
24. Gulliksen, J., Göransson, B., Boivie, I., Blomkvist, S., Persson, J., Cajander, Å.: Key principles for user-centred systems design. Behav. Inf. Technol. **22**(6), 397–409 (2003)
25. Cajander, Å.: Usability – who cares? : the introduction of user-centred systems design in organisations (2010) [cited 2020 Feb 14]. http://urn.kb.se/resolve?urn=urn:nbn:se:uu:diva-122387
26. Sandblad, B., Gulliksen, J., Åborg, C., Boivie, I., Persson, J., Göransson, B., et al.: Work environment and computer systems development. Behav. Inf. Technol. **22**(6), 375–387 (2003)
27. Gulliksen, J., Cajander, Å., Eriksson, E., Sandblad, B., Kavathatzopoulos, I.: User-centred systems design as organizational change : a longitudinal action research project to improve usability and the computerized work environment in a public authority. Int. J. Technol. Hum. Interact. **5**(3), 13–53 (2009)

Mapping the Landscape of Digitally Mediated Circular Economy Practices

Giorgia Anile[1]([✉])(iD), Luigina Ciolfi[2,4](iD), and Marica Cassarino[3,4](iD)

[1] School of Applied Psychology, Cork Enterprise Centre, University College Cork,
North Mall Campus, Cork City, Ireland
`giorgia.anile@umail.ucc.ie`
[2] Lero, The Research Ireland Centre for Software, Limerick, Ireland
`lciolfi@ucc.ie`
[3] Environmental Research Institute, University College Cork, Cork City, Ireland
`mcassarino@ucc.ie`
[4] UCC School of Applied Psychology, Cork Enterprise Centre, University College Cork,
Cork City, Ireland

Abstract. This paper investigates the method of landscape mapping in relation to digital platforms supporting Circular Economy (CE) practices in Ireland, with a particular focus on mobile applications. Through a systematic landscape mapping approach, we analyse how digital technologies mediate and enable circular practices at the community level. The research combines both academic and industry perspectives, stemming from the development of The Toy Library, a social enterprise project aimed at enabling toy sharing in local communities. Our methodology employs both bottom-up and top-down approaches to identify and analyse relevant mobile applications in the Irish market and completes the picture of the reuse sector in Ireland. A toolkit for the application of the method is also proposed. The work reveals insights about the usefulness of this approach to bridge academic and social enterprise research on the role of technology in promoting sustainable behaviours. This research contributes to the growing body of work on Sustainable Human Computer Interaction (SHCI) by providing specific insights into how digital platforms can support CE practices at the community level, while also offering practical implications for the discovery, design and implementation of future CE-focused digital initiatives.

Keywords: Landscape Mapping · Circular Economy · Digital Platforms · Social Enterprise

1 Introduction

Sustainability is a growing concern in HCI, with a growing body of work exploring the potential of digital design to encourage and support sustainable behaviours and practices [30] and the need for systems to operate sustainably in terms of digital footprint and reusability of components [9]. The work reported in this paper connects a social enterprise and academic research focusing on designing digital support for Circular

J. Abdelnour-Nocera et al. (Eds.): ARPPID 2025, CCIS 2797, pp. 69–90, 2026.
https://doi.org/10.1007/978-3-032-15516-0_5

Economy (CE) practices in Ireland at the level of local communities, starting with a systematic investigation and landscape mapping of CE mobile applications in Ireland.

As of 2019, only 9% of the world's economy is circular according to the United Nations Framework Convention on Climate Change?. The CE is gaining momentum both at the European level and in Ireland, which recently developed a Whole of Government Circular Economy Strategy [67]. The CE has started being promoted in the media, to help citizens and businesses become familiar with this new way of sharing resources. However, with a circular material use rate of just 2% in 2020 (relative to an EU average of 12.8%), Ireland has significant scope for progress, showing a deep circularity gap [15].

The Toy Library is a social enterprise project established in 2023, which aims at increasing the reuse of toys in the community, reducing plastic waste and consumption, by establishing sharing practices through a hyper-local, free digital platform. The design, deployment, adoption, and formative evaluation of The Toy Library platform are also part of an academic research project on sustainable HCI. Therefore, the methodology underpinning the project bridges academic and enterprise-based research, blending techniques that are widely used in industry contexts with theory-informed reflexive techniques to capture the academic contributions of the work. HCI work in social enterprises has occurred in relation to informing future platforms' design, particularly in developing economies and low-resource settings [11, 43, 54]. Despite an increase in interest and reflection on the non-profit sector [12], discussion of collaborations between non-profit enterprise and academia is still relatively limited in the field, where most academic-industry collaborations occur in the context of commercial product development.

In the initial phases of The Toy Library project (October 2023 to June 2024), defining the requirements and key features of the platform was informed by the first author's previous experience of many years in the UX industry and related research methods, including a mapping exercise to identify which tools and technologies are currently used by people in Ireland to engage in CE practices such as swapping and exchanging goods. The focus was mainly on mobile apps, a highly pervasive technology. Smartphone usage in Ireland is approaching 4 million users in 2023 [58]; as of 2021, Ireland's total population was 5.127 million. Mobile apps have the potential to promote large scale sustainable behaviours [71]. While the 2022 EPA report [27] mapping the reuse sector in Ireland covers a broad range of issues, it didn't go into the details of digital platforms available to citizens, and consolidated all options under a general "online" label that did not detail the most used systems and their features. With some evidence around how users of sustainability apps are more likely to translate their personal norm into pro-environmental behaviour in private and public settings [18], and how users can interact with information and communication technologies (ICTs) to co-create new processes with the potential to enhance sustainability awareness in citizens [71], this study completes the picture, providing specific insights related to the circularity of the mobile apps with which citizens engage in Ireland.

To gather these insights, we therefore leveraged the technique of landscape mapping. Landscape mapping can be defined as the systematic scouting of a specific technology within a given domain [57]. A process typically leveraged in marketing supporting product design, development and positioning [6], scanning the competitive landscape of an industry based on their function can help identify broad competitors that provide services similar to each other [49]. In the case of The Toy Library, the landscape mapping was a first step in the design process, and it helped the first author, as researcher/designer, by providing orientation in the competitive landscape of CE mobile apps, helping identify a gap in the toys category and inspiring the design of features to be included in the first iteration of the digital toy sharing platform. This study was also the first step linking the work on The Toy Library as a social enterprise to the academic research in SHCI. Following this, further research studies informed the subsequent design and launch of the platform to the public in June 2024.

In the following sections we present a review of the literature on the circular economy and on sustainable practices in HCI, we then present the method of landscape mapping and illustrate how it was applied in the context of our project. Finally, we discuss the usefulness of this approach more broadly for ongoing HCI research on CE practices as well as other community-focused initiatives. We argue that the technique of landscape mapping can benefit HCI research beyond industry contexts and help unveil insights on user awareness and perception of circular economy practices at community level, allowing, for example, the creation of research informed awareness campaigns or informing future public funding opportunities. To enable other researchers who may be exploring new product opportunities or inform the design of other services and experiences, we propose a Toolkit for guiding the use of the technique to execute a comprehensive app landscape mapping, along with a checklist that can be used to conduct similar research in other contexts.

2 Literature Review

2.1 What is the Circular Economy?

The CE emerged as an alternative model to the linear model of Take-Make-Waste [65]. This model is associated with the concept of sustainable development explored in the Brundtland report [47] and is gaining momentum both at the European and State level, with multiple initiatives being coordinated and sponsored by national governments [44]. The scope of the CE is to prevent waste and pollution, keep resources in use for as long as possible and transform waste into resources that are reused and kept in a loop of production and usage, generating more value and for a longer period. The CE has a strong connection to the Sustainable Development Goals (SDGs), as it is relevant to several goals related to pollution, resilience, inclusion, resource management and education [62]. The CE has the power to shrink global Greenhouse Gas (GHG) emissions by 39% and cut virgin resource use by 28% [15]. On a normative level, the CE sits within the sustainability paradigm [26], although the link between sustainability and the CE is still weak: a circular economy on its own is not enough, when overconsumption is at the root of sustainability challenges [64]. Moreover, industrial symbiosis (the process of re-using one industry's waste as a resource for another industry) can be sustainable but also contribute to locking-in unsustainable material systems (i.e. petrochemicals), perpetuating a need for fossil fuel extraction [69].

It is difficult to define exactly the boundaries between the CE and other sustainable economy paradigms such as collaborative consumption (CC) [37], the sharing economy (SE) [32], and the collaborative economy (CoE) [16]. A plethora of definitions are available in the literature, with the SE defined as the system through which users share with each other existing idle resources [38] while possibly getting a profit from it, with the important aspect of it happening on the internet [5], and enacting social rewards through the creation of a sense of community [4] coming together through sharing practices that promote social sustainability.

SE and CC are often used interchangeably; Hamari et. al [30, p. 2047] define CC as "the peer-to-peer (P2P) based activity of obtaining, giving, or sharing the access to goods and services, coordinated through community-based online services." This is not remarkably different from the SE definition, as both SE and CC have in common a variety of activities encompassed by the sharing, renting, or giving of existing resources from users to other users, leveraging digital platforms, whether for profit or non-profit reasons. The CE itself is also subject to a variety of definitions, some of which are inconsistent with each other. Already in 2017, Kircherr et al. [35] conducted an analysis of 114 definitions of the CE, showing the wide inconsistencies among definitions, with the CE concept sometimes mistaken as a combination of reduce, reuse and recycle activities, considered in isolation and without investigating the systemic shift needed to move away from the linear economy model.

Most scholars who analyse SE and CE business models have considered the SE to be a subset of the CE [31, 56], and in this research we embrace this view, as we conceptualise the CE as the main umbrella under which SE, CC, and CoE sit, as each of these forms of collaborative practice have one aspect in common: a use of existing resources within a community either through waste prevention or reuse, with a view to optimise the environmental, social and economic values throughout the life cycles of materials, components, and products [64]. When observing examples of CE practices, it is evident that sustainability is not as pervasive and easily demonstrable as one might think; for example, while reducing greenhouse gas emissions is a laudable goal, a more holistic and systematic analysis is needed to understand potential rebound effects from CE practices, for example shifting emissions from one part of the system to another [64]. It is also important to analyse the different types of sustainable outcomes of different CE practices: a CE model based on closed loop practices such as industrial symbiosis, creating energy from waste, is relatively easy to implement as it does not really require any dramatic change in the production lifecycle unlike another CE model with a strong emphasis on recycling and waste prevention, that however leaves consumption patterns the same, or even a model that requires more radical socio-cultural changes that shifts consumption patterns more towards a growth model, but is much harder to implement without massive paradigm shifts [64].

For example, considering SE platforms and the interactions they enable (i.e. resource sharing), when looking at the end to end journey the downstream impact of these interactions is not always positive from an environmental and/or social perspective: in the case of Uber [29], for example, it has been proven that the environmental impact of increased use of ride sharing is in fact negative (i.e. traffic congestion and/or tailpipe emissions). In other cases, such as that of Airbnb [2], the reallocation of housing enabled by the platform decreased the supply of long-term rental units, creating a negative social impact on renting communities. These rebound effects can drive a detrimental socio-environmental impact, in contrast with the sustainability factor that is so deeply ingrained in these models [48]. In short: while ideally sharing and reusing is desirable, a whole system assessment is needed to carefully understand the downstream impacts of circular practices, and, subsequently of the infrastructures and systems that facilitate them.

2.2 Digital Technology and Sustainable Practices

Digital platforms present opportunities to enable citizens' circular practices and technology can help bridging the circularity gap: digital platforms can not only orchestrate interactions between various stakeholders in the circular economy [8] but also enable the normalisation certain behaviours as citizens form habits by interacting with them. Great hopes and expectations are placed on technology to be an enabler of the CE, or a remover of its barriers [68]. Digital connectivity is expected to enable citizens and industries to co-create new forms of value. But how exactly does digitalization enable circular practices, at a functional level? What aspects of digitalization are used to perform which actions?

The range of frameworks outlined in the literature to harness different CE strategies include the well-known and prevalent R3 Model (Reduce-Reuse-Recycle), other R models such as 4Rs, 5Rs, 9Rs and 10rs [51], and the more complex ReSolve framework [24]. In this research, we adopt the 9Rs model (Fig. 1), an extension of the R3 model elaborated by Potting et.al [50] that maps each CE strategy to socio technical innovations. Liu et. al [39] use this framework as a base for mapping digital functions such as automation, data analysis and data collection to CE strategies.

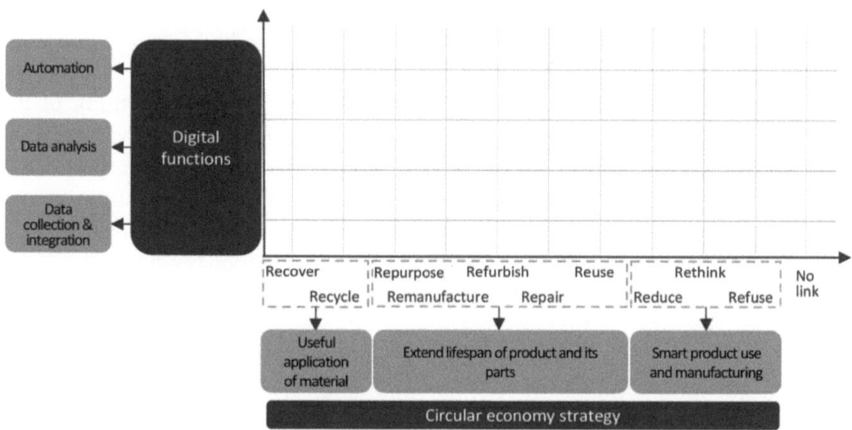

Fig. 1. R9 strategies and digital functions, from Liu et. al., 2021.

When looking at the R9 CE strategies, the technologies that enable them can be summarised as follows. First, within the function of data collection and integration sit IoT technologies, in which a physical product becomes "smart"; this enables data collection on product usage patterns, and allows the manufacturer to send maintenance when needed and inform the user on how to use the device more efficiently - this is the case of Homie [13] an initiative that developed a pay per wash model for their consumers. Another example of data collection and integration are sharing or re-commerce platforms, in which user data about idle resources is captured and shared with other users, who can avail of such resources and therefore extend their lifetime value.

Secondly, along with better data collection, within the function of data analysis, we see how in certain cases design can make the invisible visible: for example, by showing users transparent data about the usage or a certain product or service, and raising awareness around consumption, it can influence behaviours. This sits in the realm of HCI driving sustainable futures: an example of this are all those digital interactive technologies that aim to elicit behavioural changes: for example, a smart water meter that shows the user the amount of water consumed in the last shower, enabling better decision making - either through persuasive feedback or situational architecture [10], i.e. designing an "eco" mode that the user pre-select which sets a timer on the shower places the intervention "in the right place, at the right time" in relation to the consumer's everyday actions.

Finally, within the function of automation we see all those unsupervised activities that digital technologies can perform themselves, such as sorting and classifying activities, useful in smart recycling processes [52], as well as simple and repetitive tasks (such as sorting items by category). Automation can also help better capacity planning and forecasting of resource buying; for example, fruit and vegetables represent the largest source of waste in supermarkets (it's been estimated that they make up to 85% of waste in Swedish supermarkets [55]: with better automation leveraging big data, decision making around buying and pricing perishable items in supermarket can significantly reduce food waste [20].

Overall, we see that digital platforms are conceptualised in different ways, ranging from more to less technical definitions. In our research, we build on the definition of Koh and Fichman [36], which define digital platforms as two-sided networks, facilitating interactions between distinct but interdependent groups of users; we think of digital platforms for the CE in the same way, adding the condition that the group of users co-create value and drive positive social impact through their interactions. While mobile apps are only a type of digital platform (websites in which similar interactions take place would be included in the category) the scope of this research is mostly focused on these for two reasons: firstly, mobile apps exist within more clearly defined boundaries, residing in specific spaces such as the Google PlayStore for Android devices, or the Apple Appstore for iOS devices. Secondly, while the EPA report mapping the reuse sector in Ireland had breadth [27], it didn't go into the details of digital platforms available to citizens and consolidated all options under an "online" umbrella. With the evidence around how users of sustainability apps are more likely to translate their personal norm into pro-environmental behaviour in private and public settings [18], this research completes the picture. While we acknowledge the limitation of this focus, which potentially excludes websites leveraged for CE practices, we think that the narrower focus allows greater accuracy in assessing each application.

Due to their widespread adoption, digital platforms have an important role as mediators of the CE - digitalisation can make processes in organisations more efficient, helping to minimise waste and transaction costs [1]. While in their 2018 paper Sutherland and Jarrahi [59] summarise the roles of digital platforms specifically in relation to the SE, we believe some of those affordances, namely match-making, extending reach, trust building and facilitating collectivity, are equally applicable to the realm of the CE. For example, match-making which enables the matching of demand and offer is a common quality of marketplace-type applications; reach, on the other hand, is extended by the creation of wide networks where users co-create value, with the output of user generated content increasing proportionally with the growth of the user base, and vastly outperforms what a traditional firm could produce [17]. Digital platforms also enable the building of trust by providing rating or user review systems [32], encouraging the interaction amongst anonymous users who do not know each other. Finally, facilitating collectivity is also an important aspect of digital platforms for the CE: in different ways, these platforms bring users together working as communities of practices [66], sharing resources that would otherwise remain idle, mobilising them to connect with each other and leverage technology to build new, "real life" connections with like-minded users in their community, with a natural consequence of establishing more sustainable behaviours. In the SantaCoin case study [60], the digital currency ideated for a festival seamlessly integrated with the participant's regular practices, allowing them to create an alternative, parallel economy.

3 Methodology

We conducted a study aimed to map the landscape of mobile apps enabling CE for citizens in Ireland; this was the first step in understanding the problem space for the creation of a peer-2-peer digital platform to enable toy sharing in Irish communities, The Toy Library. The scope of this study was to provide orientation to the researcher/designer, identifying the most common systems being used by citizens, and the functions offered by the existing mobile apps they use to practice circularity. This research also allowed the researcher/designer to identify a gap in the landscape of such mobile applications, which The Toy Library aimed to fill. At the time of final submission of this article (August 2025), The Toy Library had already become a well-established social enterprise counting 2310 users, with 341 toys being listed on the platform in several local communities in Ireland.

Landscape mapping is the systematic scouting of a specific technology within a given domain [57]. This method has been used in different disciplines to map mobile applications related to food [40, 42], health, and specifically pregnancy [40], oncology [63], and COVID [45, 46], as well as tourism [7]. In HCI, studies using landscape mapping focus on functional reviews of mobile apps, for example related to mindful eating [28] or on the issues of privacy policies [70] also in relation to period tracking apps [23]. The initial scanning of the digital landscape was conducted leveraging the top 200 ranked apps for Google Playstore and Apple Appstore. We defined inclusion and exclusion criteria to identify mobile apps relevant to our research scope.

To capture the landscape of mobile apps in Ireland, we leveraged both a "bottom up" approach - in which we first explored the top ranked mobile apps on the Irish market on a specific day, and identified the ones in which CE practices were taking place, and then a "top down" approach in which - through a selection of keyword based queries - we searched on the Google Play store and the Apple store for mobile apps that possessed the same criteria. Inclusion criteria: mobile apps designed with CE practices in mind, as per the R9 framework (for example enabling recycling, reusing, remanufacturing, etc.). This framework was used to gain a background understanding of CE practices and inform the landscape mapping in the scanning phase but was not part of the core research questions. Exclusion criteria: apps typically categorised under the sharing economy umbrella, such as "ride sharing" apps - as in the Irish market they are equivalent to taxi services - and "house sharing" apps - as apps like Airbnb have become equivalent to B&B business.

For the "bottom up" approach, we collected the data on three specific days (20th, 21st and 22nd of December 2023). Our data set was hosted on the Google Play Store (which hosts Android mobile apps) and the Apple store (for iOS mobile apps). To extract the data, we used the website data.ai intelligence (formerly known as the Annie app), which is an analytics platform that extracts public facing information from Google Play and Apple stores. On the days specified, above, data was reviewed from the Google PlayStore and Appstore top ranked apps listing[1] and recorded in a spreadsheet, collecting the name of the app, ranking position, and a link to the app's page. The charts provided by data.ai show the relative popularity of each application on a specific market (in this case, Ireland), on a specific day. The data was securely stored on the university cloud based storage service, and being defined as "public data points", this information (mobile app ranking) is allowed for research and publication purposes by data.ai, according to their data usage policy [19].

For the "top down" approach, a list of keywords related to the CE was identified (sharing, share, freecycle, waste, sell, buy, swap, second hand, preloved) and used to search for applications on the two stores. These keywords were selected based on the most frequent occurrences through the author's organic discovery of second hand/preloved freecycling group in her local Facebook community. After having conducted the keyword-based search, results were collected on a spreadsheet, including the name of the app, and a link to its detail page. Following that, a quality check was conducted to assess the relevance of the app in the Irish market, as the apps that were produced by the queries were often not really "actively functioning" in the Irish market, even if they were publicly available (this is possibly due to the fact that developers can publish an app globally, and they take that chance even if the app is targeting a different market). Each relevant app detail page was scanned for quality checks to identify, for example, a foreign currency mentioned in the apps' screenshots, and if in further doubt, it was installed on the researcher's device and its functionality on the Irish market was personally checked. The different steps completed for both the bottom-up and top-down approach were captured and collated to formulate a toolkit for future landscape mappings.

This approach helped identify more mobile apps than possible using only one of the two analytical methods and paint a broader picture of mobile applications used for

---

[1] For the Google Playstore, the data was collected on the 20th of December, Ireland, top 200 free apps for all Android devices, and the data was extracted at this link. For the Apple Appstore, the data was collected on the 21st of December, Ireland, top 200 free apps, for iPhone, extracted at this link.

CE practices in Ireland. The quality control on the keyword-based query results ensured the identified apps were actually being used in Ireland. Landscape mapping provided a comprehensive picture of CE related mobile apps, as the criteria used to surface the top 200 ranked apps and the criteria used to surface apps following a keyword query are different: the first is influenced by popularity (i.e. user engagement with the app), while the second is heavily influenced by the relevance to the users' query.

4 Landscape Mapping Findings

More than one third (36.5%) of the top ranked 200 apps on the Google Playstore on the data collection day were games; on the Apple Appstore, games represented 15.5% of the top 200 ranked. Shopping was the second most popular category: it represented 9.50% of the top ranked 200 apps on Google Playstore, and 14.5% of the top ranked 200 apps on the Apple Appstore on the data collection day. In the top ranked 200 apps on the Google Playstore on the data collection day, only one was specifically designed with CE practices in mind: Too Good To Go - End food waste. However, it is common knowledge that CE practices also take place on social media apps (with the most well-known in Ireland being Facebook Groups). Social media apps on which CE practices take place that appeared in the top ranked 200 apps on the Google Playstore were: Facebook, Whatsapp, Telegram, Instagram, TikTok. In the top ranked 200 apps on the Apple Appstore on the data collection day only two were specifically designed with the CE in mind: Too Good to Go - End Food Waste and Depop - Buy and Sell Clothing. Overall, the bottom-up approach did not yield many results in terms of CE related apps: this may be because the results are "diluted" by the overwhelming presence of gaming and shopping apps in the top ranked charts. Or it could simply show a lack of awareness and engagement with existing CE apps.

The highest ranked shopping app on both the Google Playstore and the Apple Appstore was "Temu - Shop Like a Billionaire". Temu is a Chinese-owned online store that launched in the last year and has "taken over the internet" for its popular artificially cheap prices. Temu has achieved great popularity internationally but has been criticised for selling poor quality items and for its "crowdsourced marketing", using consumers to promote the app, providing them with credits to be spent on the online shop. Items are shipped from China everywhere in the world. Arguably, from an environmental perspective, Temu is the opposite of a CE app, as noted by several critics [26]: cheaply produced items shipped from China using cargo planes, making it practically and financially inconvenient to return a wrong item, increasing the chance that this would end up as waste.

Following the initial scanning of the landscape, we focused our research using keyword based queries on the Google Playstore and the Apple Appstore (sharing, share, freecycle, waste, sell, buy, swap, second hand, preloved). The keyword search produced more results, however having captured the data it was evident that many of the apps officially available on the Irish market did not have a real user base in Ireland and had been designed with other markets in mind: we screened those out of our search results. This approach resulted in seventeen mobile apps (Fig. 2) for giving or buying/selling items (with some apps allowing both options), across different categories: from general marketplace or general items to more specific categories such as food, fashion, sports, tech, and vehicles, with fashion being the category that produced more results across all categories.

Fashion apps for buying/selling second-hand designer clothes have the widest space in the market. This is important, as the fashion industry is one of the most unsustainable ones; already in 2018, it was responsible for 20% of global wastewater, with 85% of textiles ending up in landfill instead of being reused [61]. While some organizations in the fashion industry have started adopting circular business models (for example, luxury brand Stella McCartney allowing the resale of used garments on their own platform), third party marketplace apps (like Depop) play an important role in the circular fashion economy, allowing users to buy and sell used clothes, with some apps specifically targeting the luxury fashion niche (Siopaella in Ireland and Vestiaire Collective globally) - promoting trust building with their users by providing them with a validation of the authenticity of the luxury items put on sale on their marketplaces.

The only apps designed specifically for giving away unused resources were Olio, Trashnothing, and Go Zero Waste. These are citizen to citizen apps (or P2P). Within Olio, users can choose between food and non-food. The app is geolocated, so it encourages giving in local neighbourhoods. Certain features (such as an ad free experience and being able to see listings on a map) are reserved to "supporters" of the app, who can subscribe for €32.99 yearly. Olio also allows users to volunteer with supermarkets and redistribute leftover items within their community, to achieve giving goals (such as adding 7 listings in 7 days to get a special badge) and to reduce their carbon footprint through actions such as deleting unused photos from their phone (see Appendix 1). Trashnothing, on the other hand, only allows users to give items away to other users but is completely free to download and use.

Another notable app to prevent food waste is Too Good To Go: this is more centred on a business to citizen model, with businesses signing up to it and selling leftover items that would otherwise be discarded at discounted prices. Bakeries, restaurants and supermarkets create "surprise bags" and sell them to citizens for a fraction of the price, however citizens cannot choose contents, and agree to collect the bags at a specific time of the day (see Appendix 2).

While we did not focus our attention on a specific "R" in the R9 Framework (see Fig. 2, adapted from Potting et. al. [50]) when scoping our research, the results show that all the Apps emerged from our landscape mapping refer to the R3: "reuse" strategy, with the only difference that some follow a P2P model, and others a B2C model (while others, like Olio, created a B2C2C model, in which a business - namely a supermarket - gives items away to a consumer - called "Food Waste Hero" -, who takes responsibility to redistribute them to other consumers). None of the available apps present a B2B model. (see Appendix 3).

Finally, as there is increasing evidence that commercial social networks are the go-to platform for giving/swapping/buying and selling in communities worldwide, Facebook was included in the selection of apps in our research. As of November 2023, there were 3.6 million Facebook users in Ireland, accounting for 71.4 percent of the country's population [58]. In the last decade, Facebook has evolved from being a social network to becoming a global platform for online sociality [53]. The website circularliving.ie

[16] consulted in December 2023, provided citizens with a directory of links to avoid waste and dispose (or acquire) items, listing several resources for freecycling, broken down by county. As of December 2023, most of those resources (excluding mentions of Olio, Freecycle.org and the app Go Zero Waste Dublin), were Facebook groups. The overwhelming presence of Facebook as a platform for circular economy practices is somewhat problematic and known as "the platform paradox" [53]: this illustrates how - despite Facebook being objectively mis-aligned with the core values and ethos of online solidarity groups, and despite its dubious data management practices - the social network is still the lowest effort/easier to adopt solution to facilitate at least some of the interactions in each group, due to some fundamental aspects such as its extensive market penetration.

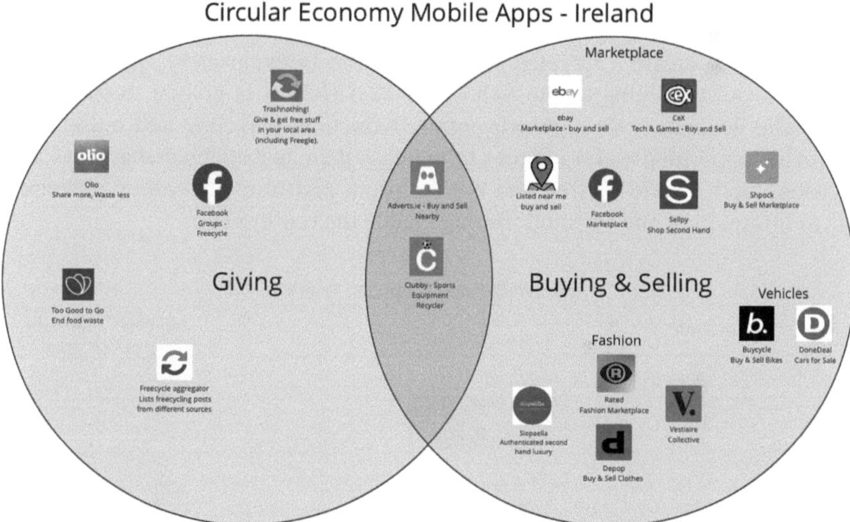

Fig. 2. Landscape of CE related mobile apps in Ireland

5 Discussion: Towards a Landscape Mapping Toolkit

Overall, the study showed that CE platforms in Ireland remain scarce and poorly discoverable, with low rankings in App stores. Most of the platforms identified through the landscape mapping operate for profit, with Olio being semi-nonprofit and Trashnothing! being the only free item recirculation app. Other platforms like Facebook Freecycle and Too Good 2 Go monetize through user data or reduced-price sales, indicating opportunities for nonprofit CE solutions. Additionally, App store searches yielded irrelevant results, requiring time-consuming verification processes that may discourage users; better quality control of the apps made available to regional App stores would user experience for citizens who wish to practice circularity. From a social responsibility perspective, the only "government backed" mobile app emerged from our research was the "Waste Less" app (funded by Hong Kong's government), designed to help citizens locate recycling points; similar tools could be designed by local authorities to support reuse initiatives. Finally, Facebook's role as the main freecycling platform can be problematic from a data-privacy and user experience perspective.

Meanwhile, Temu's popularity as a fast-fashion retailer demonstrates the need for better consumer education about environmental impacts. Organizations like the EPA could have a more active role in informing citizens about the consequences of purchasing from apps that are located outside of the European Union, and that do not adhere to European regulations, data security practices, and have significant environmental impact [3], while also using dark patterns (deceptive or manipulative design techniques) in their user interface [51].

The deep dive in the world of mobile apps for CE practices unearthed a gap in the existing offerings tailored to peer to peer sharing of resources from citizens, and a scarcity of non-profit organizations providing such services, as most mobile apps are based on a for-profit model which ultimately requires user data monetization. It also showed a gap in relation to toys, the category we were investigating with The Toy Library, highlighting an opportunity to create a targeted web application to exclusively allow peer 2 peer sharing of toys. According to the SDG goal 12.5 [62], it is pivotal to "substantially reduce waste generation through prevention, reduction, recycling and reuse". Mobile apps provide opportunities for citizens to increase their sustainable behaviours, and for this reason, there should be free and not for profit platforms that allow citizens wide access to information and interactions that enable the reuse sector.

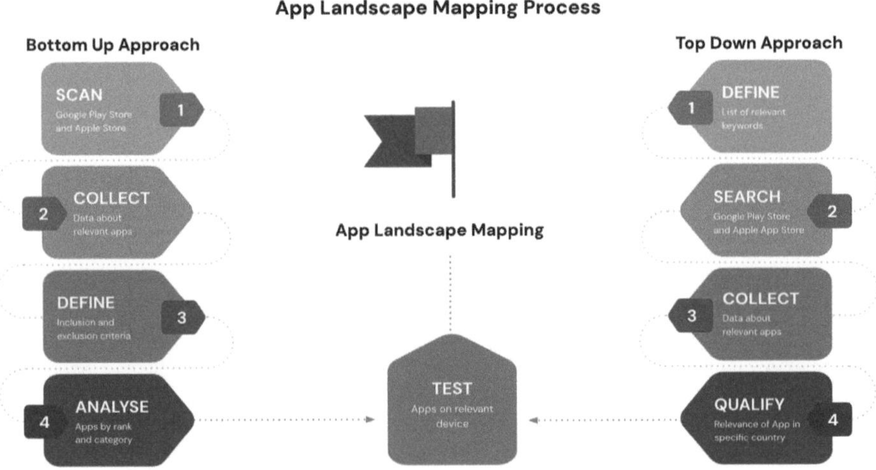

Fig. 3. Mobile app landscape mapping process

Conducting a landscape mapping exercise can be a good starting point for researchers who are exploring new product opportunities, as it can provide directional insights on existing gaps in the market, while also informing the design of future product or experiences based on the analysis of the existing applications and the functions they allow. For example, our in-depth exploration of Olio allowed us to discover the neighbourhood discovery function, which ended up being one of the most popular features in the proof of concept for The Toy Library, allowing users to discover items in the proximity of their own location, amplifying the sustainability impact of the platform (Fig. 3).

5.1 Landscape Mapping Toolkit

The toolkit includes a visual representation of the steps of the technique to execute a comprehensive app landscape mapping - including both the bottom and up and top-down approaches, along with a checklist that can be used to conduct similar research in another context or refined in case of additional requirements.

Researchers who wish to replicate this approach to map the landscape of mobile apps in the context of their work, can use the following checklist to inform the research design (Table 1).

Table 1. Checklist for mobile app landscape mapping

App Landscape Mapping - Checklist	
Phase 1 - Bottom-Up Approach	Phase 2 - Top-Down Approach
Scan - Google Play Store and Apple App Store for top 200 ranked Apps; it is possible to leverage third party tools such as data.ai intelligence (formerly known as the Annie app), an analytics platform that extracts public facing information from the Google Playstore and the Apple App store. Define a specific date range and stick to it	**Define** - list of keywords relevant to your research questions. This can be an iterative process, with keywords being refined throughout (i.e. for Circular Economy Apps: sharing, share, freecycle, recycle, etc.)
Collect - data from the Google Play Store and App Store top ranked apps listing and record it using a method of choice; record app name, ranking position, and a link to the app's page	**Search** - Google Play Store and Apple App Store leveraging the keywords previously identified. Refine and iterate. Which keywords work best and achieve results most relevant to research questions?
Define - inclusion and exclusion criteria for the analysis: these depend on your research questions (app category - i.e. mobility, food, or other - business model - i.e. b2b, b2c, p2p; platform type -i.e. marketplace vs freecycle)	**Collect** - data about relevant Apps. Record the same information as in phase 1 to ensure consistency
Analyse - apps by rank and category: which category has the biggest presence in the top ranked apps (i.e. games vs shopping, etc.)	**Qualify & Test** - are the selected Apps not simply available but truly functioning in the relevant country? (hints to look out for: currency, language, etc.). Test functioning of Apps in relevant devices (iOS, Android). Does the App have a significant user base (i.e. are there many user generated entries, listings, etc.)

6 Expanding the Discussion on Social Enterprise Research in HCI

Discussions about the application of the landscape mapping method and the related case study of The Toy Library show interesting insights in relation to the under representation in the discipline of design for social good and sustainable HCI, and of social enterprise research more in general. This was also noted in the exploration of relevant literature for the present article, which we further address below. In light of this study and of our wider work, we argue that the HCI space linking academic research and industry in terms of both interests and approaches needs to be expanded with the inclusion of alternative forms of enterprise.

Being a social enterprise, The Toy Library does not belong "neatly" in the commercialisation world: it came to market with the speed and agility of a commercial product as a service, but it doesn't belong to the for-profit paradigm. Social enterprises are a significant reality: they employ over 40 million people worldwide [14] and have a growing role in addressing Sustainable Development Goals (SDGs).

Despite the rapid growth of social enterprises worldwide, academic engagement at the intersection of Human-Computer Interaction and social entrepreneurship remains minimal. Indeed, a review of ACM, IEEE, and Scopus databases using keywords such as "HCI" and "Social Enterprise" returned fewer than 150 publications over the past 28 years, many of which are tangentially related, or focus on broader Information and Communication Technologies for Development (ICT4D) contexts rather than HCI frameworks specific to social enterprises.

In contrast, searches for "HCI" and "e-commerce" yielded thousands of papers (specifically 3178), highlighting a stark disparity. The keywords "HCI" and "start-up" similarly produced results in the thousands (1,651). This gap is further underscored by the absence of sessions in major HCI conferences (such as CHI or CSCW) dedicated explicitly to social enterprises, suggesting that the field is underexplored despite its growing societal relevance. In fact, while these conferences and others include many workshops connected to social justice, fairness, environmental care, and responsible technology, none are focused explicitly on social enterprise as a research domain or design context.

However, the context of the present study, The Toy Library, is an example of how rigorous design research was paired with agile design practices, typical of industry environments, while also enabled by business mentors and social enterprise investors who supported the project financially. The human cantered design (HCD) approach was fundamental to "design things right", but the business acumen and flexibility driven by the collaboration with industry practitioners was fundamental for the success of the platform. Cases such as this open an interesting space for HCI to examine design approaches which connect well known processes of industry research with an increasingly important space of responsible innovation.

For instance, by keeping an eye on the market and understanding the landscape of mobile applications for the circular economy before moving into the design phase, the team at The Toy Library paired rigorous research with agile design practices and business insight, following a process that is common in industry. The difference between the development process of The Toy Library, spanning between the worlds of academia, industry, and social enterprise, and many examples of prototypes that were "born and raised" solely in academic vs. industry contexts, is striking.

Many prototypes arising from HCI research start and end with extremely limited real-world data beyond lab settings. The well-documented disconnect between HCI and industry fields of interaction (and industrial) design - is arguably systemic throughout

HCI [21]. HCI prototypes often fail to succeed due to poor usefulness in their real world application - an aspect that is often disregarded in favour of understandability and usability [33]. There is also a concern that HCI innovations rarely develop into commercial products [31], and that user centered design in HCI lacks attention to business factors and long-term uptake of technology in society [25].

A further argument for greater bridging of HCI and the world of social enterprises is the opportunity to further HCI research on platform design, particularly by proposing alternative business and operational models [41]. Radically different from industry-based research in the commercial paradigm, the case of The Toy Library shows how social enterprises open up distinct opportunities for advancing this. While commercial ventures are largely driven by a for profit model, social enterprises are driven by social impact, care, and community. This difference in motive is fundamental, as it shifts the research agenda from designing for efficiency and consumption to designing for care and cooperation. With certain HCI research indeed auspicating new economic models of platform development (i.e. the commons) [41], greater attention to the world of social enterprises and social innovation would significantly push forward this aspect of the HCI research agenda.

Finally, the issue of how project impact is measured must be addressed. In academia, success is still primarily gauged by the number and prestige of publications, with lesser regard for tangible, real-world outcomes and impact—arguably the only metric that truly matters for social enterprises. We believe that fostering closer collaboration between academia and social enterprises would enable meaningful knowledge exchange, empowering the field of Sustainable HCI to drive greater and more lasting social change.

7 Summary of Contributions and Conclusions

This study offers several contributions to HCI research and practice bridging academic and non-academic contexts. Firstly, it shows the value of an industry-based research method for product design across contexts: one of the challenges of Sustainable HCI is the disconnect with industry fields of interaction (and industrial) design – which DiSalvo et. [22] argue is systemic throughout HCI. HCI prototypes often fail to succeed due to poor usefulness in their real-world application – aspect that is often disregarded in favour of understandability and usability [34]; additionally, it has been a repeated concern that HCI innovations rarely develop into commercial products [33]. An industry-based approach that enables the researcher to identify the existing applications and potential gaps / unmet needs in the existing market is an advantage in informing the decision to move from discovery to design. In our specific case, as of the 21st August 2025, The Toy Library counts 2310 users in the whole Republic of Ireland, with 341 toys being shared between families in the same community. This is evidence that the platform addresses real user needs and a gap in the existing mobile/web apps offering in relation to toy sharing.

Secondly, the study completes the picture of the reuse sector in Ireland. The analysis aims to connect the dots between the CE and mobile apps currently used by citizens to practice a specific function (circularity) in a specific area (Ireland). To the best of our knowledge, no other studies focused on this specific intersection between the CE and mobile apps; the 2022 EPA report [27] addressed the reuse sector but grouped all the resources identified under an "online" umbrella. Our study completes the picture focusing on mobile apps and unearths additional platforms with "atypical" business models (i.e. Olio and their B2C2C model). Finally, it has been distilled into a re-applicable model (toolkit) that academic researchers can leverage when exploring product design, to make sense of the landscape of mobile apps enabling specific relevant functions. This is useful when in the discovery phase of product design, to quickly identify existing functions in a specific problem space and can even be used to conduct market research and ideate solutions that are currently unaddressed in the market.

We also acknowledge certain limitations. The research captures the results of a specific moment in time (December 2023) – results which could vary significantly by the introduction of new mobile apps in the relevant area (i.e. since then, Vinted – the most famous second-hand marketplace for clothes in Europe, has launched in the Irish market). Furthermore, for the top-down approach, the keywords-based research was based on the first author's own organic discovery of existing resources for CE in Ireland, but this selection of keyword does not pretend to be comprehensive or even unbiased, therefore the researchers' own subjective experience has influenced the queries that produced the results further analysed. Finally, we acknowledge that the only publicly available data is the ranking of the apps released by Google Playstore and Apple Appstore, and it is not clear how reliable and valid the data is.

In conclusion, this paper presented a study applying the method of landscape mapping, which is an established approach to product design and development in industry, to The Toy Library, a project bridging research in academic and social enterprise contexts to develop a Circular Economy community platform. We have shown how this technique can be useful for the growing professional practice of Sustainable HCI, and we proposed a reusable toolkit that can be used by stakeholders engaged in this field and wishing to either understand and/or add to the existing landscape of digital platforms fostering CE practices in a particular area.

Finally, we argue that the dearth of social enterprise perspectives in the field of HCI is striking, and needs addressing. Social enterprises are structured to prioritise social and environmental value over profit, making them a living counter-example to the commercial paradigms that dominate both industry and design research. Without such perspectives, our critique of exploitative design risks remaining abstract, lacking engagement with existing alternative models that sit outside of the commercial paradigm. If the field aims to bridge academia and industry and is serious about reimagining design's role in society, and encouraging better knowledge transfer to and from academia, they must create space for social enterprises to be visible, heard, and taken seriously.

With the hope that sustainable HCI research will increasingly translate into tools adopted and used by relevant communities, we suggest that methods drawn from product and UX design can make a valuable contribution to the process, particularly in supporting social enterprises and other not-for-profit initiatives engaged in research. We hold the aspiration that social enterprises will gain greater representation at HCI venues and within the field as a whole.

Acknowledgments. This publication has emanated from research conducted with the financial support of Taighde Éireann – Research Ireland under Grant number 18/CRT/6222. For the purpose of Open Access, the author has applied a CC BY public copyright licence to any Author Accepted Manuscript version arising from this submission.

Appendices

Appendix 1 – Olio

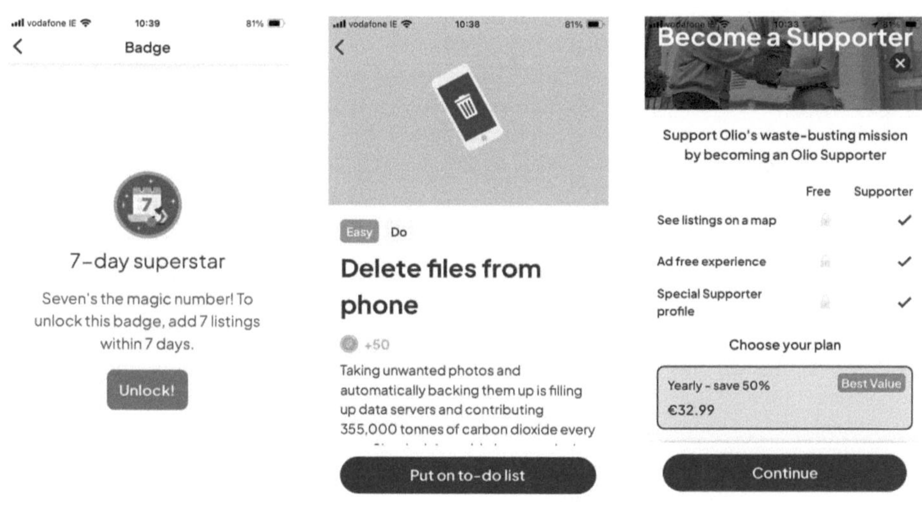

Appendix 1 - Olio User Experience

Appendix 2 – Too Good To Go

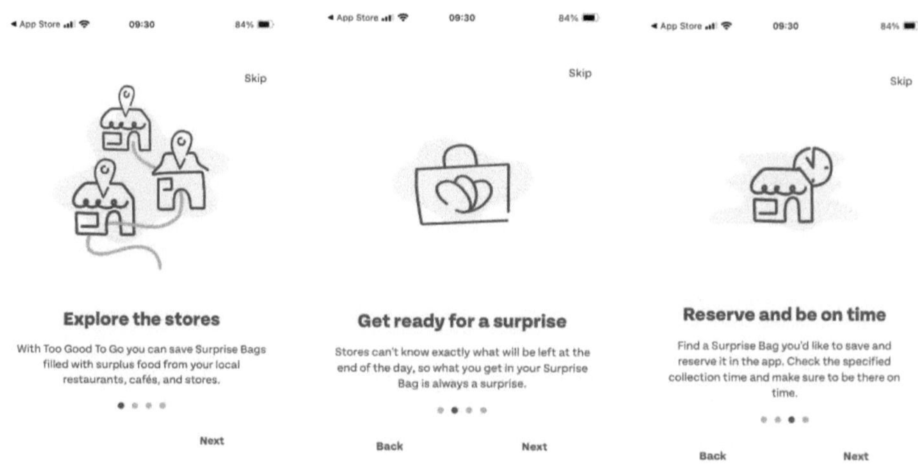

Appendix 2 - Too Good To Go User Experience

References

1. Antikainen, M., Uusitalo, T., Kivikytö-Reponen, P.: Digitalisation as an enabler of circular economy. Procedia CIRP **73**, 45–49 (2018). https://doi.org/10.1016/j.procir.2018.04.027
2. Barron, K., Kung, E., Proserpio, D.: The Effect of Home-Sharing on House Prices and Rents: Evidence from Airbnb. SSRN Scholarly Paper (2020). https://doi.org/10.2139/ssrn.3006832
3. Becker, R.: Mapping out the Media Landscape of TEMU's Market Entrance in the European Union (2024). https://www.diva-portal.org/smash/record.jsf?pid=diva2%3A1860051&dswid=6849
4. Belk, R.: Why not share rather than own? Ann. Am. Acad. Pol. Soc. Sci. **611**(1), 126–140 (2007). https://doi.org/10.1177/0002716206298483
5. Belk, R.: You are what you can access: Sharing and collaborative consumption online. J. Bus. Res. **67**, 1595–1600 (2014). https://doi.org/10.1016/j.jbusres.2013.10.001
6. Bergen, M., Peteraf, M.A.: Competitor identification and competitor analysis: a broad-based managerial approach. Manag. Decis. Econ. **23**, 157–169 (2002). https://doi.org/10.1002/mde.1059
7. Birenboim, A., Bulis, Y., Omer, I.: A typology of tourism mobility apps. Tour. Manage. Perspect. **48**, 101161 (2023). https://doi.org/10.1016/j.tmp.2023.101161
8. Blackburn, O., Ritala, P., Keränen, J.: Digital platforms for the circular economy: exploring meta-organizational orchestration mechanisms. Organ. Environ. **36**, 253–281 (2023). https://doi.org/10.1177/10860266221130717
9. Blevis, E.: Sustainable interaction design: invention & disposal, renewal & reuse. In: Proceedings of the SIGCHI Conference on Human Factors in Computing Systems, pp. 503–512. Association for Computing Machinery, New York, NY, USA (2007). https://doi.org/10.1145/1240624.1240705
10. Boll, S., Bidwell, N., Väänänen, K., Hassenzahl, M.: A human-computer interaction perspective to drive change towards sustainable future (2023) : https://www.dagstuhl.de/23092. Accessed 18 Oct 2025
11. Bopp, C., et al.: Disempowered by data: nonprofits, social enterprises, and the consequences of data-driven work. In: Proceedings of the 2017 CHI Conference on Human Factors in Computing Systems (CHI 2017), pp. 3608–3619. Association for Computing Machinery, New York, NY, USA (2017) https://doi.org/10.1145/3025453.3025694
12. Bopp, C., Voida, A.: Voices of the social sector: a systematic review of stakeholder voice in HCI research with Nonprofit organizations. ACM Trans. Comput.-Hum. Interact. **27**, 2, Article 9, 26 pp. (2020). https://doi.org/10.1145/3368368
13. Bressanelli, G., Saccani, N., Perona, M., Baccanelli, I.: Towards circular economy in the household appliance industry: an overview of cases. Resources **9**, 128 (2020). https://doi.org/10.3390/resources9110128
14. British Council, & Social Enterprise UK. More in common: The global state of social enterprise. British Council (2022). https://www.britishcouncil.org/sites/default/files/more_in_common_global_state_of_social_enterprise.pdf. Accessed 18 Oct 2025
15. Circularity Gap Report. https://www.circularity-gap.world/2021. Accessed 27 Jube 2024
16. Circularliving.ie. https://web.archive.org/web/20230102010646/https://circularliving.ie/freecycle-groups-ireland/. Last accessed 2023/12/28
17. Cusumano, M.: Technology strategy and management. The evolution of platform thinking. Commun. ACM **53**, 32–34 (2010). https://doi.org/10.1145/1629175.1629189
18. D'Arco, M, Marino, V.: Environmental citizenship behavior and sustainability apps: an empirical investigation. Transform. Govern.: People, Process Policy **16**, 185–202 (2022). https://www.emerald.com/tg/article-pdf/16/2/185/2358078/tg-07-2021-0118.pdf

19. Data AI Usage Policy. https://www.data.ai/en/legal/data-usage-policy/#:~:text=All%20use%
20of%20such%20data,to%20the%20respective%20partner's%20policies. Accessed 14 Jan
2025
20. De Souza, M., et al.: A digitally enabled circular economy for mitigating food waste: understanding innovative marketing strategies in the context of an emerging economy. Technol.
Forecast. Soc. Chang. **173**, 121062 (2021). https://doi.org/10.1016/j.techfore.2021.121062
21. Diefenbach, S., Kapsner, A., Laschke, M., Niess, J., Ullrich, D.: Technology for behavior
change – potential, challenges, and ethical questions: an interdisciplinary experts discussion.
i-com **15**, 195–201 (2016). https://doi.org/10.1515/icom-2016-0025
22. DiSalvo, C., Sengers, P., Brynjarsdóttir, H.: Mapping the landscape of sustainable HCI. In:
Proceedings of the SIGCHI Conference on Human Factors in Computing Systems, pp. 1975–
1984. ACM, Atlanta Georgia USA (2010). https://doi.org/10.1145/1753326.1753625
23. Dong, Z., Wang, L., Xie, H., Xu, G., Wang, H.: Privacy analysis of period tracking mobile apps
in the post-roe v. wade era. In: Proceedings of the 37th IEEE/ACM International Conference
on Automated Software Engineering, pp. 1–6. Association for Computing Machinery, New
York, NY, USA (2023). https://doi.org/10.1145/3551349.3561343
24. Ellen MacArthur Foundation. Towards a circular economy: Business rationale for an acceler-
ated transition. https://www.ellenmacarthurfoundation.org/towards-a-circular-economy-bus
iness-rationale-for-an-accelerated-transition. Accessed 29 Dec 2024
25. Frohlich, D.M., Sarvas, R.: Critiques of user-centered design in HCI: Innovation and business.
CHI EA 2011 Extended Abstracts on Human Factors in Computing Systems, pp. 713–728
(2011). https://doi.org/10.1145/1979742.1979670
26. Geissdoerfer, M., Savaget, P., Nancy Bocken, Bocken, N., Hultink, E.J.: The circular economy – a new sustainability paradigm? J. Clean. Product. **143**, 757–768 (2017). https://doi.
org/10.1016/j.jclepro.2016.12.048
27. Gibson, C., et al.: Qualifying and Quantifying the Reuse Sector in Ireland. https://www.epa.
ie/publications/research/epa-research-2030-reports/Research_Report_405.pdf. Accessed 29
Jan 2024
28. Guluzade, L., Sas, C.: Functionality and user review analysis of mobile apps for mindfulness
eating and eating disorders. In: Proceedings of the 2024 ACM Designing Interactive Systems
Conference, pp. 1350–1371. Association for Computing Machinery, New York, NY, USA
(2024). https://doi.org/10.1145/3643834.3661521
29. Haider, M.: To Uber or Not to Uber: That is the Question (2015). http://stream1.newswire.
ca/media/2015/09/29/20150929_C6395_PDF_EN_508957.Pdf. Accessed 22 Jan 2024
30. Hamari, J., Sjöklint, M., Ukkonen, A.: The sharing economy: why people participate in
collaborative consumption. J. Am. Soc. Inf. Sci. **67**, 2047–2059 (2016). https://doi.org/10.
1002/asi.23552
31. Henry, M., et al.: The battle of the buzzwords: a comparative review of the circular economy
and the sharing economy concepts. Environ. Innov. Soc. Trans. **38**, 1–21 (2021). https://doi.
org/10.1016/j.eist.2020.10.008
32. Ikkala, T., Lampinen, A.: Monetizing network hospitality: hospitality and sociability in the
context of airbnb. In: Proceedings of the 18th ACM Conference on Computer Supported
Cooperative Work & Social Computing, pp. 1033–1044. ACM, Vancouver BC Canada (2015).
https://doi.org/10.1145/2675133.2675274
33. Isaacs, E.A., Tang, J.C.: Technology transfer: so much research, so few good products.
Commun. ACM **39**, 23–25 (1996). https://doi.org/10.1145/234215.234463
34. Jones, W., Spool, J., Grudin, J., Bellotti, V., Czerwinski, M.: 'Get real!': what's wrong with
hci prototyping and how can we fix it? In: CHI '07 Extended Abstracts on Human Factors in
Computing Systems, pp. 1913–1916. Association for Computing Machinery, New York, NY,
USA (2007). https://doi.org/10.1145/1240866.1240922

35. Kirchherr, J., Reike, D., Hekkert, M.: Conceptualizing the circular economy: an analysis of 114 definitions. SSRN Scholarly Paper at (2017). https://doi.org/10.2139/ssrn.3037579

36. Koh, T.K., Fichman, M.: Multihoming users' preferences for two-sided exchange networks. MIS Q. **38**, 977–996 (2014). https://doi.org/10.25300/MISQ/2014/38.4.02

37. Leismann, K., Schmitt, M., Rohn, H., Baedeker, C.: Collaborative consumption: towards a resource-saving consumption culture. Resources **2**, 184–203 (2013). https://doi.org/10.3390/resources2030184

38. Light, A., Miskelly, C.: Platforms, scales and networks: meshing a local sustainable sharing economy. Comput. Supported Coop Work **28**, 591–626 (2019). https://doi.org/10.1007/s10606-019-09352-1

39. Liu, Q., Trevisan, A.H., Yang, M., Mascarenhas, J.: A framework of digital technologies for the circular economy: Digital functions and mechanisms. Bus. Strateg. Environ. **31**, 2171–2192 (2022). https://doi.org/10.1002/bse.3015

40. Lupton, D.: 'All at the tap of a button': mapping the food app landscape. Eur. J. Cult. Stud. **24**, 1360–1381 (2021). https://doi.org/10.1177/1367549421105557

41. Lyle, P., Sciannamblo, M., Teli, M.: Fostering common-fare: Infrastructuring autonomous social collaboration. In: Proceedings of the 2018 CHI Conference on Human Factors in Computing Systems (CHI '18, Paper 452, pp. 1–12). Association for Computing Machinery (2018). https://doi.org/10.1145/3173574.3174026

42. Mauch, C.E., et al.: Mobile apps to support healthy family food provision: systematic assessment of popular, commercially available apps. JMIR Mhealth Uhealth **6**, e11867 (2018). https://doi.org/10.2196/11867

43. Mehra, A. et al. Prayana: a journey towards financial inclusion. In: Proceedings of the Ninth International Conference on Information and Communication Technologies and Development (ICTD '17), Article 26, pp. 1–5. Association for Computing Machinery, New York, NY, USA (2017). https://doi.org/10.1145/3136560.3136591

44. Mhatre, P., Panchal, R., Singh, A., Bibyan, S.: A systematic literature review on the circular economy initiatives in the European Union. Sustain. Product. Consumpt. **26**, 187–202 (2021). https://doi.org/10.1016/j.spc.2020.09.008

45. Micheli, M., et al.: A European approach to COVID-19 apps? A landscape analysis of apps stores in the initial stages of the health crisis. First Monday (2022). https://doi.org/10.5210/fm.v27i3.12412

46. Nebeker, C., et al.: Digital exposure notification tools: a global landscape analysis. PLOS Digital Health **2**, e0000287 (2023). https://doi.org/10.1371/journal.pdig.0000287

47. Our Common Future: From One Earth to One World - A/42/427 Annex, Overview - UN Documents: Gathering a body of global agreements. http://www.un-documents.net/ocf-ov.htm. Accessed 29 Dec 2024

48. Pearce, D.W., Turner, R.K.: Economics of natural resources and the environment. JHU Press (1989)

49. Peteraf, M.A., Bergen, M.E.: Scanning dynamic competitive landscapes: a market-based and resource-based framework. Strateg. Manag. J. **24**, 1027–1041 (2003). https://doi.org/10.1002/smj.325

50. Potting, J., Hekkert, M., Worrell, E., Hanemaaijer, A.: Circular economy: measuring innovation in the product chain. PBL Netherlands Environmental Assessment Agency 2 Copernicus Institute of Sustainable Development, Utrecht University (2017). https://dspace.library.uu.nl/handle/1874/358310

51. Reike, D., Vermeulen, W.J.V., Witjes, S.: The circular economy: new or Refurbished as CE 3.0? — exploring controversies in the conceptualization of the circular economy through a focus on history and resource value retention options. Resources Conserv. Recycl. **135**, 246–264 (2018). https://doi.org/10.1016/j.resconrec.2017.08.027

52. Reis, J.S., da, M., et al.: Striding towards sustainability: a framework to overcome challenges and explore opportunities through industry 4.0. Sustainability **13**, 5232 (2021). https://doi.org/10.3390/su13095232

53. Rossitto, C., et al.: Chapter 5. Why are we still using facebook? the platform paradox in collaborative community initiatives. In: Teli, M., Bassetti, C., (eds.) Becoming a Platform in Europe – On the Governance of the Collaborative Economy, pp. 90–109. Now Publishers (2021). https://doi.org/10.1561/9781680838411.ch5

54. Saigal, A.K., Saigal, A.: Saathimobile and the rapid deployment of prototypes to build applications for social enterprise in the developing world. In: Proceedings of the 1st International Conference on Wireless Technologies for Humanitarian Relief (ACWR '11), pp. 351–356. Association for Computing Machinery, New York, NY, USA (2011). https://doi.org/10.1145/2185216.2185311

55. Scholz, K., Eriksson, M., Strid, I.: Carbon footprint of supermarket food waste. Resour. Conserv. Recycl. **94**, 56–65 (2015). https://doi.org/10.1016/j.resconrec.2014.11.016

56. Schwanholz, J., Leipold, S.: Sharing for a circular economy? an analysis of digital sharing platforms' principles and business models. J. Clean. Prod. **269**, 122327 (2020). https://doi.org/10.1016/j.jclepro.2020.122327

57. Spitsberg, I., Verti, M.J., Brahmandam, S., Coulston, G.W.: Capitalizing on emerging technologies: a path to creating opportunities in new markets. Res. Technol. Manag. **58**, 17–27 (2015). https://doi.org/10.5437/08956308X5804263

58. Statista. Ireland monthly number of Facebook users 2024. https://www.statista.com/statistics/1017375/facebook-users-ireland/. Accessed 29 Jan 2024

59. Sutherland, W., Jarrahi, M.: The sharing economy and digital platforms: a review and research agenda. Int. J. Inform. Manage. **43**, 328–341, ISSN 0268-4012 (2018). https://doi.org/10.1016/j.ijinfomgt.2018.07.004

60. Teli & Bassetti. Becoming a platform in europe: on the governance of the collaborative economy. Now Publishers (2021). https://doi.org/10.1561/9781680838411

61. United Nations Climate Change. UN Helps Fashion Industry Shift to Low Carbon | UNFCCC. https://unfccc.int/news/un-helps-fashion-industry-shift-to-low-carbon. Accessed 29 Dec 2024

62. United Nations Economist Network (UNEN). https://www.un.org/sites/un2.un.org/files/circular_economy_14_march.pdf. Accessed 29 Dec 2024

63. Upadhyay, V.A., Landman, A.B., Hassett, M.J.: Landscape analysis of oncology mobile health applications. JCO Clin. Cancer Inform. 579–587 (2021). https://doi.org/10.1200/CCI.20.00156

64. Velenturf, A.P.M., Purnell, P.: Principles for a sustainable circular economy. Sustain. Product. Consumpt. **27**, 1437–1457 (2021). https://doi.org/10.1016/j.spc.2021.02.018

65. Wautelet, T. Exploring the role of independent retailers in the circular economy: a case study approach (2018). https://doi.org/10.13140/RG.2.2.17085.15847

66. Wenger, E.: Communities of practice: learning as a social system. Syst. Think. **9**, 2–3 (1998). https://thesystemsthinker.com/communities-of-practice-learning-as-a-social-system/. Accessed 18 Oct 2025

67. Whole of Government Circular Economy Strategy 2022 – 2023 'Living More, Using Less'. https://www.gov.ie/en/publication/b542d-whole-of-government-circular-economy-strategy-2022-2023-living-more-using-less/#. Accessed 22 Jan 2025

68. World Economic Forum. Intelligent assets: unlocking the circular economy potential (2016). https://www.ellenmacarthurfoundation.org/intelligent-assets-unlocking-the-circular-economy-potential. Accessed 29 Jan 2025

69. Wu, Q., et al.: Pro-growth giant business, lock in, sustainable urban development and effect on local political economy: the case of petrochemical industry at Nanjing. J. Clean. Product. **107** (2015). https://doi.org/10.1016/j.jclepro.2015.03.046

70. Xiang, A., Pei, W., Yue, C.: PolicyChecker: analyzing the GDPR completeness of mobile apps' privacy policies. In: Proceedings of the 2023 ACM SIGSAC Conference on Computer and Communications Security, pp. 3373–3387. Association for Computing Machinery, New York, NY, USA (2023). https://doi.org/10.1145/3576915.3623067
71. Yanamandra, R., Ramesh, A.: Motivating The Stakeholders through a contest based mobile application for promoting and rewarding sustainability initiatives **15**, 30–40 (2019). https://doi.org/10.37383/SBJ14021903

Cultural Nuances in Game Speech: The Social Science Insights Challenge Transferred to AI-Mediated Localisation

Rebeca Caroline Acco$^{(\boxtimes)}$ (iD)

SEGA of Europe, London, UK
`rebeca.c.acco@gmail.com`

Abstract. This paper analyses the application of Interactive Design in overcoming challenges related to transferring cultural nuances in game dialogue to AI-driven localisation practices, with a particular emphasis on user experience and the integration of technology in gaming. The findings indicate that AI-assisted localisation faces significant obstacles, especially in translating context-dependent elements such as idioms, humour, and wordplay, which can result in awkward, inaccurate, or potentially offensive interpretations. Additionally, capturing emotional tone, slang, and subtleties in character dialogues necessitates human intervention to maintain the immersive experience of the game. The paper also reflects on my professional point of view as a Localisation Specialist at SEGA of Europe, detailing the difficulty of preserving cultural authenticity while incorporating AI tools into localisation workflows.

Keywords: Cultural Authenticity · AI Localisation · Game Speech · Adaptive Localisation · Ai-mediated Localisation · Player Engagement · Speech Nuance · Artificial Intelligence in Localisation · Game Localisation

1 Introduction

In the rapidly evolving gaming industry, the process of adapting game content for different regions and cultures has become vital. The importance of localisation in gaming extends beyond mere translation; it incorporates cultural adaptation and the immersion of intrinsic individual experiences, ensuring that in-game content aligns with local customs, ethics, transient trends, historical facts, idioms, and societal norms at all times. Zorrakin-Goikoetxea, I. (2022) [1] considers that transcreation, which is a form of translation, distances itself from the form and meaning of the source text to some extent, in order to adapt to the cultural needs of the target market. In this way, localisation enhances player immersion and engagement, as gamers are more likely to connect with content that feels native to their cultural context. She highlights the perspective of developers and a sample of players, exploring opinions and the extension of concept around audiovisual translation in communicating the same message in a different sociocultural context, where translators must determine whether cultural references will be understood in the target culture.

J. Abdelnour-Nocera et al. (Eds.): ARPPID 2025, CCIS 2797, pp. 91–103, 2026.
https://doi.org/10.1007/978-3-032-15516-0_6

As developers and publishers aim to reach global audiences, ensuring that games resonate culturally and linguistically with diverse player bases is essential. Simultaneously, the integration of Artificial Intelligence (AI) into localisation practices is transforming how games are tailored for various markets, enhancing efficiency in the overall workflow, as much as significantly changing and setting the rules for a new global demand. The AI integration into localisation processes raises several debates inherent in traditional methods in what concerns scalability, efficiency, consistency, accuracy, cultural sensitivity and legal concerns. In the scope of AI-mediated localisation within the gaming industry, the application of interaction design (IxD) principles brings a crucial framework to enhance user experience.

What I have experienced is that despite AI's advantages, AI-mediated localisation is not without challenges, mainly because of understanding context-specific translations, such as idioms, humour, or wordplay, which can lead to awkward, incorrect or even offensive interpretations. Also, emotional resonance, capturing the emotional tone, slangs and subtleties of character dialogues for example necessitate a human touch to preserve the game's immersive quality.

Building on my background as a graphic designer and Animator, I have consistently applied the knowledge gained during my Bachelor's in Animation Design throughout my career. I focused on conceptualising and executing creative work tailored to specific niches, incorporating branding methodologies and audience-centered design principles to overcome a wide variety of customer related challenges and demands in Brazil. Over time, my expertise found a new dimension in the Localisation Quality Assurance (LQA) field within the gaming industry in London, where I engaged with AI-driven processes and user experience, but now with languages.

As a language specialist of SEGA of Europe's Localisation department, I act as a safety net for translation issues post-review for the Brazilian Portuguese language. I supervise text nuances, slangs, dialects, speech tones, grammar rules, idiomatic expressions, vocabulary, and terminology adaptations to reflect cultural references accurately. Although AI has been recently incorporated into our workflows, which comes with new concerns and challenges, it also compensates with considerable agility in our internal processes, especially considering the growing demand due to exponential market expansion across multiple territories. This poses a permanent change to our roles, opening the door to a hybrid position, orbiting editing, supervision and translation duties, with AI being a crucial assistant.

In terms of academy-industry partnership, my perspective is that industry professionals and academic researchers could collaborate in addressing existing challenges by conducting deep research on various methodologies for AI-mediated localisation processes, and how to safely approach it. This collaboration can offer valuable insights into how Large Language Models (LLMs) function, that could potentially be adapted to localisation purposes, surfing on market released models, where companies such as OpenAI, META or Google already spent heavy resources on. I will explore possible solutions in the conclusion section of this paper.

This case study brings a solely personal perspective, where I use my experience to make a comparative among traditional and AI-mediated localisation, highlighting social science concepts, real industry strategy solution insights to unpredictable challenges, and how the optic of interactive design can assist humans and AI in adapting skills and resources to current new work requirements, increasing reliability and efficiency with the use of AI in project planning and to aid companies' workflows, meeting the increasing global demand. I conclude this paper by examining the implications, challenges, opportunities, and some aspects of AI's future potential for efficiently adapting to the localisation and QA practices.

2   A Brief Social Science Insight

Understanding cultural and social language contexts is vital for game localisation, as it is not just simple word-by-word translation. Linguistic anthropology examines how language reflects culture, ensuring that language aligns with target audience norms. It means adapting dialogue, terminology, and even character speech patterns to align with the cultural expectations of players. For example, in Japanese RPGs, the localisation team carefully adapts honorifics, formal speech, and slang to preserve the game's cultural integrity while making it accessible to non-Japanese-speaking players. Without such adjustments, players may miss subtle social cues or misunderstand character relationships.

Sociolinguistics studies language variation across social contexts like region, class, and identity, and applying its principles can help to adapt dialogues and narratives to resonate with diverse player groups. In game localisation, this is crucial for ensuring that characters speak in a way that matches their backgrounds. A noble character in a medieval RPG for example should not use the same slang as a teenager of the 21st century. Similarly, Fehrmann, D. (2021) [2] explains how in games like Final Fantasy XIV, localisation teams focus on adapting characters' tone of voice. This approach ensures that characters' speech patterns resonate with their backgrounds and personalities, maintaining consistency across diverse players' emotional experience.

By applying social science insights, localisation teams can create gaming experiences that feel natural, immersive, and engaging for players worldwide, preserving the original tone, humour, and emotional impact across languages. Yu, K. (2024) [3] emphasises that localised content significantly impacts player engagement and satisfaction. Games that effectively adapt to local cultures and languages provide a more immersive and enjoyable experience, leading to broader market acceptance.

3   Cultural Nuances in Language

Language is inherently tied to culture, and words or phrases often carry meanings that cannot be directly translated into another language without losing their essence.

Consider the expression "not my cup of tea", which can exemplify how language reflects cultural nuances. This idiom in English conveys a specific sentiment about something not being to one's taste, usually in a light, non-confrontational manner. In other languages, however, there may be no equivalent expression that communicates this sentiment with the same cultural context. In Brazil however, where Portuguese is predominantly spoken, culture is deeply connected to its extensive coastline and natural environment. Consequently, the expression is adapted to reflect this connection, resulting in phrases such as "This is not my beach" or "This is not my vibe". When using

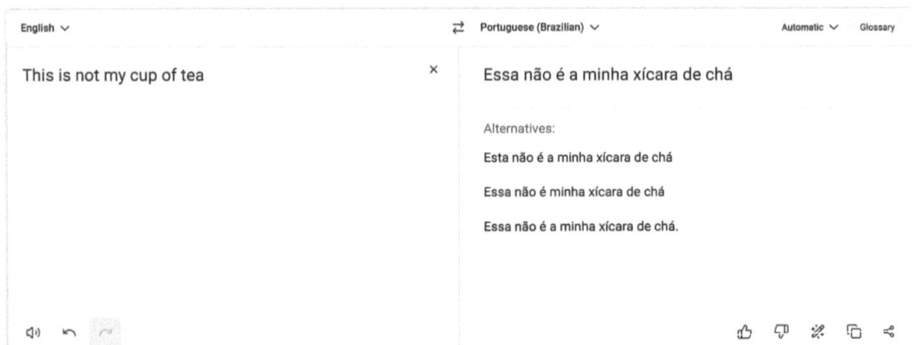

Fig. 1. DeepL translator tool, web version, screenshot taken on the 20th of April 2025

DeepL translation tool for example, the AI fails to understand the contextual meaning, providing a literal translation, as observed in Fig. 1:

In the French language, as a comparison, the term would translate to "Ce n'est pas ma tasse de thé" same as English, but more as a cultural recognition rather than having a specific French context, as it is known to be recent in the French language [4].

When referring to politeness and social hierarchies, one of the biggest localisation challenges, the Japanese language levels of politeness and formality are integral. The language changes its basic lexicon and subtle grammar features depending on the social context, from casual conversations with close friends to hyper-formal interactions with superiors, like CEOs. Mishandling these nuances can lead to a loss of authenticity or even offense, thereby affecting the gaming experience [5].

And last, in regard of cultural symbols and traditions, Lewin, K. (2005) [6] says that games often incorporate cultural symbols, traditions, and values that may not resonate universally. This process involves extensive research and adaptation of items, holidays, and writing systems to ensure the game feels authentic to the new target audience.

Furthermore, humour—especially puns and wordplay—relies on linguistic features that can vary by individuals, region, neighborhood, city, country, niche, culture, age, and generation, also shifting through forms as of homonymy, homophony, homography, and paronymy.

4   Traditional Challenges in Game Localisation

As game localisation goes beyond translation, requiring cultural nuances adaptation, linguistic accuracy, and technical adjustments to maintain authenticity, challenges permeate cultural sensitivity, UI constraints, voice-over synchronisation, and regulatory compliance.

In terms of Cultural sensitivity, the symbols, themes, or narratives acceptable in one culture may be inappropriate or offensive in another. For instance, according to Plante, C. (2025) [7] in the game "Wolfenstein II: The New Colossus," National Socialist German Workers' Party (NSDAP) symbols, including their leader's moustache, were altered or removed in the German version to comply with local laws and cultural sensitivities. Linguistic nuances are also another key point, where languages differ in structure, idioms, and idiomatic expressions. Translating humour, slang, or idiomatic expressions requires a deep understanding of both the source and target languages to maintain the original's intent and impact. Technical constraints differences, such as in text length between languages can lead to issues with interface design, voice-over synchronisation, and on-screen text display. Additionally, Regulatory compliance highlights the importance on different countries, varying regulations regarding content such as violence, gambling, religion and political themes. Ensuring a game complies with local laws is essential to avoid bans or legal issues, however this is too vast of a topic to explore within this paper and should be covered by another dedicated research.

5   Unpredictability and Decision Making

As a comprehensive process of adapting a video game to meet the linguistic, cultural, and regulatory requirements of a specific target market, localisation processes encompass cultural adjustments, visual changes, and considerations primarily based on previous experiences with the primary objective of an optimised interaction design for improved end-user engagement. There are numerous possibilities that require a range of strategic decisions and critical thinking, and such challenges can sometimes materialise as unprecedented scenarios.

Due to the nature of unpredictable events of game projects, it is utmost important to illustrate the necessity of continuous human oversight in localisation. This section will touch on two cases, highlighting the complexities and intricacies involved in the complex process of localisation.

Leone, M. (2005) [8], details the localisation of Cyberpunk 2077, illustrating the scale and complexity of adapting a game for multiple languages and cultures. Nearly half of the 5,000-person team worked on translating and adapting the game, stressing the resources required to address cultural nuances effectively. One significant challenge faced by the localisation team was managing late script changes, which required corresponding adjustments across multiple languages and necessitating additional voice recording sessions. These "pickups" were particularly demanding, as they aimed to maintain the narrative's strength while adhering to tight schedules. Additionally, the introduction of a Ukrainian language option in the 2.0 update led to unforeseen issues when anti-Russian statements appeared in the translation, highlighting the challenges in controlling content across vast localisation efforts.

Carpenter, N. (2025) [9] explores the intricate localisation process behind the game "Chants of Sennaar", focusing on the creation and implementation of fictional languages and word puzzles. In the article's interview with the translators of the game, the strategies and efforts they employed were based on a thorough understanding of their target audience. For instance, since not every player is proficient in foreign languages, some translation approaches focused on being beginner-friendly and accessible to players. The Japanese translator mentions the challenge of having players act as interpreters, using pictures to form sentences. The translation was neutral and used simple words to help players figure out terms, considering word order in each language. Tips and hints were included for players who might forget grammar rules.

It is undeniable that these decisions made by humans illustrate that this process requires a deep integration of the game UI, cultural background, a thorough understanding of the target audience, exceptional knowledge of user experience aligned to company values, culture and vision; game design acknowledgement, access to a vast database of past localisation problem-solving from several previous titles, context in world politics and a creative mindset focused on the human learning curve process, altogether.

6 Artificial Intelligence and Challenges in Cultural Context

Artificial Intelligence is increasingly used to enhance efficiency in not just localisation workflows but also translating and adapting game content across many industries. While AI can handle straightforward translations, and perform a series of advantages as of speed, scalability, consistency of style and terminology across a massive volume of content, while efficiently focusing on cost reduction around increased demands, it struggles with context-specific nuances, idioms, or cultural references, necessitating human intervention to ensure quality, cultural relevance and avoid problems.

Despite the considerable advancements in Natural Language Processing (NLP) and Machine Learning, AI can still struggle to understand the deeper layers of social sciences and human communication. In localisation, context is key, and AI tools generally focus on direct word-for-word translations based on statistical patterns learned from vast datasets. For instance, an AI-driven translation tool can recognise the phrase "Not my cup of tea" as a simple negation, but some of the AI tools could not capture the subtle, culturally rooted sense of politeness and avoidance of conflict that accompanies this phrase in English-speaking cultures.

As of a practical example, incorporating "not my cup of tea" in AI in a language like Polish, there might be no direct equivalent, and an AI tool can translate it as a literal phrase or give a valid option but bring the wrong context, missing the nuanced sentiment within a peculiar situation, also considering their sense of importance in historical context and customs.

Again, DeepL translator tool provided literal translations as observed in Fig. 2:

Fig. 2. DeepL translator tool, web version, screenshot taken on the 20th of April 2025

As per Polish, these expressions could vary between for example "To nie dla mnie", as to "This is not for me.", a simple and direct way to express disinterest; "To nie moja działka" as "This is not my field.", used when something is outside your area of expertise; or "To nie moje klimaty", as to "This is not my vibe", a more informal way to say something doesn't suit your taste.

I also conducted two types of tests: one focused on isolated English expressions, and the other on a full story. The full story included the phrase "This is not my cup of tea", along with several other English expressions, to examine the target expression within a detailed and high context descriptive text, using different nuances and tones. The test was reviewed by a SEGA of Europe Polish Language Specialist, who provided feedback on the level of satisfaction in what concerns quality, grammar, context, and language felt natural and human-like. It was noticeable in every five lines, there were three same expressions, it looked there was a lack of vocabulary and an inability to use other words to describe the situation to some extent, due to repetition, as seen in Table 1:

Table 1. Polish expressions sample by ChatGPT 4o mini from the 18th of April 2025

	English	Localisation by AI	Specialist's Comments
1	Barry said "**it's not his cup of tea**" to live a conventional life	Barry powiedział, **że to nie jego bajka**, ta cała konwencjonalność	It looks similar but we should avoid repetition and sound more natural
2	Terry made a face like he'd licked a lemon. "**Definitely not my cup of tea**", he muttered, shuddering, this time with genuine revulsion	Terry wykrzywił się jak po cytrynie.—**Zdecydowanie nie moja bajka**—mruknął z odrazą	They are talking about Mrs. Dunlop that is not in Terry's taste, therefore we can use another translation for this expression
3	Shaz looked at her phone. "*Oh, bugger all's happening now*". I'm off to paint toenails and listen to other people's dirty laundry "**Now that's my cup of tea**", she grinned, disappearing into the salon	Shaz zerknęła na telefon.—*Nic się nie dzieje.* Idę robić pedicure i słuchać cudzych brudów **— O, to już moja bajka**—rzuciła z uśmiechem, znikając w salonie	Translation changed to "*this is something for me*" as she is talking about things in a positive way. Also, there is an incorrect translation highlighted in italic, after the asterisk

Similarly for Korean, a test involving multiple tools showed that AI can struggle with context-dependent expressions. Korean, as an Asian language, has several peculiarities when compared to English or Latin-based languages. For example, as opposed to the Subject-Verb-Object (SVO) structure primarily observed in Romance languages, Korean necessitates the Subject-Object-Verb (SOV) word order. In addition, honorifics, politeness, and relative seniority play an imperative role in rendering the Korean language highly dependent on context. Lastly, case marking particles in Korean are essential for indicating the grammatical roles of words within a sentence. Unlike English, where word order often determines the function of words, Korean relies on these particles to clarify whether a word is the subject, object, topic, etc.

In a case study involving a native and expert in the Korean language, many expressions were given as examples to four different AI tools for translation, from where each tool was prompted to provide the five best interpretations. As a sample, I have picked the expression **"가슴 시리다"**, which according to the Korean expert, it translates in English as "an acute emotional pain that makes one feel as if they have frost in their heart that makes it shiver".

An example of the results can be observed in Table 2 (italic considered best output):

Table 2. Korean expressions sample by 4 AIs from the 17th of April 2025

ChatGPT 4o mini	Gemini 2.0 Flash	Perplexity 2.42.1	DeepL Translator
It makes my heart ache	*My heart aches*	My heart feels frozen with pain	Chesty
There's a chill in my chest I can't shake	There's a coldness in my heart	I feel a deep chill in my heart	Breastfeeding
It cuts right through the heart	I feel gutted	*My heart is aching with a bitter coldness*	Chestnut
It's that kind of sadness that lingers in your chest	I've got a heavy heart	I have a heart-wrenching feeling that cuts like ice	
Makes the heart go all cold, doesn't it?	My heart is breaking	My heart is pierced by a cold sorrow	
Score 7/10	**Score 5/10**	**Score 9/10**	**Score 0/10**

The Korean expert provided the scores to assess the accuracy of these AIs in translating from Korean to English. He stated that Perplexity proved to be the most narrative, whilst not losing the reference to "chill through the heart" from the Korean source text. Both ChatGPT and Gemini did an acceptable job at delivering the nuance in the source text yet end up either being too loquacious or too straight to the point. DeepL completely misunderstood the source text and additional information and presented irrelevant lexical items.

Another key challenge arises from games that incorporate local puns and jokes. AI faces significant obstacles in this area. While AI can process language, it often struggles with the subtleties and cultural nuances inherent in humour. This limitation can lead to translations that miss the mark, resulting in a loss of the original joke's impact or, worse, causing confusion or offense. Translating local puns and jokes in video games presents significant challenges, as humour can be deeply embedded in niche, cultural and linguistic contexts. Relying on wordplay, they inevitably often lose their intended effect when organically translated directly into another language [10]. The difficulty increases when humour stems from phonetic similarities, historical allusions, or double meanings.

AI can fail to recognise the layers of interpretation involved, as for example in English, the phrase "letting the cat out of the bag" conveys revealing a secret, while in German, the equivalent is "die Katze aus dem Sack lassen", which maintains a similar meaning. However, in Chinese, a literal translation would be nonsensical, requiring an alternative such as "说漏嘴"(shuō lòuzuǐ), meaning "to speak carelessly and reveal a secret". When it comes to regional humour, these challenges become even more pronounced. This complexity extends into individual humour preferences, where jokes can resonate differently based on personal experiences, cultural background, or even generational trends. AI, which primarily relies on statistical analysis and pre-existing datasets, may struggle to navigate these intricate variations. As a result, without human intervention, AI-localised jokes risk feeling either forced, confusing, or, in the worst case, entirely unfunny to the target audience.

Additionally, adapting fundamentally different language systems, such as Japanese, is naturally challenging due to differences in writing systems and cultural contexts. Kanji characters often carry complex meanings that require additional space when translated, complicating accuracy and readability. User interface (UI) design is strongly impacted, as space constraints and text expansion must be carefully managed. Therefore, AI-based translation tools, which lack the visual context awareness of the UI that human developers possess, increase the risk of error if adaptive localisation is not planned.

7   The Future with AI in Localisation

AI is revolutionising localisation by enhancing the entire workflow, not just automating translations. Duyar A. (2025) [11] expresses that it speeds up timelines, improves accuracy, and redefines how businesses approach localisation. The potential for AI-human collaboration in game localisation workflows is transformative, offering a blend of efficiency, accuracy, and cultural relevance. This collaborative approach leverages AI's ability to handle repetitive tasks such as initial translations and terminology management, freeing human translators to focus on refining content for cultural authenticity and maintaining the game's original tone, terminology and intent. AI technologies, particularly Neural Machine Translation (NMT) and generative AI, have significantly enhanced translation accuracy and speed, allowing for faster localisation processes and cost reductions.

Duyar highlights how AI systems use advanced algorithms and machine learning to process large volumes of content quickly and efficiently. They analyse context, predict translations, and suggest cultural adaptations. Neural networks in Machine Translation, like NMT, are a key innovation for the localisation practice. These systems leverage large datasets to look way more natural and context appropriate. AI excels in automation by streamlining workflows, managing terminology, and considerably ensuring consistency in translation projects.

In the evolving landscape of game development, AI is becoming a pivotal tool in localisation. However, while AI has advanced in processing and translating languages, it sometimes falls short in grasping cultural nuances. The International Achievers Group (2024) stresses that AI operates based on patterns of data and lacks the lived experiences that inform cultural sensitivity, also indicating that LLMs inherit cultural biases from their training data, as shown in a University of Sydney study on GPT-3 reflecting U.S. values, leading to translations that reinforce stereotypes or exclude minority perspectives. These aspects underscore the crucial need for exploring AI-human collaboration in game localisation workflows [12].

8 Conclusion

Due to the AI struggle with contextual understanding and cultural nuances, human oversight becomes critically essential to maintain authenticity, balancing AI and human expertise, while keeping it economically competitive. However, the AI tools have revolutionised the processes by speeding up workflows, enhancing localisation efficiency by handling repetitive tasks, allowing humans to focus on more complex tasks such as cultural adaptation, reference research, creative strategies and quality assurance. Advancing with AI in localisation requires integrating social science perspectives to provide training with diverse datasets, which improves its ability to handle idioms, humour, and context-specific expressions. Additionally, human-centered AI design prioritises user feedback and iterative design, which leads to more ethical and effective AI-driven localisation.

8.1 Exploring Possible Solutions and Improvements

This paper explores the needs of a hybrid system, where the key for successful and effective AI-mediated localisation centers on the integration of interaction design principles, social science insights, and the collective efforts of researchers, linguist specialists, QA and Localisation professionals, and developers, as a multidisciplinary collaboration among academia and industry.

I would like to emphasise the integration of human input into AI models on:

- **Context-Aware Mechanisms** – Incorporating deeper context-aware mechanisms, such as **sentiment analysis** (a technique in NLP, a branch of AI that focuses on helping computers understand, interpret, and generate human language; it helps the machine to find out whether text is positive, negative, neutral, or how strongly a sentiment is expressed) or **speaker-intention models** (a task in NLP that focuses on identifying the purpose behind speaker's words, whether it is a request, a command, a question, or being sarcastic), which could allow AI systems to detect tones and undertones.
- **Localised Corpora for Training Data** – Corpora are big data sets of real-world language. Bilingual corpora are types of corpora that contain the same content in two different languages. Usually, each sentence or phrase in one language is directly aligned with its translation in another language. These are useful for training translation systems like AI models, because the system learns how words and phrases in one language map to another. Expanding the range of bilingual corpora to include everyday conversations, slang, and regional variations could make AI systems more capable of understanding and translating informal language. This will help the system better handle colloquialisms, slang, metaphors, abbreviations and idiomatic expressions.
- **Collaborative Localisation Specific Platforms** – Encouraging collaborative translation platforms that combine AI with contributions from native speakers can help bridge the gap in tone and cultural context. Also, AI-based QA tools for LQA could automatically review and check translations to maintain consistency and prevent errors during translation and QA in different stages of the project, establishing different filtered layers of AI processes. They leverage technologies like Translation Memory and NMT to provide real-time feedback, improving the AI's accuracy over time.

Furthermore, industry actors can contribute with empirical knowledge in what concerns multilateral negotiations and legal compliance regarding practical daily life actions and real consequences due to human decision making and emotions around the matter to change a multinational environment. However, the ability to engage in long-term exploration is often limited by time constraints and the immediate demands of business operations. Academic institutions, on the other hand, are well-positioned to undertake rigorous research, pushing practice further and helping guide companies towards evidence-based decision-making, conserving resources and improving outcomes. This initial case study represents just an early step in what can be a much broader research trajectory focused on localisation challenges and AI collaboration.

The role of design and research in-between industry-academia should not be reduced to a simple pipeline where findings are transferred from one sphere to another. Instead, it operates as a form of boundary spanning, mediating between institutional pressures, technical systems, user expectations, and disciplinary frameworks. The "gap" between research and practice is not simply a lack or a delay, but a structural space where negotiation, translation, and adaptation take place. Engaging in that space is key for advancing localisation practices, particularly when AI is involved. Technologies emerge within systems of labour, accountability, and economic constraint which means that every design choice reflects priorities and infrastructures.

Such a perspective underscores the importance of situating localisation not just in terms of language processing, voice or graphics, but also in terms of social systems and institutional conditions. In practice, this requires continuous attention to user needs. These needs are variable, shaped by ethnicity, profession, age, culture, language, regulation, gender, and accessibility requirements. Addressing this complexity demands clear definitions and adaptive models of usability that can accommodate both short-term effectiveness and long-term sustainability. When coupled with methods that combine qualitative inquiry and quantitative measurement, such approach ensures a more reliable understanding of user experience. Empathy and accessibility are the foundation elements of design that enable trust in AI systems.

Hybrid approaches allow AI to function as a tool that supports rather than replaces human input. Improving user feedback mechanisms plays a critical role in this process, feedback loops should be provided to deepen relational trust between humans and systems.

Another challenge that lies in the relationship between academia and industry is that each side operates with different temporalities and priorities: academia invests in long-term, exploratory research while industry can be, in a way, mostly driven by short-term or more immediate constraints and performance metrics. Yet, my vision is that both can complement one another when they attempt to adapt, even if partially, to each other's rhythms. Industry can offer empirical data, contexts of application, and resources, while academia provides foresight, critical frameworks, and methodological depth. For this collaboration to succeed, however, researchers must also communicate in ways that resonate with business stakeholders, by engaging with the language of efficiency, compliance, profitability, and internal policies.

My perception is that localisation represents a fertile ground for collaboration. By for example potentially systematically gathering benchmark data from AI powered translation tools, mapping needs across cultural and linguistic contexts, and designing adaptive workflows, localisation research can expand beyond its traditional departmental boundaries to influence broader organisational practices. This has the potential to create significant efficiencies, reducing costs and avoiding communication failures across countries and time zones. At the same time, it enhances inclusivity and user experience by recognising the nuances of diverse global audiences.

Attention should be given to linguistic fidelity and to the technical and regulatory details that shape usability, such as handling of string codes, line breaks, compliance conventions, and legacy assets including glossaries, terminologies, and voice tones. Comparative studies across prompting techniques and framework solutions will be important for understanding how multiple AI systems can operate collaboratively. Further studies can help clarify not only technical performance but also broader questions of governance, accountability, and ethical responsibility. Ultimately, the advancement of AI-mediated localisation will not be determined solely by technical innovation but by the cultivation of trust, empathy, and adaptive collaboration. The speed of technological change is undeniable, yet it is the "speed of trust" that will determine how effectively these systems are adopted, integrated, and sustained. Research and practice must therefore be understood as intertwined forms of mediation, continuously negotiating between infrastructures, policies, cultural contexts, and utmost important, the user needs.

This paper contributes to laying the groundwork for such inquiry by situating localisation and AI collaboration. It advocates for a collaborative, interdisciplinary approach to innovation, one that recognises the productive potential of the research–practice gap and treats it as a space for co-creation. By approaching localisation as a boundary-spanning practice, it becomes possible to design systems that are more trustworthy, inclusive, and sustainable, ensuring that technological progress aligns with the diverse realities of its global users.

Acknowledgments. Special thanks to Stuart Wright, Kashif Iqbal and Professor Jose Abdelnour Nocera for making this opportunity possible. Also, a special mention to Firas Al Sekran, Krzysztof Piotrowicz, Lucile Minard, Melanie Fuchs and Tianyu Zhou and the expert in Korean (who wishes to be anonymous) for their brilliant assistance in verifying the accuracy of excerpts in this paper.

References

1. Zorrakin-Goikoetxea, I.: Transcreación y adaptación cultural en videojuegos: proceso, producto y recepción. TRANS. Revista de Traductología **26**, 213–231 (2022)
2. Final Fantasy Portal Site, Final Fantasy XIV Localization Team Interview! Part 2 (2021). https://na.finalfantasy.com/topics/266. Acessed 10 April 2025
3. Yu, K.: An analysis of cultural adaptation in video game localization – a case study of cyberpunk 2077: phantom liberty. In: (eds.) Proceedings of the 2nd International Conference on Social Psychology and Humanity Studies, Lecture Notes in Education Psychology and Public Media, vol. 37, pp. 242–252. EWA Publishing (Oxford) (2024)
4. Expressio.fr, Les expressions françaises décortiquées (2024). https://www.expressio.fr/expressions/ce-n-est-pas-ma-tasse-de-the. Accessed 13 April 2025

5. AsiaLocalize, The Challenges of Japanese Game Localization (2024). https://asialocalize. com/blog/game-localization/. Accessed 13 April 2025

6. Polygon, To release Animal Crossing in the West, Nintendo 'had to change everything' (2025). https://www.polygon.com/animal-crossing/484661/animal-crossing-localizat ion-book-excerpt. Accessed 14 April 2025

7. Polygon, Who shaved Hitler's mustache? The localizer (2025). https://www.polygon.com/ gaming/506037/video-game-localization-explained. Accessed 15 April 2025

8. Polygon, Nearly half of Cyberpunk 2077's 5,000-person team worked on localizing the game (2025). https://www.polygon.com/gaming/506323/cyberpunk-2077-localization-data. Accessed 15 April 2025

9. Polygon, How to translate a game with no words (Chants of Sennaar) (2025). https://www. polygon.com/gaming/510006/chants-of-sennaar-localization-process-fictional-language. Accessed 16 April 2025

10. Terra Translations, The Translation of Humor and Its Challenges (2021). https://terratransla tions.com/2021/03/24/the-translation-of-humor-and-its-challenges/. Accessed 16 April 2025

11. MotaWord, AI in Modern Localization – Benefits, Challenges, and Best Practices (2025). https://www.motaword.com/fr/blog/ai-in-modern-localization-benefits-challe nges-and-best-practices. Accessed 17 April 2025

12. International Achievers Group, The Challenges of Preserving Cultural Nuance in AI-Generated Content (2024). https://internationalachieversgroup.com/localization-ai/the-challe nges-of-preserving-cultural-nuance-in-ai-generated-content/. Accessed 17 April 2025

Case Report: Designing an AI Agent to Enhance Patient Education and Administrative Support Within an NHS Hospital Healthcare Setting

Richard M. H. Lee[1,2](✉) 📵, Aglaia Gantzopoulou[1,3] 📵, Jose Abdelnour-Nocera[3] 📵, Thomas Bainton[1] 📵, Oliver Chan[1] 📵, Olivia Li[1] 📵, David O.' Kelly Loesberg[2] 📵, Alicja Sidorowicz[2,4] 📵, and Miles Parnell[2,5] 📵

[1] Chelsea and Westminster Hospital, London, UK
richard@occiai.com
[2] Occi AI Ltd, Hampshire, UK
[3] University of West London, London, UK
[4] Moorfields Eye Hospital, London, UK
[5] Kingston Hospital, Kingston, UK

Abstract. Artificial Intelligence (AI) has the potential to revolutionise healthcare by improving patient engagement, streamlining administrative workflows, and alleviating both the patient experience and reducing the burden on healthcare staff. However, designing an AI system that addresses both patient education and administrative support while navigating real-world constraints faced by the National Health Service (NHS) requires a careful balance of innovation, practicality, and human-centred design. This case study examines the design and deployment of OcciAI, a conversational AI agent (Chatbot) at Chelsea and Westminster Hospital NHS Foundation Trust in London (England) that integrates personalised patient education with administrative assistance through patient questionnaires into a single, user-friendly system. The study illustrates opportunities for stronger collaboration between academia and the Healthcare industry, emphasising the benefits of bridging research and practice in Interaction Design to enhance UX (User Experience) and accessibility.

Keywords: Interaction design · Artificial intelligence · Chatbot · UX

1 Introduction

The first outpatient appointment is an important milestone that facilitates the journey to secondary care and managing complicated health conditions, acting as a gateway into diagnostics, treatment pathways, and care management [14]. National data has shown that the average Did Not Attend (DNA) rate for first outpatient appointments has been 8.7%, which costs the NHS (National Health Service) England approximately £1 billion. This creates a significant financial burden for a healthcare system already under strain [6]. Reducing the number of patients who do not attend new outpatient appointments is critical to improving health outcomes. This will allow patients to receive an earlier diagnosis and access specialist expertise and treatments [12, 14].

© The Author(s), under exclusive license to Springer Nature Switzerland AG 2026
J. Abdelnour-Nocera et al. (Eds.): ARPPID 2025, CCIS 2797, pp. 104–112, 2026.
https://doi.org/10.1007/978-3-032-15516-0_7

In recent years, as technology advances, Artificial Intelligence (AI) has become increasingly prevalent [15]. Conversational agents (AI Chatbots) allow users to communicate with computers using natural language processing (NLP) [7]. AI chatbots can mimic human conversations, allowing them to automate services and reduce effort. This makes them increasingly popular in a variety of fields, including healthcare [13].

OcciAI is an AI-driven patient information portal designed by two consultant ophthalmologists to simplify the outpatient appointment process and provide patients with greater understanding before their appointment. Patients access the portal to receive personalised, AI-generated videos explaining their condition and treatment options, available in multiple languages. An integrated AI chatbot addresses further questions, and additional information is summarised and uploaded to the patient's electronic health record. OcciAI aims to reduce inefficiencies in outpatient care, improve surgery conversion rates, and address healthcare inequalities by offering multilingual support, ultimately leading to better patient outcomes and efficient usage of clinician time.

It should be noted, however, that interaction design is a complex discipline, and challenges arise regarding implementation in the real world. The fundamental challenge to overcome is the disparity of perspectives among academics, healthcare professionals, User Experience (UX) designers, and patients [3]. Despite the various design approaches that have been proposed over the years, researchers and practitioners are often viewed as separate islands, and better Industry-Academia collaboration is needed [9].

This case study examines the design and deployment of OcciAI at Chelsea and Westminster Hospital NHS Foundation Trust (London, United Kingdom). It explores how it could be applied in the NHS context, addressing its specific challenges, such as resource constraints, diverse patient populations, and complex organisational structures. It emphasises the benefits of bridging research and practice in Interaction Design to enhance UX (User Experience) and accessibility.

2   Background: Addressing Dual Pain Points

In healthcare systems worldwide, including the NHS (National Health Service), patients encounter two primary challenges:

2.1   Educational Gaps

Alignment between patients' and clinicians' perspectives on health status is not always possible [8]. Due to limited consultation time and inaccessible information, patients often struggle to understand medical terminology, treatment options, and pre-/post-operative instructions. Consequently, clinicians and researchers cannot assess the outcomes of patients affected by these barriers comprehensively or reliably, which may adversely affect their health [8]. This can lead to confusion, poor adherence to treatment plans, and increased non-attendance, resulting in the demand for follow-up care.

2.2   Administrative Overload

Informatics has been identified as an essential component of Medicine, contributing to transforming healthcare systems. However, that causes a high workload for medical staff

[2]. Routine administrative processes, including collecting routine patient information, strain healthcare staff and patients. Long waiting times, unclear processes, limited capacity, and limited staff availability exacerbate these issues, particularly in under-resourced healthcare settings [1].

OcciAI was designed to tackle these dual pain points by offering a unified solution that empowers patients to understand their healthcare journey while streamlining the collection of routine patient information.

3 Design Approach

The literature recognises the challenges in designing healthcare solutions that should be addressed to make new technology usable and acceptable [10, 11]. In the context of user-centred design in the NHS (National Health Service), the challenges come up at different stages, including the approval process of ethics, user recruitment and stakeholder involvement, eliciting needs from users associated with sensitive and personal issues, and bringing together different disciplines [11]. In order to ensure effective participation of users and stakeholders, the time, logistics, and financial implications must be carefully planned at the beginning of a project [11].

The development of OcciAI followed an iterative, user-centered methodology that emphasised accessibility, empathy, and scalability.

3.1 Research and Ideation

The design process began with extensive research to understand the needs of patients and healthcare providers. Discussions were held with NHS stakeholders, including clinical and administrative staff, to identify common frustrations during a patient group meeting arranged in early 2025. Key insights highlighted the importance of optimising patient education and improving the collection of routine patient information, with a particular emphasis on creating a system capable of supporting non-native speakers.

The team then undertook journey mapping of the NHS patient pathway, from the point of referral (via optometrists or general practitioners) through to the pre-operative appointment. This process helped identify critical touchpoints where OcciAI could provide meaningful assistance and enhance the overall patient experience.

Once patient data collection begins as part of the pilot, data management will follow strict security and ethical guidelines. Data collection will be limited to only those elements essential to the conduct of the pilot. Access to data will be role-based, with each team member able to view only the information relevant to their role, supported by strong authentication methods such as NHS passwords or multifactor authentication. A comprehensive record will be maintained of all dataset accesses and modifications.

All identifiable data will be encrypted both "at rest" (when stored in databases or servers) and "in transit" (when transmitted over networks). Data will be stored only in secure locations, such as approved NHS or accredited cloud environments. Direct identifiers, including names, NHS numbers, and addresses, will be removed or replaced prior to analysis.

Clear definitions of responsibilities, access rights, and security measures will be set out in data-sharing agreements between the NHS hospital and any team members from universities or external partners involved in the pilot. Furthermore, any analysis of sensitive datasets will take place exclusively within a secure environment to ensure compliance with data protection standards.

3.2   Interaction Design and Prototyping

OcciAI was designed as an integrated conversational AI system capable of handling both educational and administrative tasks. Key features included:

- Personalised Education: OcciAI provides patients with educational AI driven videos based on their reason for referral. The video content is easily customisable to the hospital and available in multiple languages to promote equality and diversity within the NHS.
- Conversational Interface: OcciAI's natural language processing (NLP) capabilities enabled intuitive, conversational interactions. Patients could ask, "What is a cataract?" or "What will happen during surgery?" in a language of their choice and receive clear, actionable responses in the same language.
- Multi-Modal Interaction: Occiai provides both text and visual interactions to accommodate patients with different communication preferences or accessibility needs. An inclusive usability testing, in which the participants have special access needs, such as voice interaction, is being planned for late 2025 based on feedback from discussions conducted so far. For example, visual aids and multilingual support were particularly useful for non-native speakers and patients with low literacy levels. Following the initial deployment of the pilot, OcciAI will also aim to enhance accessibility for people with disabilities in accordance with the Web Content Accessibility Guidelines.

3.3   Usability Testing and Iteration

OcciAI is in the process of arranging a pilot study within the surgical suite of Chelsea and Westminster Hospital in London, United Kingdom, scheduled to begin in 2025. The primary aim of this pilot is to evaluate the system's usability and effectiveness in a real NHS environment.

A key component of the pilot will involve user testing with NHS patients to gather feedback that will inform further optimisation of the software design. This process will help ensure that the interface remains simple to use while enhancing the quality and accuracy of AI-generated responses.

The pilot will also be implemented across multiple specialties within the surgical suite, which caters to eight different clinical areas. Specifically, the study will focus on three specialties—ophthalmology, gynaecology, and trauma and orthopaedics. By targeting multiple disciplines, the pilot aims to determine whether the theoretical benefits of OcciAI within an NHS setting can be replicated across a range of patient demographics and clinical conditions.

4   Application in the NHS: Challenges and Opportunities

Applying OcciAI in the NHS requires addressing unique constraints and challenges while leveraging opportunities for impact:

4.1   Challenges in the NHS Context

- Resource Constraints: NHS resources are often stretched, with staff shortages and limited funding for new technologies [16]. OcciAI addresses this by reducing staff administrative workload, freeing up time for patient care.
- Integration with Existing Systems: In the digital era of the NHS, digital health records permit the whole record (or relevant information from it) to be shared quickly, securely, and in a standard way between health professionals to support patient care, achieving 'integrated' electronic health records, such as GP (General Practitioner) records or the NHS app [5]. OcciAI was designed to integrate with the NHS App, ensuring interoperability and minimising disruption to existing workflows.
- Digital Literacy and Inclusivity: A significant proportion of NHS patients may have limited digital literacy or lack access to technology. Thus, in the design of any service, it is essential to consider digital inclusivity, ensuring no one is left behind [4]. OcciAI's multi-modal design, including planned voice interactions and offline functionality, ensures inclusivity for these populations.
- Trust and Data Security: Patients and NHS staff must trust OcciAI to handle sensitive medical and financial data. Robust encryption, compliance with GDPR (General Data Protection Regulation), and transparent privacy policies were built into OcciAI's design to address these concerns. OcciAI worked with a third party to ensure we were compliant with the NHS Data Security and Protection Toolkit.
- Sustainability and ethical considerations: AI systems can be highly energy and water intensive, particularly during training and continuous use. As part of the NHS's commitment to net-zero emissions, this project prioritises energy efficiency with lightweight, fine-tuned models hosted on green infrastructure. It is designed to minimise computational waste, with periodic efficiency reviews and lifecycle assessments.

4.2   Challenges in the Design Process

Applying recommended interaction design methods and processes within an NHS context presented both unique challenges and valuable opportunities.

The NHS places a strong emphasis on patient safety, data privacy (including GDPR compliance), and equitable access. These priorities can limit the flexibility to iterate quickly or adopt experimental design approaches that are more common in commercial technology development. To address this, the project team outsourced governance and compliance aspects to a company with extensive experience in healthcare regulation. This partnership allowed the team to develop and refine the product at pace while maintaining full compliance with all necessary NHS and legal requirements.

Another key challenge arose from the wide variability in user demographics, which included patients from diverse age groups, levels of digital literacy, and cultural backgrounds. Designing intuitive and universally accessible interactions required careful consideration of these factors. To support this process, the team presented their work at the Hospital's Quality, Equality and Health Inequality Impact meeting in December 2024, where approval was granted to progress to the next stage of implementing OcciAI within the Trust. In January 2025, a patient participation group involving 10–15 individuals of varying ages, genders, and ethnic backgrounds was held. Feedback from this session demonstrated strong support for the platform, with participants recognising its potential to enhance patient engagement and improve clinical pathways.

These challenges also revealed significant opportunities to bridge the gap between interaction design theory and real-world healthcare practice. The NHS's commitment to evidence-based methods can be leveraged to validate AI-driven solutions through participatory design and co-creation with clinicians and patients. Engaging stakeholders early in the design process helps ensure that AI systems align with clinical workflows, thereby improving adoption and overall utility. Additionally, the use of AI video avatars offers a means to overcome communication barriers by personalising interactions, providing multilingual support, and simplifying complex medical information for patients.

4.3 Opportunities for Impact

- Reducing Waiting Times: By providing patients with information prior to their appointment, this ensures that patients understand the important of attending their appointment and also allows patients to decline referral if they do not wish to proceed with treatment. This will help to reduce non-attendance and enhance clinic efficiency.
- Improving Health Literacy: By simplifying complex medical information, OcciAI empowers patients to take a more active role in managing their health, reducing the need for repeat consultations. With OcciAI, complex medical terminology is translated into clear, accessible language that is tailored to the level of literacy of the individual. With the chatbot, patients can make informed decisions about their treatment and recovery by interacting with a conversational, on-demand explanation of diagnoses, medications, procedures, and aftercare instructions. By improving comprehension, patients are able to gain greater confidence, adhere to care plans, and are less likely to rely on clinicians for repetitive clarifications.
- Supporting Underserved Communities: OcciAI's multilingual support and inclusive design make it particularly beneficial for underserved and diverse populations within the NHS. OcciAI is designed with inclusivity in mind, providing multilingual support and culturally sensitive communication so that the diverse patient populations within the National Health Service may be better served. Using an AI agent, individuals from marginalised or underserved communities - including non-native English speakers, recent migrants, and those without access to traditional health education resources - receive accurate, empathetic health information that is easily understood. Ultimately, this will result in greater equity in care, more confident engagement of patients with healthcare services, and a reduction in disparities in access to healthcare, quality of care, and satisfaction with care. The accessibility and responsiveness of OcciAI support the NHS' commitment to delivering inclusive, patient-centered care.

4.4 Outcomes and Reflections

Key Successes

- Empowered Patients: OcciAI aims to enhance health literacy and administrative confidence.
- Streamlined Operations: By automating routine queries, OcciAI aims to reduce administrative workloads, freeing up NHS staff for more complex tasks.
- Enhanced Accessibility: The system demonstrates strong usability across diverse NHS patient groups, including older adults, non-native speakers, and individuals with disabilities. The OcciAI system is designed for ease of use and accessibility, so that patients of all ages, languages, and abilities can interact effectively with it. To support older adults less comfortable with digital technologies, the chatbot offers simplified navigation, a clear visual design, and voice interaction. With the system, non-native English speakers can communicate in plain language and avoid miscommunications. In addition, OcciAI aims to adhere to accessibility standards such as WCAG, providing features like alternative text font, and adjustable text sizes. A broad range of accessibility needs is addressed by OcciAI, ensuring that all patients have equal access to health care.

Challenges and Solutions

Implementing OcciAI within the NHS presented key challenges that required targeted solutions. Scalability was a major consideration, as rolling out the system across multiple NHS Trusts demanded a balance between customisation and adaptability to different local infrastructures. For complex patient queries, OcciAI includes an escalation process that seamlessly transfers unresolved issues to human staff, ensuring patient satisfaction and maintaining trust in the system.

5 Broader Implications for Interaction Design

OcciAI offers valuable insights for Interaction Design in complex, resource-constrained environments like the NHS:

1. Human-Centered Design in Public Systems: Designing for public healthcare systems requires balancing user needs with operational constraints, such as scalability and resource limitations. Human-centered design principles ensure that OcciAI's technology meets the needs of diverse users with different levels of health literacy, clinical staff under pressure, and administrative teams managing high workloads, while being intuitive, empathic, and responsive. In addition to budget constraints, infrastructure variability, and interoperability requirements, the system is built with operational realities in mind. This solution is designed to be scalable, easy to deploy, and maintainable to ensure widespread adoption across NHS sites. Using user feedback, iterative testing, and co-design with NHS stakeholders, OcciAI aligns digital innovation with public health's values of accessibility, equity, and sustainability.
2. Empathy at Scale: OcciAI's conversational tone and multi-modal design illustrate how AI systems can deliver empathetic, patient-centered experiences at scale.

3. Collaborative Innovation: The success of OcciAI underscores the importance of partnerships between academia and industry in addressing real-world challenges through
design.

6 Conclusion

OcciAI demonstrates the transformative potential of AI in healthcare, particularly within
complex systems like the NHS. By integrating patient education and administrative
support into a single, unified system, OcciAI empowers patients, reduces staff workload,
and enhances the overall healthcare experience.

The collaborative partnership between academia and industry will be instrumental
in OcciAI's success, blending user-centered design principles with practical insights to
create an innovative and scalable solution. In the NHS context, OcciAI's potential to
reduce waiting times, improve health literacy, and support underserved communities
offers a roadmap for the future of AI-driven healthcare.

As the NHS continues to face growing demand and resource constraints, OcciAI
represents a critical step forward in delivering equitable, efficient, and patient-centered
care.

Acknowledgments. .

Disclosure of Interests.   RL and MP are co-directors of OcciAI Ltd.

References

1. Carr, A., Smith, J.A., Camaradou, J., Prieto-Alhambra, D.: Growing backlog of planned
surgery due to covid-19. BMJ. **n339** (2021). https://doi.org/10.1136/bmj.n339
2. Doleman, G., Duffield, C.: Administrative applications. In: Hussey, P. and Kennedy, M.A.
(eds.) Introduction to Nursing Informatics, pp. 233–265. Springer International Publishing,
Cham (2021). https://doi.org/10.1007/978-3-030-58740-6_9
3. Duffy, A., Christie, G.J., Moreno, S.: The challenges toward real-world implementation of
digital health design approaches: narrative review. JMIR Hum. Factors. **9**, 3, e35693 (2022).
https://doi.org/10.2196/35693
4. Heaslip, V., Holley, D.: Ensuring digital inclusion. Clin. Integrat. Care **17**, 100141 (2023).
https://doi.org/10.1016/j.intcar.2023.100141
5. Honeyman, M., Dunn, P., McKenna, H.: A digital NHS? (2016)
6. Kiruparan, P., Kiruparan, N., Debnath, D.: Impact of pre-appointment contact and short message service alerts in reducing 'Did Not Attend' (DNA) rate on rapid access new patient
breast clinics: a DGH perspective. BMC Health Serv. Res. **20**, 1, 757 (2020). https://doi.org/
10.1186/s12913-020-05627-2
7. Kuhail, M.A., Alturki, N., Alramlawi, S., Alhejori, K.: Interacting with educational chatbots:
a systematic review. Educ. Inf. Technol. **28**(1), 973–1018 (2023). https://doi.org/10.1007/s10
639-022-11177-3
8. Long, C., Beres, L.K., Wu, A.W., Giladi, A.M.: Patient-level barriers and facilitators to completion of patient-reported outcomes measures. Qual. Life Res. **31**, 1711–1718 (2022). https://
doi.org/10.1007/s11136-021-02999-8

9. Marijan, D., Sen, S.: Industry-academia research collaboration and knowledge co-creation: patterns and anti-patterns. ACM Trans. Softw. Eng. Methodol. **31**(3), 1–52 (2022). https://doi.org/10.1145/3494519

10. Moody, L.: User-centred health design: reflections on D4D's experiences and challenges. J. Med. Eng. Technol. **39**(7), 395–403 (2015). https://doi.org/10.3109/03091902.2015.1088086

11. Moody, L., Long, A., McCarthy, A.: Design for health and dignity: user and stakeholder involvement in design for urinary continence. Adv. Hum. Aspects Healthcare Med. 58 (2021) https://books.google.co.uk/books?hl=en&lr=&id=SWhYBAAAQBAJ&oi=fnd&pg=PA58&dq=Moody,+L.,+Long,+A.,+and+McCarthy,+A.,+2014,+Design+for+Health+and+Dignity:+User+and+Stakeholder+Involvement&ots=PLNwzqjo8o&sig=M1gPW-hIA0xnSoe9AbT5t6JeDro&redir_esc=y#v=onepage&q&f=false

12. NHS England. Reducing did not attends (DNAs) in outpatient services 2023 [updated August 15 2023; cited 2023 November 6]. https://www.england.nhs.uk/long-read/reducing-did-not-attends-dnas-in-outpatient-services/

13. Oh, K.-J, Lee, D., Ko, B., Choi, H.J.: A Chatbot for psychiatric counseling in mental healthcare service based on emotional dialogue analysis and sentence generation. In: 2017 18th IEEE International Conference on Mobile Data Management (MDM), pp. 371–375. IEEE, Daejeon, South Korea (2017). https://doi.org/10.1109/MDM.2017.64

14. Sung, B., et al.: Identifying barriers to outpatient appointment attendance in patient groups at risk of inequity: a mixed methods study in a London NHS trust. BMC Health Serv. Res. **24**, 1, 554 (2024). https://doi.org/10.1186/s12913-024-10947-8

15. Tlili, A., et al.: What if the devil is my guardian angel: ChatGPT as a case study of using chatbots in education. Smart Learn. Environ. **10**, 1, 15 (2023). https://doi.org/10.1186/s40561-023-00237-x

16. Warner, M., Zaranko, B.: NHS funding, resources and treatment volumes, IFS Report, No. R236, ISBN 978-1-80103-114-1, Institute for Fiscal Studies (IFS), London (2022). https://doi.org/10.1920/re.ifs.2022.0236

Human by Design: Integrating Human-Centred Principles in Augmentation Technologies

Aryaman Jacob[1]([✉]) [iD] and Apala Lahiri Chavan[2] [iD]

[1] Independent design Researcher, London, United Kingdom
jacob.aryaman@gmail.com
[2] Co-Founder – HFI APAC and Chief of Technical Staff, Fairfield, IA 52556, USA

Abstract. Human Augmentation Technologies (HAT) are rapidly advancing, promising to extend physical, sensory, and cognitive capabilities. However, their development often remains technology-driven, overlooking the human, social, and ethical dimensions critical to real-world integration. This paper argues for a Human Centred Design approach to HAT, one that foregrounds lived experience, contextual awareness, and inclusive participation. Through a review of the current HAT landscape and a case study of the Second Skin project, which engaged manual workers in the co-design of a wearable augmentation prototype, the paper demonstrates how embodied, participatory methods can reveal user insights and challenge dominant narratives around efficiency and surveillance. Building on this foundation, the paper proposes a set of design principles tailored to the complex demands of augmentation emphasising empathy, ethical reflection, adaptability, and systemic awareness. By reorienting design processes around human values and societal context, this work contributes to shaping augmentation futures that are not only innovative but also equitable, sustainable, and attuned to the realities of those they aim to serve.

Keywords: Human Augmentation Technologies · Human-Centred Design · Inclusive Design · Ethical Technology · Wearable Technology

1 Introduction

Human augmentation technologies (HAT) encompass a broad range of innovations designed to extend or enhance human physical, sensory, or cognitive capabilities, either temporarily or permanently. These technologies include wearable devices such as exoskeletons, sensory aids like advanced prosthetics and implants, and even emerging gene-editing techniques that modify biological functions [6, 7, 16]. As the boundary between humans and machines increasingly blurs, HAT promises profound impacts on health, productivity, and everyday life.

While human augmentation technologies hold transformative potential, their development has largely followed a technocentric path, one that prioritises technical innovation and performance over the nuanced realities of users and the complex systems they inhabit. This trajectory is not unique to HAT but reflective of a broader pattern in emerging technologies, where engineering-led solutions often underemphasise social, ethical,

J. Abdelnour-Nocera et al. (Eds.): ARPPID 2025, CCIS 2797, pp. 113–126, 2026.
https://doi.org/10.1007/978-3-032-15516-0_8

and experiential dimensions [1, 4, 9, 24]. As a result, augmentation systems are often designed for users rather than with them, risking poor adoption, exclusion, and unintended consequences [18]. Such challenges call for a reorientation towards Human Centred Design (HCD) principles, an approach that prioritises users lived realities, values, inclusivity, and embeds ethical reflection throughout the design process.

This paper investigates the question: How can HCD principles be effectively applied to the development of human augmentation technologies to ensure they are ethical, inclusive, and contextually relevant? This research question emerges from the growing concern that augmentation technologies are being developed in isolation from the users they aim to support [6, 20]. By examining a real-world case study, the paper explores how embedding user insight into the design of wearable systems can lead to more responsible and human-aligned technological futures that are not only innovative but also sustainable, ethical, and socially responsible. By adopting a holistic perspective that considers the dynamic interplay between humans, technology, and environment, designers and developers can better anticipate challenges, foster equitable access, and ensure that augmentation technologies genuinely enhance human well-being in ways they want.

In the sections that follow, the article outlines the current landscape of HAT, the necessity of HCD and key principles to guide future development.

2   HCDs Role in Designing for a Better Future

In the context of Human Augmentation Technologies, distinguishing between Human-Centred Design and User-Centred Design (UCD) is critical. While both share the goal of improving technology for people, UCD traditionally emphasises usability and efficiency, whereas HCD expands the scope to include ethics, social values, and long-term sustainable systemic impacts. As shown in Table 1, this distinction matters because HAT intervenes directly in the body and identity of users, demanding a framework that goes beyond functional optimisation toward responsibility, inclusiveness, and care.

Augmentation technologies and any future technology that is made in relation with the human body would need to have robust guard-rails to guide the conceptualisation, design, development, and integration of such solutions for the benefit of all. HCD has contributed to such endeavours and would be an appropriate starting point for designing for HAT.

3   Landscape of HAT

3.1   Influences and Popular Culture

The concept of human augmentation has long captured the imagination of popular culture, featuring prominently in science fiction media such as Cyberpunk 2077, Star Wars, The Expanse, and Neuromancer. These narratives often explore technologically enhanced bodies, envisioning scenarios where implants, prosthetics, or exosuits push humans beyond natural limitations. Far from mere entertainment, such depictions play

Table 1. Comparing Human-Centred Design (HCD) and User-Centred Design (UCD) in Human Augmentation Technologies

Aspect	Human-Centred Design	User-Centred Design
Focus	Holistic: considers human experience, context, ethics, and systems [1, 19, 24]	Narrow: optimises usability and task performance [19, 20]
Approach	Ethnography, participatory methods, iterative prototyping [8, 9, 23]	Personas, scenarios, usability testing [19, 20]
Scope	Broad ecosystem: users, caregivers, environment, long-term impacts [8, 9, 23]	Direct user–device interaction, short-term use [19]
Ethics	Embeds values: equity, autonomy, societal responsibility [10, 24]	Limited ethical reflection; focuses on acceptance [19]
Participation	Co-design with diverse stakeholders [12, 20]	Users mainly involved in testing/validation [19]
Relation with HAT	Inclusive, context-sensitive augmentation (e.g. ergonomic exosuits) [6, 7, 17, 24]	Functional, efficient devices but risks overlooking social context [18, 20]

a significant role in shaping public expectations and influencing the trajectory of technological development. Scholars have noted that speculative fiction acts as a form of "design fiction," creating imaginaries that inform both public discourse and the ideation phase within innovation and design communities [3, 21].

While these cultural imaginaries may seem distant from reality, advances in wearable technologies, neural interfaces, and bioengineering are steadily narrowing the gap between fiction and practice. Already, exoskeletons are being adopted in industrial and rehabilitative contexts, such as in logistics and physiotherapy [4], while sensory augmentation tools like cochlear implants and haptic feedback systems are increasingly integrated into everyday assistive technologies. Although the mainstream visibility of more radical augmentations such as robotic limbs with AI-driven feedback loops is still limited, early-stage research and niche applications suggest that wider adoption may not be far off [24].

3.2 Existing Paradigms

As seen in Fig. 1, these technologies encompass both life-altering clinical enhancements like disease management, to more expressional alterations for social enhancements. In both research and application, human augmentation technologies are often conceptualised across three interrelated domains: sensory, motor, and cognitive augmentation.

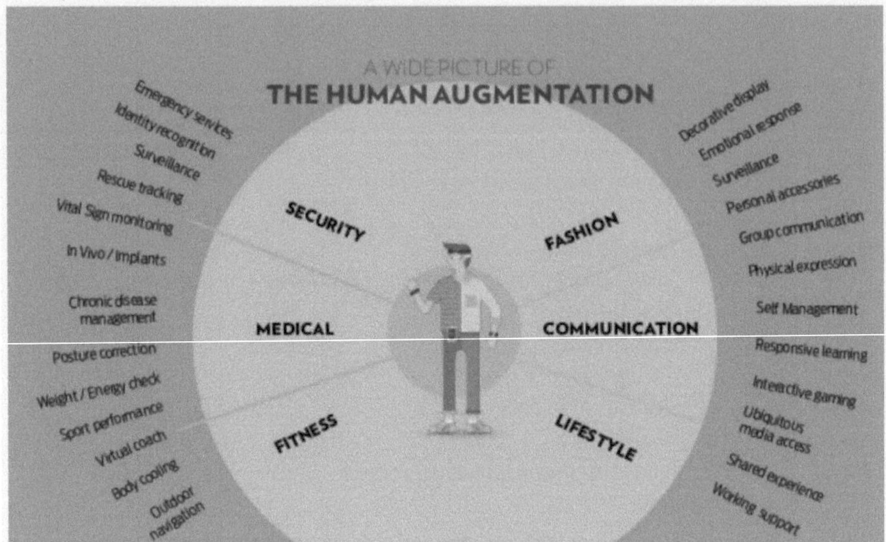

Fig. 1. Different forms Human Augmentation can take in the future [22]

- Sensory augmentation involves enhancing perception, such as vision, hearing, or tactile feedback, through devices like visual prosthetics or sensory substitution interfaces.
- Motor augmentation targets physical movement and strength, evident in technologies like robotic limbs, exosuits, and supernumerary robotic limbs [18].
- Cognitive augmentation refers to the enhancement of memory, attention, or decision-making through tools such as neurofeedback systems, brain–computer interfaces (BCIs), or AI-assisted cognitive aids [6, 24].

Together, these categories help delineate the ways HAT can interface with the human body, enabling targeted innovations across healthcare, work, mobility, and beyond. However, As Villa et al. argue, focusing solely on sensory–motor–cognitive capabilities risks reducing users to passive recipients of technological intervention rather than active agents embedded within complex social, cultural, and ecological networks [24].

To fully grasp the implications of human augmentation, we must go beyond the technological lens and examine how these innovations intersect with social values, power structures, and lived experience. As such, it becomes increasingly important to frame the landscape of HAT not just in terms of capability expansion, but also in relation to societal norms, ethical imperatives, and the relational contexts in which technologies are adopted and experienced.

Moving beyond these abstractions, it is crucial to examine a concrete example where human-centred design methods are applied. The following case study of the Second Skin project demonstrates how embedding user insight and embodied inquiry at every stage can yield augmentation solutions that resonate with the complex realities of physically demanding professions.

4 Case Study: Second Skin

4.1 Context

The case explored in this paper is the Second Skin project, a research-led thesis and design initiative that examines how wearable augmentation technologies can support the embodied experiences of physically demanding professions. The project was selected as a case because it engages directly with the lived expertise of blue-collar workers, whose voices are often excluded from discussions on emerging tech and it sought to implement conceptual technology, like wearable devices, into a novel workspace. Workers embodied knowledge and work routines present a unique and underrepresented perspective for designing augmentation systems that are ethical, inclusive, and practical.

4.2 Method and Process

The project employed a Human Centred Design approach and a collaborative design process (co-design) that brought together electricians, carpenters, university technicians and warehouse staff, whose bodily routines, safety needs, and sensory feedback loops were central to shaping the design.

The research began with contextual inquiries and observational studies in work environments where physical strain, repetitive motion, and environmental exposure were part of daily practice. Informal interviews and shadowing sessions revealed nuanced insights into how workers perceived fatigue, posture, pressure points, and sensory overload; factors that often go unaddressed in conventional wearable tech design. These early engagements informed the design brief and led to a participatory process where practitioners became co-creators rather than mere end users.

Workshops were conducted with these professionals to co-design concepts for the Second Skin prototype. Through bodystorming (sketching on the body) and rapid material prototyping, participants explored how wearables might augment awareness, offer feedback, or intervene during physically intensive tasks. Collaborators also evaluated early functional mock-ups, offering grounded feedback on comfort, flexibility, interference with workflow, and perceived usefulness.

Traditional HCD methods were adapted to inform experiential and embodied knowledge, allowing for design decisions to emerge not just from dialogue, but from firsthand interaction and bodily intuition. For instance, an electrician's feedback on toolbelt usage and cold temperatures influenced material choices and sensor placement. A warehouse worker's insight into shift-based fatigue cycles shaped the logic behind passive versus active haptic alerts.

4.3 Synthesis

Existing HATs, all in various stages of development, were mapped in accordance with the "closeness" to the body and close they are to be market ready (Fig. 2). While many are in their nascent stages, either as college project (Vision Project) or might still be at an experimental research stage (3rd Thumb), many have entered the market without us directly labelling them as augmentation technologies, like Telescopes or Prosthetics.

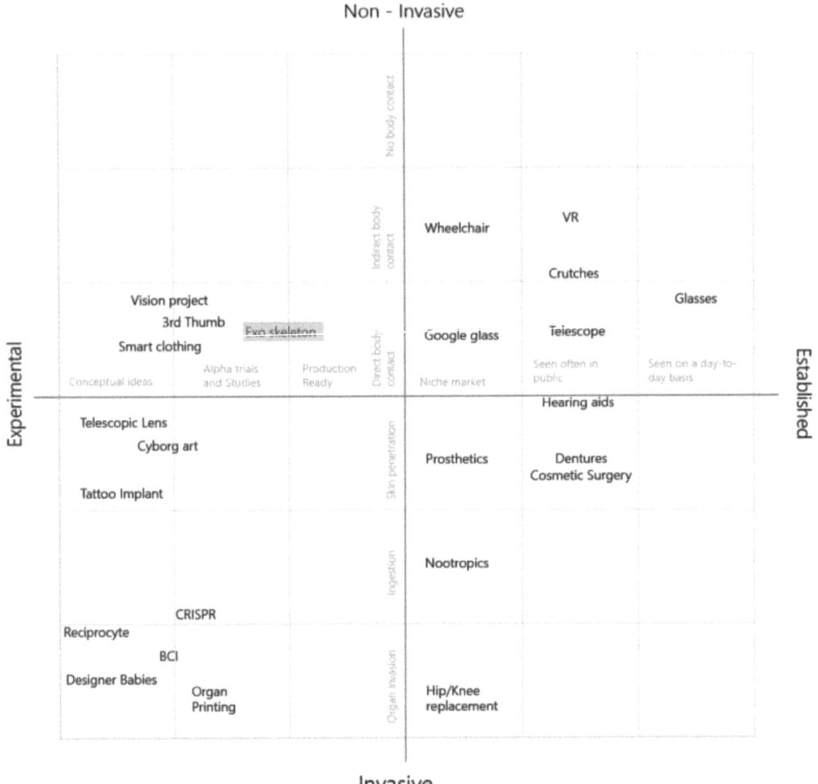

Fig. 2. Relationship between Established and Invasive nature of HAT

Exo-skeletons stood out as one such technology that is being rapidly adopted in workplace environments to help assist with load, transportation and support [7, 13, 17]. Its main application for now is seen in medicine for rehabilitating patients after hip/knee surgery or partly restoring limb functions for people who use wheelchairs, or in the military. In order to understand gaps in relation with the body itself, several of the examples from Fig. 2 were mapped to human body parts, establishing relationships between specific body functions, the type of HAT and number of affected areas.

In both research and application, human augmentation technologies are often conceptualised across three interrelated domains: sensory, motor, and cognitive augmentation [13]. Figure 3 builds on this by overlaying existing research prototypes, illustrating coverage gaps but also the large coverage area by exo-suits. For these reasons exo-suits as a HAT showed promise in workplace application. It also connects with most of the body to provide strength, support and rehabilitation. Following this structured approach within a design framework and outlook helped narrow down an area of intervention that had strong conceptual foundation and impact on the user's body.

By grounding the intervention in both biomechanical need and user context, the exo-suit not only delivered strength and support but also set the stage for richer conversations about the worker's experience. These findings helped further interactions with blue-collar

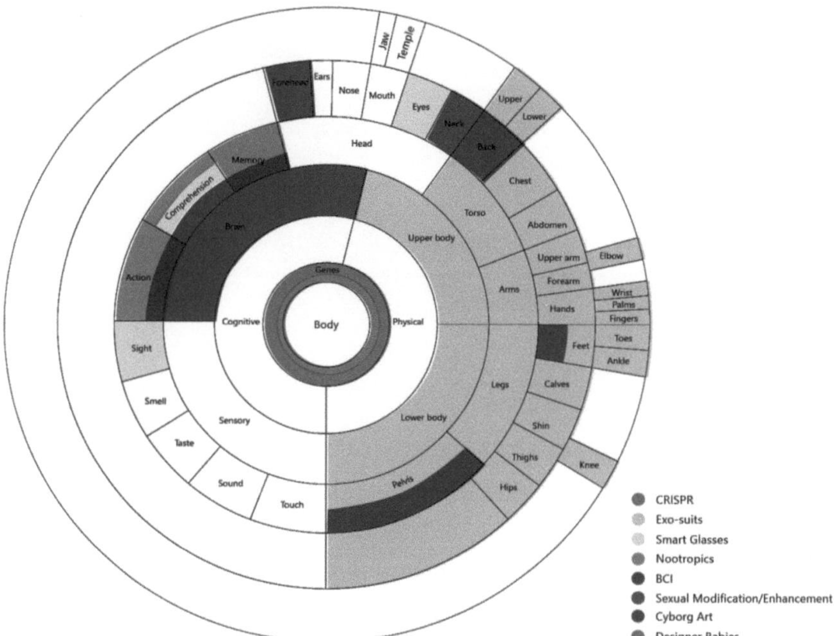

Fig. 3. Overlay of some existing devices in relation to the human body

workers which revealed that workers did not want to be "fixed" or monitored, rather they wanted a partner in their labour.

Here, it was also important to establish exo-suits as a form of wearable device that people would need to wear and remove for specific work.

4.4   Insights and Reflection

One of the most profound insights gained from this collaborative process was the importance of dignifying physical labour through design. Rather than framing wearable tech as a tool to correct or monitor behaviour, participants viewed it as a partner in their daily rhythms, a perspective that only emerged through deep engagement and mutual respect. This challenged dominant narratives of efficiency and surveillance in wearable design, and emphasized augmentation as a means of support, awareness, and care. As seen in Fig. 4, a blue-collar worker, like an electrician, can wear the sleeve while performing repetitive tasks. The sleeve itself is designed to be non-intrusive (it doesn't add barriers to performing tasks) while also providing support, targeted heating for comfort when workers experience pain, and made using breathable, comfortable materials like cotton.

For the Interaction Design community, the Second Skin project underscores the value of including skilled manual workers and frontline practitioners as design collaborators, not just as test subjects. It also demonstrates how HCD can evolve to include embodied, context sensitive, and socially grounded practices. Ultimately, the project advocates for a more inclusive and responsive design ethic; one that listens to the body, honours lived expertise and creates with rather than for those who wear our technologies.

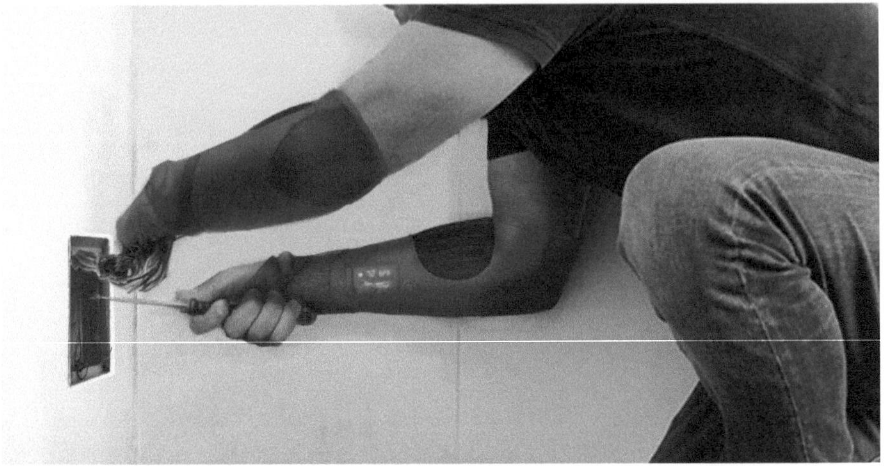

Fig. 4. Conceptual depiction of Second Skin being used in the field

The Second Skin project served as both a proving ground and a provocation for revealing the potential of wearables to support embodied labour, and the limitations of traditional HCD frameworks when applied to complex, emergent domains like human augmentation. Insights from this collaboration informed a deeper examination of how interaction design methods might be reoriented to better address the ethical, experiential, and systemic dimensions of augmentation. Drawing from this experience, the following section outlines key principles and process considerations for designing HAT in ways that are attuned to lived realities, bodily nuance, and social responsibility.

5 Principles and Processes in Human-Centred Design for HAT

Human Centred design has matured significantly, providing structured, evidence-based approaches to developing technologies that truly meet human needs. The value of systematic design processes in conceptualising and creating future technologies has been well documented [1, 19]. Yet, current frameworks often lack the breadth needed for emerging fields like HAT, which require designers to balance complex human, technological, ethical, and environmental factors.

To navigate the unique demands of HATs, this checklist draws on both established and emerging frameworks in interaction design, including ISO 9241-210 principles [19], sustainable and appropriate design methodologies [22], and value-sensitive design [9, 23]. These principles are not arbitrarily selected but reflect recurring priorities across HCD literature, such as context-awareness, iterative development, inclusivity, and ethics, that are critical when designing for the body and identity. Their value was demonstrated in the Second Skin project, where practitioner engagement, prototyping, and environmental considerations led to more grounded and respectful design decisions [12].

By offering a synthesised yet actionable framework, the checklist functions both as a conceptual tool and a practical guide for navigating the socio-technical complexity of HAT development for future designers and engineers.

5.1 Human Centred Design

This principle encompasses multiple components essential for grounding design in real human experiences:

- Empathy and understanding through immersive research methods, such as ethnography and interviews, to capture the nuanced lived realities of users [19]. In Second Skin, shadowing electricians revealed critical posture and repetitive movement discomforts that shaped sensor placement [12].
- Participatory Research Methods that actively involve users and stakeholders in the early research phase, gathering diverse perspectives without necessitating direct involvement in design decisions [20]. People often suggest innovative ways they have used to solve specific problems for themselves, which in turn can be distilled into useful features rather than going off assumptions.
- Iterative Testing and Feedback to refine prototypes based on actual user interaction and evolving needs, ensuring responsiveness and usability over time [14]. Second Skin underwent four in-situ prototype cycles, each improving upon materiality or comfort [12].

5.2 Contextual and Environmental Awareness

Designers should consider the social, cultural, and physical environments in which HAT will be deployed. This understanding supports solutions that are appropriate for local contexts and sustainable within their environmental settings [22]. In Second Skin, extreme cold temperatures led us to select a combination of phase-change materials and battery-powered heating elements while also providing adequate insulation [12]. Figure 3's overlay of exo-skeletons in relation to multiple body parts underscores the importance of assessing environmental fit which drives context-aware design.

5.3 Iterative Prototyping

Repeated cycles of design, testing, and refinement allow early detection of usability issues, enhance stakeholder engagement, and mitigate risks associated with complex technologies. Through iterative prototyping, designs evolve based on authentic user feedback, resulting in products that better meet user expectations and adapt to real-world conditions [14]. For example, early Second Skin mock-ups created with cardboard and fabric quickly revealed arm girth differences between workers, prompting a switch to modular Velcro attachments and stretchable fabric [12].

5.4 Ethical Reflection and Responsibility

Ethics should be embedded throughout the design process, with proactive attention to privacy, equity, autonomy, and potential societal impacts [4, 10, 23]. In Second Skin, participants collectively rejected continuous data logging in favour of event-triggered haptic alerts, demonstrating how early ethical discussions guided the choice to preserve worker autonomy [12].

5.5 Flexibility and Adaptability

Given the diversity of human bodies, behaviours, and contexts, HAT should be designed with modularity and adaptability in mind, capable of evolving alongside users and their changing needs [20]. This would work not only for the product itself, but also for the ecosystem created around it.

5.6 Inclusive Design

Technologies must be accessible and usable by people across varied abilities, ages, genders, and socio-economic backgrounds. Inclusive design aims to reduce barriers and prevent technology from reinforcing existing inequalities [4, 8]. A later trial of Second Skin with female warehouse staff confirmed that adjustable straps and non-gendered sizing are critical for universal adoption [12].

5.7 Inclusivity Beyond the Human

Designers should extend ethical considerations to the environment, animals, and ecosystems affected by technology development and deployment, acknowledging humans' interconnectedness with broader ecological systems [22]. In the Second Skin project, all materials were chosen for recyclability and low-impact manufacturing, aligning with sustainable design goals [12]. Furthermore, finding inspiration from nature has led to great advancements in design, like the front shape of the Shinkansen which was inspired by the Kingfisher bird that helped trains in Japan to glide smoothly through tunnels and produce less noise while doing so.

6 Discussion

HAT systems are inherently complex socio-technical systems that affect people, devices, environmental, and social factors that cumulatively influence each other in unpredictable ways [11]. In practice, the checklist should be applied early and repeatedly throughout the design process. For example, project teams can use it during the initial research and ideation phase to map out needs and constraints and then revisit it in each prototyping cycle to ensure no critical human or contextual factor is overlooked. By aligning with principles of iterative, HCD and systems thinking, the checklist helps designers and engineers take "small and simple steps" to address large problems [11].

6.1 When to Use

The checklist is most valuable at the conceptualization and early design stages of a HAT project. It guides teams to consider user needs, context, ethics and sustainability from the outset before committing to a single technical solution. It can also be used at key decision points (e.g. after a research sprint or prototype test) as a practical audit: teams review each checklist item to see if issues like user comfort, data privacy, or environmental impact have been addressed.

In essence, it functions both as a brainstorming framework and as a project milestone gate. By flagging concerns early (for example, ensuring ergonomic fit for diverse body shapes or assessing workplace safety implications), teams reduce the risk of costly redesigns later. Industry examples underscore this need: for instance, the Skelex 360 industrial exoskeleton, designed for overhead assembly work, was rapidly refined through continuous prototyping to accommodate *multiple body types* and enable full range of motion [5]. Using the checklist early would have similarly highlighted those ergonomic and inclusivity challenges from the start.

In many situations creating first in order to meet business goals outweighs considerate designing and through this checklist we can start considering how we may continue to design good products and services in a more equitable fashion.

6.2 Type of Problem

The checklist is tailored for augmented-work design problems, i.e. solutions aimed at extending or enhancing human physical or cognitive capabilities. These problems often involve tasks that are physically strenuous (lifting, reaching, repetitive motion) or precision-oriented, where technology can assist humans to work better or safer. Importantly, HAT problems combine technical innovation with human factors: designers must balance mechanical or software performance against human comfort, social acceptance and ethics.

This checklist is not just for well-defined usability fixes, but for wicked, socio-technical challenges where the "right" solution may not be obvious. For example, a factory exoskeleton project faces both an engineering task (building a supportive frame) and a human one (ensuring workers feel safe, empowered, and fairly treated). Research shows that even promising exoskeletons "are not a fix-all technology" and are most effective when closely matched to specific tasks (e.g. static lifting vs. dynamic movement) [2, 15]. Thus, this checklist suits problems where human needs, organizational practices, and environmental constraints must all be integrated into the design, or for wicked socio-technical challenges, where the "right" solution may not be obvious [11].

6.3 Intended Users

The primary users of this checklist are designers, engineers, and multidisciplinary development teams who are creating HAT products. It serves as a tool for professionals (and advanced students) to reflect on the human side of high-tech projects. For example, a mechanical engineer prototyping a wearable arm exosuit can use the list to remember to consult with end-users and consider ethics, rather than focusing only on actuator performance. The checklist can also guide team meetings or design reviews, ensuring that ergonomists, ethicists or field partners (e.g. occupational health experts) have input on key decisions. In short, anyone responsible for HAT design and deployment can use this as a design thinking map to keep the project user-centred, equitable and sustainable.

6.4 Context of Use

While the checklist is broadly applicable to any human-facing technology, it is especially relevant in workplace and industrial contexts. In blue-collar settings workers perform physically demanding or repetitive tasks that HAT can help alleviate, like shown in the case study [2, 15]. These environments pose specific design constraints (e.g. extreme temperatures, safety regulations, long shifts) and user characteristics (workers of different ages, genders, abilities, possibly low tech-literacy). For instance, an overhead-reach exoskeleton must be durable for factory use and easily adjustable to fit both male and female workers. Studies in occupational exoskeletons highlight that comfort and ease of use are critical to worker acceptance [2]. In practice, this means using the checklist to drive decisions, like choosing breathable, recyclable materials for harsh conditions, or adding modular straps for size adjustment (as was done in practice with a "Second Skin" prototype for electricians). The checklist also applies in healthcare or daily-living contexts where augmentation is used (e.g. prosthetic devices or cognitive aids), but its emphasis on job-related tasks and environments makes it particularly useful for industrial designers. In all these contexts, the goal is to produce technology that truly fits the real-world setting rather than assuming a one-size-fits-all solution.

7   Conclusion

Human augmentation technologies hold transformative potential to extend human capabilities, but they also raise complex ethical, social, and environmental questions. Moving beyond a purely technology-driven approach, human-centred design places empathy, inclusivity, and ethical reflection at the core of development. This shift ensures that augmentation technologies align with real human needs, respect dignity and autonomy, and consider broader systemic impacts.

By engaging diverse stakeholders and understanding context, designers can create adaptable, equitable solutions that anticipate unintended consequences and foster sustainable innovation. As the line between human and machine blurs, a human-centred design ethos becomes essential to guide augmentation technologies toward enhancing human well-being in just and compassionate ways.

The choices made today in designing these technologies will shape the future of humanity. Embracing responsibility with critical insight and care is key to realizing augmentation's promise as a positive force for society.

Acknowledgments. This study would not have been possible without the guidance of Dr Apala Lahiri Chavan on ethical human-centered design principles. I would like to thank the organiseres of ARPPID 2025 conference for providing a space to exchange crucial ideas across academic and industry practices, the guest speakers and chairs for facilitating engaging thought-provoking conversations between the panelists, and peers that made the conference engaging and rich. Lastly, I want to thank all the participants in the Second Skin case study for helping steer the project based on real use-cases.

Disclosure of Interests. The authors have no competing interests to declare that are relevant to the content of this article.

References

1. Anastassova, M., Mégard, C., Burkhardt, J.M.: Prototype evaluation and user-needs analysis in the early design of emerging technologies. In: Human-Computer Interaction. Interaction Design and Usability, pp. 383–392. Springer, Berlin Heidelberg (2007). https://doi.org/10.1007/978-3-540-73105-4_42
2. Baltrusch, S., van Dieën, J.H., van der Have, A., van der Helm, F.C.T., van der Kooij, H., Kingma, I.: The effect of passive back-support exoskeletons on functional performance in healthy individuals. Appl. Ergon. **103**, 103800 (2023). https://pubmed.ncbi.nlm.nih.gov/36478728
3. Bleecker, J.: Design fiction: a short essay on design, science, fact and fiction. Near Future Laboratory (2009). https://drbfw5wfjlxon.cloudfront.net/writing/DesignFiction_WebEdition.pdf
4. Chavan, A.L.: Another culture, another method. Human Factors International White Paper (2005). https://www.humanfactors.com/downloads/whitepapers/another-culture-another-method.pdf
5. Core77 Design Awards: The ultimate exoskeleton for overhead work. https://designawards.core77.com/tools-work/95045/The-Ultimate-Exoskeleton-for-Overhead-Work. Accessed 10 Sept 2025
6. De Boeck, M., Vaes, K.: Human augmentation and its new design perspectives. Int. J. Design Creativity Innov. **12**(1), 61–80 (2024). https://doi.org/10.1080/21650349.2023.2288125
7. de Looze, M.P., Bosch, T., Krause, F., Stadler, K.S., O'Sullivan, L.W.: Exoskeletons for industrial application and their potential effects on physical workload. Ergonomics **59**(5), 671–681 (2015). https://doi.org/10.1080/00140139.2015.1081988
8. Greenhalgh, T., Shaw, S., Bound Alberti, F., Wrigley, J., Papoutsi, J.: Narrative change in health research: a conceptual framework for the co-production of research. Health Res. Policy Syst. **17**(1), 1–17 (2019). https://doi.org/10.1186/s12961-019-0484-9
9. Greenhalgh, T., et al.: Beyond adoption: a new framework for theorizing and evaluating nonadoption, abandonment, and challenges to the scale-up, spread, and sustainability of health and care technologies. J. Med. Internet Res. **19**(11), e367 (2017). https://doi.org/10.2196/jmir.8775
10. Hansson, S.O. (ed.): The ethics of technology: methods and approaches. Rowman & Littlefield International, London (2017)
11. Interaction Design Foundation: Complex socio-technical systems. Interaction-design.org. https://www.interaction-design.org/literature/topics/complex-socio-technical-systems. Accessed 10 Sept 2025
12. Jacob, A.: Second Skin. Master's thesis, Glasgow School of Art (2023). https://drive.google.com/file/d/1R9diuzYj13scz5pcMxmiJRappFlxaZ-Z/view?usp=drive_link
13. Jurczak, M.: This is how exoskeletons were born and are used in logistics. Trans.INFO, October 18 (2019). https://trans.info/thisis-how-exoskeletons-were-born-and-are-used-in-logistics-163321
14. Kelley, B.: The role of prototyping in human-centered design. BradenKelley.com, July (2021). https://bradenkelley.com/2021/07/the-role-of-prototyping-in-human-centered-design-2/

15. McFarland, T., Fischer, S.: Considerations for industrial use: a systematic review of the impact of active and passive upper limb exoskeletons on physical exposures. IISE Trans. Occup. Ergon. Hum. Factors **7**(3–4), 322–347 (2019). https://doi.org/10.1080/24725838.2019.168 4399

16. Ministry of Defence (UK), Bundeswehr Office for Defence Planning: Human Augmentation – The Dawn of a New Paradigm: A Strategic Implications Project. UK Ministry of Defence / German Federal Ministry of Defence (2021). https://assets.publishing.service. gov.uk/government/uploads/system/uploads/attachment_data/file/986301/Human_Augmen tation_SIP_access2.pdf. Accessed 10 Sept 2025

17. Raisamo, R., Väänänen-Vainio-Mattila, A., Salminen, T.: Human augmentation: current approaches and future challenges. In: Proceedings of the 21st International Conference on Human-Computer Interaction, pp. 131–143. ACM, New York (2019). https://doi.org/10.1145/3340764.3340807

18. Ritter, F.E., Baxter, G.D., Churchill, E.F.: Foundations for designing user-centered systems: what system designers need to know about people. Springer, London (2014)

19. Roper, S., Micheli, M., Vahter, K.: Understanding the impact of user-centred design on product innovation. Enterprise Research Centre Research Paper 41 (2016). https://www.enterpriseresearch.ac.uk/wp-content/uploads/2016/05/ERC-ResPap41-RoperMicheliLoveVahter.pdf

20. Sanders, E.B.-N., Stappers, P.J.: Co-creation and the new landscapes of design. CoDesign **4**(1), 5–18 (2008). https://doi.org/10.1080/15710880701875068

21. Saracco, R.: The future of human augmentation. IEEE Future Directions (2017). https://future.ieee.org/2017/11/27/the-future-of-human-augmentation/

22. Sianipar, C.P.M., Yudoko, G., Dowaki, K., Adhiutama, A.: Design methodology for appropriate technology: engineering as if people mattered. Sustainability **5**(8), 3382–3394 (2013). https://doi.org/10.3390/su5083382

23. Vallor, S.: Technology and the virtues: a philosophical guide to a future worth wanting. Oxford University Press, Oxford (2016)

24. Villa, P., Alparone, L., Mainardi, L.: Human augmentation: a review on current state and challenges. Front. Robot. AI (2023)

Hardly Any Sliders in Real-World Apps: A Library of Algorithmic Affordances to Bridge the Research-Practice Gap in Human-AI Interaction

Aletta Smits[1,4]([✉]) [ID], Karine Cardona[2] [ID], Marissa Berk[3] [ID], Bart Jan Hoekman[1] [ID], Tamara Marantika[3] [ID], Tomas Meeuwse[4] [ID], Suzanne van Rossen[5] [ID], Danielle Sent[3,6] [ID], and Koen van Turnhout[3] [ID]

[1] Hanze University of Applied Sciences Groningen, Groningen, Netherlands
a.m.smits@pl.hanze.nl
[2] Appealy Design, Groningen, Netherlands
[3] HU University of Applied Sciences Utrecht, Utrecht, Netherlands
[4] Utrecht University, Utrecht, Netherlands
[5] Avans University, Breda, Netherlands
[6] Eindhoven University of Technology, Eindhoven, Netherlands

Abstract. Algorithmic affordances—interactive mechanisms that allow users to exercise tangible control over algorithms—play a crucial role in recommender systems. They can facilitate users' sense of autonomy, transparency, and ultimately ownership over a recommender's results, all qualities that are central to responsible AI. Designers, among others, are tasked with creating these interactions, yet state that they lack resources to do so effectively. At the same time, academic research into these interactions rarely crosses the research-practice gap. As a solution, designers call for a structured library of algorithmic affordances containing well-tested, well-founded, and up-to-date examples sourced from both real-world and experimental interfaces. Such a library should function as a boundary object, bridging academia and professional design practice. Academics could use it as a supplementary platform to disseminate their findings, while both practitioners and educators could draw upon it for inspiration and as a foundation for innovation. However, developing a library that accommodates multiple stakeholders presents several challenges, including the need to establish a common language for categorizing algorithmic affordances and devising a categorization of algorithmic affordances that is meaningful to all target groups. This research attempts to bring the designer perspective into this categorization.

Keywords: Interactive AI · Research-Practice Gap · Pattern Library

J. Abdelnour-Nocera et al. (Eds.): ARPPID 2025, CCIS 2797, pp. 127–142, 2026.
https://doi.org/10.1007/978-3-032-15516-0_9

1 Introduction

1.1 Responsible AI at an Interactional Level

Recommender systems and decision support systems (DSS) increasingly influence both personal lives and professional practices. As their adoption grows, so do efforts to ensure these applications operate responsibly— that is, in ways that are fair, trustworthy, lawful, non-malicious, sustainable, and supportive of autonomy, privacy, and dignity [1–3]. The majority of these efforts focused on the data and algorithmic levels: curating higher-quality datasets [4–6], tuning algorithms for greater fairness [7–9], or incorporating cognitive variables such as attrition into model calculations [10].

An additional, equally powerful way to create responsible recommender systems is through the interactional level [11]. Here, two dominant approaches have emerged: Explainable AI (XAI) and Interactive AI (IAI) [12–15]. XAI aims to enhance users' understanding of an AI's output by providing local explanations (why a specific recommendation was made) and global explanations (how the system generally functions) [14]. Such explanations help users develop more accurate mental models of the algorithm, increasing interpretability, perceived transparency, and trust, all essential components of Responsible AI.

IAI offers users not just explanations but also algorithmic affordances [16, 17]): human-ai interactions that provide users with tangible control over the algorithm [18–21]. These affordances move from passive understanding to active influence, enabling users to directly shape outputs or decision processes. Figure 1 illustrates this concept using Amazon's checkout flow as an example:

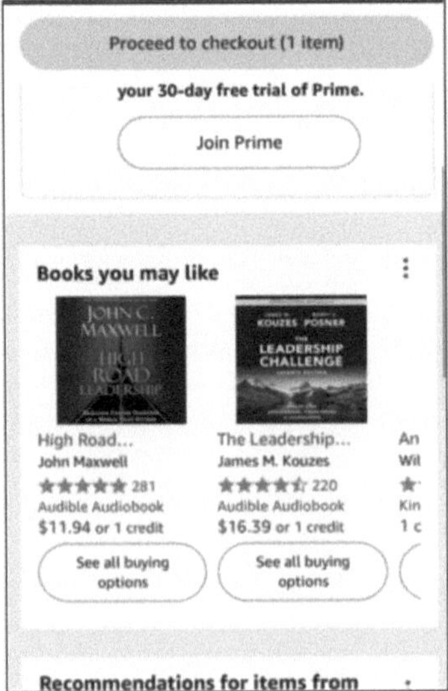

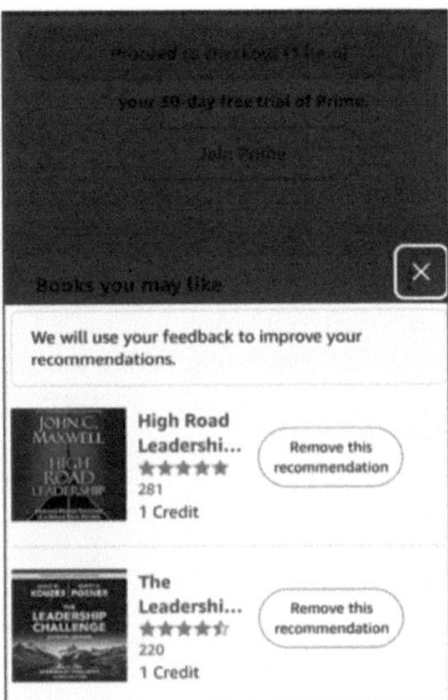

Fig. 1. Real world example of algorithmic affordances (input): Amazon's checkout flow, where the user is invited to curate the recommended items.

In this checkout workflow, users are consistently shown a set of recommended items—products they "may like" (left-hand image). While users cannot disable the display of these recommendations, they can curate the list (right-hand image) by removing unwanted suggestions. Via this interaction, the user provides information to their user model and course-corrects future calculations. Such interactions, too, have been demonstrated to increase qualities central to Responsible AI, such as a user control, transparency, agency and autonomy (see e.g. [18, 22–24]).

Figure 2 presents a second example of an algorithmic affordance. In this experimental music recommender interface, presented in a study by Jin et al. [25], users can adjust the influence of the parameters 'location' and 'activity' on the algorithm's music selection. With a slider ranging from 0 to 100, users can set the relative weight of these factors. While it is not possible to opt out of using these variables, since the algorithm will always consider them in its calculation, users do control how heavily each is weighted in the recommendation process. In this case, users do not influence the input of the algorithm (as was the case in the first example), but rather the algorithmic processing of that input.

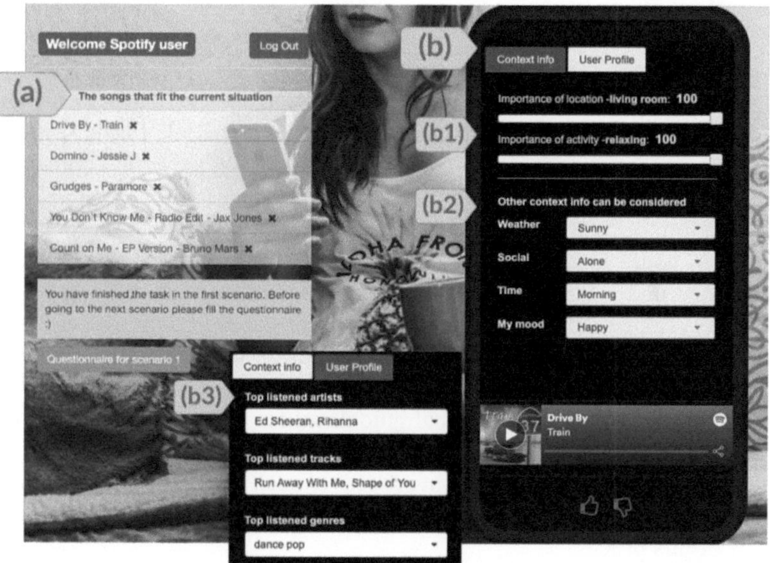

Fig. 2. Academic example of algorithmic affordances (process): sliders (**in b1**) help the user select how much 'location' and 'activity' should be weighted in the recommendation process [25]

1.2 A Research-Practice Gap: From Designers to Academia

While data scientists develop the algorithms that generate explanations or process the user input, designers, UX and UI designers play a crucial role in determining which explanations and interactions are needed in specific contexts and how they should be implemented. These design choices directly influence the extent to which users experience control, trust, and other qualities central to Responsible AI [20]. In both XAI and IAI, designers are thus key contributors to the development of responsible recommender systems.

However, many designers report lacking the resources necessary to design effective explanations and interactions. A recent global survey on Interactive AI (IAI) conducted among 198 professional designers, identified several reasons for this information gap [26]. First, many more experienced design professionals indicated that they were not trained to design for AI. Design curricula have only recently begun incorporating topics in their curricula such as "designing with" and "designing for AI" and are still figuring out how to do so effectively [26]. Second, academic research on interaction design for interactive AI only sparsely bridges the research-practice gap.

Designers provide the following reasons for this gap. In the first place, they indicate that they lack the time and resources to systematically locate, evaluate, and apply academic findings to their work [27]. Secondly, even when they do attempt to search for relevant literature, they are frequently unaware of the dominant academic terminology, so they simply do not find the relevant papers [28–30]. For instance, while a designer might search for information on algorithmic affordances that enable a user to provide 'feedback' on an item, the academic literature may instead use the term 'critiquing' [29]. Thirdly, their search for relevant papers is further complicated by the dominance of technically focused papers which far outnumber design-oriented studies on AI. Finally, when designers do locate relevant research, it is often context-specific and consequently, they hesitate to generalize or apply it to their own projects [27]. As a result, many fall back on familiar solutions in their active repertoire [31]: they consciously or unconsciously replicate algorithmic affordances from widely used platforms such as Netflix and Spotify in their work [27, 32, 33]. Designers do acknowledge the limitations of this approach but feel they have little alternative [27].

As a solution, designers suggest that "a wiki-type guide of solutions", "with current examples" could assist in designing algorithmic affordances [27], both to support their conceptual understanding better and to use them as a basis for innovation. What they seek is a systematically structured pattern library of algorithmic affordances: well-documented, contextualized, and up to date, featuring examples from both academic and commercial sources [27]. These examples should be richly described, including ethical considerations [34] and practical guidelines for addressing users' varying level of algorithmic literacy [35, 36].

This paper presents the development process of such a pattern library for algorithmic affordances in recommender systems, including the challenges encountered during the first phases of this process.

2 A Pattern Library of Algorithmic Affordances

2.1 Intermediate Knowledge in a Boundary Object

When designers express a need for a pattern library of algorithmic affordances, they are, in effect, articulating a need for *intermediate knowledge* [37]. Intermediate knowledge is defined as knowledge that exists between theory and practice [31, 37, 38]: it is neither overly abstract nor merely a collection of isolated, context-specific examples. Rather, it is concrete enough to be actionable while remaining abstract enough to inform and inspire design innovation [33, 39, 40]. Other forms of intermediate knowledge include design heuristics [41] and portfolios [37, 42].

Pattern libraries have proven to be effective interventions in various contexts [43], consistently strengthening the professional practices in which they are used [44–48]. The patterns included in the library, as Alexander [49] put it, formally document "good solutions to recurring design problems in specific contexts". As such, they serve as a structured means of communicating design solutions, providing practitioners with concrete resources to systematically improve both the quality and quantity of their work.

A pattern library of algorithmic affordances also has the potential to function as a boundary object [50]. Boundary objects are entities that serve different purposes across domains, such as education, professional practice, and research, while being commonly recognized as the same object by all stakeholders. They facilitate collaboration, support knowledge exchange [51] and contribute to the development of a shared vocabulary [52]. A pattern library of algorithmic affordances could, therefore, serve distinct functions within each domain: as a pedagogical tool for educators, a source of inspiration and innovation for the professional practice, and as an additional dissemination platform for researchers. In this way, a pattern library can establish a lasting connection between research, education, and industry.

2.2 The Construction of a Pattern Library

To develop a pattern library of algorithmic affordances, a consortium was established consisting of five applied universities in the Netherlands, four international research universities, two professional associations, 18 design professionals and three public organizations. The participating designers represent a diverse range of backgrounds, including various nationalities (Vietnam, South Korea (2), Russia, Iran, Turkey, India (3), Netherlands (2), UK, US, France, China (3), Brazil), religions, and gender (4 male, 14 female). At the time of the study, all live in the Greater Amsterdam area. Their professional experience ranges from 3–15 years, and their formal backgrounds include design, engineering and psychology. In addition to the professionals, a group of international graduate students supported the project by contributing to the collection of algorithmic affordances examples (32 of the 177 examples). The diversity of the collector group ensured that we examined a wide range of real-world applications, representing various cultures and age groups.

The project is organized into six work packages, as illustrated in Fig. 3. Work package 1 focused on collecting a broad set of algorithmic affordance examples from both academia and commercial platforms. Participating designers then engaged in a series of card-sorting exercises to categorize a subset of these examples. Their sorting decisions serve as a basis for the categorization structure of the pattern library. Work package 2 will examine how the interactions in collected examples impact user experience. Insights from both Work Packages 1 and 2 will lead to a prototype of the pattern library, that will subsequently be tested in Work package 3. In this Work package three case studies, provided by the public organizations in our consortium, will explore the use of the pattern library in the design process.

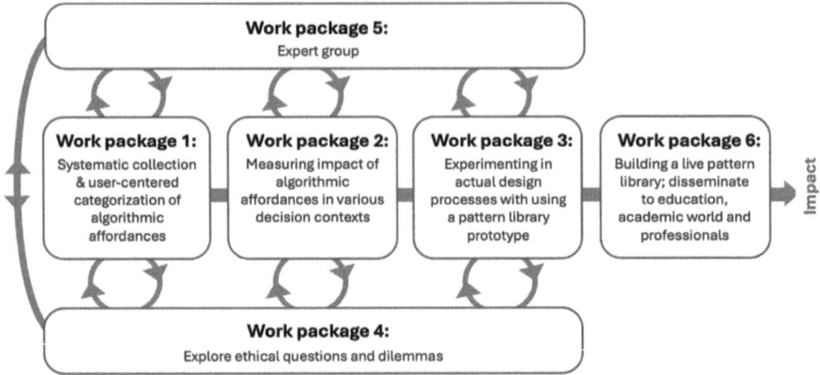

Fig. 3. The construction of a pattern library of algorithmic affordances

Work package 4, which runs in parallel to the first three, focuses on the ethical dimensions of algorithmic affordance. This includes the identification and analysis of dark patterns [53] and placebo controls [54]. Preliminary research for this work package suggests that, when applied unethically, the very mechanisms intended to support responsible AI may in fact undermine it. For example, Vaccaro et al. (2018) show how a mechanism that pretends to provide users with control over their social media feed was clearly not connected to the algorithm [54]. As a result, the interaction had no real impact on the system's calculations. Participants in the user study, however, still reported a greater sense of control when this toggle was available to them.

Finally, the project as a whole is overseen by an expert board (Work package 5) consisting of academic experts, design methodologists, ethicists and industry professionals. The resulting publicly accessible pattern library of algorithmic affordances will be supported by a series of dissemination activities targeting academia, education, and professional practice (Work package 6). At the time of writing, the project has started Work Packages 2 and 3.

3   WP1: Systematic Collection and Categorization of Examples

A critical requirement for a pattern library of algorithmic affordances in recommender systems is that its structure is accessible to all stakeholders (education, professional practice and academia). Work Package 1 (WP1) aims to establish such a structure through the following steps:

1. **Collection of examples:** the collection of examples from both real-world applications and experimental interfaces studied in academic research.
2. **Open card-sorting sessions:** Conducting open card-sorting exercises with professional designers using a randomly selected subset of examples. Participants group examples based on their own logic, while think-aloud protocols are collected to uncover the reasoning behind their decisions.
3. **Development of preliminary categories:** Analyzing the results of the open card-sorting sessions to derive an initial set of categories for organizing the pattern library.

4. **Closed card-sorting validation:** Testing the preliminary categorization through a series of closed card-sorting sessions, again involving professional designers.
5. **Final validation via global survey and expert interviews**: Conducting interviews with members of the expert board and distributing a large-scale internationally distributed only survey targeting designers and academics to validate and refine the final categorization(s).

The establishment of a structure for the pattern library may seem redundant, given that a well-established and widely used framework for categorizing algorithmic affordances already exists. However, it is in fact one of those occasions where academics' and practitioners' frames of reference clash. In academic research, the dominant categorization of algorithmic affordances is based on an input-process-output-model [12, 17, 18, 55]. In this framework, users can interact with the algorithm in three primary ways:

1. **Providing input**: Users supply information to the algorithm, such as preferences (see Fig. 1).
2. **Controlling the process**: Users define how the algorithm should process the provided information, for example, by adjusting its weighting (see Fig. 2).
3. **Exploring the output**: Users manipulate how results are presented without altering the underlying recommendations. For instance, in Fig. 4, the user can reorder the recommended results based on different parameters.

Fig. 4. Real world example of algorithmic affordances (output): sorting the results in an e-commerce website based on relevance, and other variables

However, as the next section will demonstrate, in a project aimed at bridging academia and practice, this categorization proves to be inadequate. A new—or at least supplementary—framework is needed.

3.1 Academic Versus Real-World Algorithmic Affordances

The input-process-output (IPO) framework can be considered an algorithm-centric classification model: it organizes algorithmic affordances according from the perspective of the algorithm. While this categorization, as do all classification systems, suffers from the problem of fuzzy edges [56], it generally functions well and is widely accepted within academia [18, 55, 57, 58].

However, designers appear to find this model confusing and not useful for organizing concrete examples. This disconnect between the two perspectives first became clear during a workshop that prepared for this project, held in 2023. Researchers and practitioners collaboratively sorted 40 algorithmic affordance examples [29]. While academics naturally applied the algorithm-centric model, practitioners favored more user-centric categorizations [28, 29, 59]. The same issue resurfaced during the open card sorting sessions in WP1 of the current project.

For the open card sorting activity we randomly selected 80 original contributions from the full dataset. These were reviewed by two teams of three researchers each, who screened the submissions to verify whether they constituted valid algorithmic affordances. Submissions that did not involve any form of user interaction with the algorithm were excluded. For example, one discarded case involved an automatically generated list of recommendations displayed during checkout that users could not curate or modify. In total, 65 of the 80 examples (81%) were classified as proper algorithmic affordances.

Contributors also completed a standardized metadata form for each example, documenting the date of collection, application name, and the device used (e.g., mobile, tablet). In addition, each participant classified their example according to the IPO model. These classifications were later compared with classifications made by the research team (see Table 1; the asterisked cells include respectively 1 and 3 academic examples; the other examples in this subset come from real-world applications).

Table 1. Collectors' classifications of the algorithmic affordances

Research classification	Collectors' classification				
	Input	Process	Output	Not certain	Total
Input	23	10	1	13	47
Process	4*	5*	1	2	12
Output			2	5	7

Table 1 demonstrates two points. First, the majority of the identified algorithmic affordances in real-market apps can be classified as providing control over *input*. This finding is notable when contrasted with the results of an ongoing systematic literature review of empirical studies on algorithmic affordances [60], which shows that most academically studied algorithmic affordances fall within the process category (e.g., weighting variables) or the output category (e.g., interactive visualizations such as those in Fig. 5, or counterfactual interactions) [29].

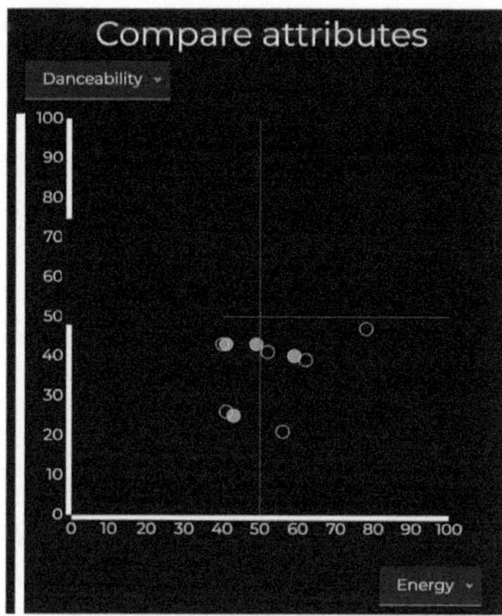

Fig. 5. Academic example of algorithmic affordances (exploration of output): visualization that helps a user determine to what extent music tracks meet two different criteria (in this case danceability and energy). The user can adjust the criteria (Millecamp et al. 2019) [61]

This discrepancy suggests two possibilities: either the interactions celebrated in academic research as interactions that provide users with more satisfactory results fail to cross the research-practice gap, or they do reach the professional practice but, despite their promising experimental results, are tested and ultimately discarded in real-world applications. This lack of process-oriented algorithmic affordances in commercial apps also aligns with observations that slider-based interactions, frequently used in empirical studies to give users control over algorithmic weighting, are rarely found in the real world. When sliders do appear in the dataset, they are typically used as filters rather than as mechanisms to influence the weighting of variables. Similarly, the limited presence of output-oriented interactions in real-world systems is reflected in the absence of complex visualizations, such as those shown in Fig. 5, that would allow users to explore and interrogate recommended results.

Secondly, although all collectors were introduced to the input-process-output model and confirmed their understanding of the framework, Table 1 clearly reflects the difficulties they experienced in applying this algorithm-centric classification. Designers categorized 30 out of 66 affordances correctly (45%), expressed uncertainty about 20 (31%) and misclassified 16 (24%). The distinction between input and process proved particularly challenging, with 10 process-examples being classified as input and 4 input-examples being classified as process.

This confusion is understandable. Consider the example in Fig. 6. In this example the user gives Booking.com's algorithm permission to generate personalized recommendations. The contributor classified this example as an input-example. However, technically, no new information is being provided to the algorithm. Instead, the algorithm is simply instructed to begin using data which it already had access to. According to the IPO-framework, this affordance would be classified as a process affordance. From a user-centered perspective, however, one could argue that the user is initiating profiling and thus contributing input. This ambiguity illustrates the tension between algorithmic and user perspectives in affordance classification.

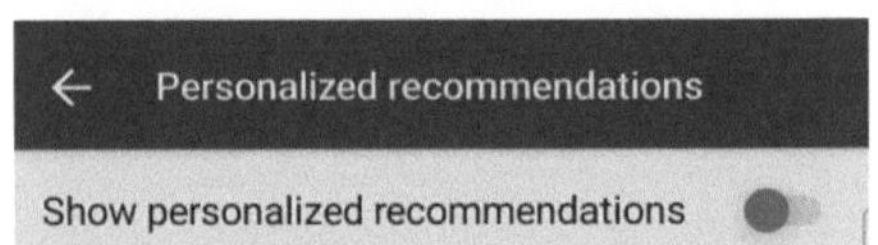

Fig. 6. Booking.com's algorithmic affordances that allows a user to control whether or not they receive personalized recommendations

3.2   User-Centered Structures of Algorithmic Affordances

When asked to reflect on the classification discrepancies discussed above, the participating designers confirmed a preference for a more user-centric categorization model. To support the development of such a model, we conducted four open card-sorting sessions (both online and offline) involving a total of 13 designers. Participants were presented with a set of 65 cards and were asked to (1) group the cards into categories, and (2) articulate their reasoning aloud while creating and labeling categories, assigning cards to categories, or revising category labels and card assignments.

The resulting think-aloud protocols were thematically coded by a team of 6 coders, in three rounds, with discussions in between rounds. Themes emerging from the constant comparison included, among others, 'immediacy of the results', 'duration of the effect', 'profile-building', 'level of control' and 'user journey'.

The first classification model that emerged from the thematic analysis is referred to as the USER INTENT-model. It is a user-centered categorization structured across two dimensions: (1) temporal impact, distinguishing between long-term effects (carrying over multiple sessions) and short-term effects (confined to a single session); and (2) target of impact, differentiating between actions that affect a profile (for a user or a session) and those that affect items (Fig. 7).

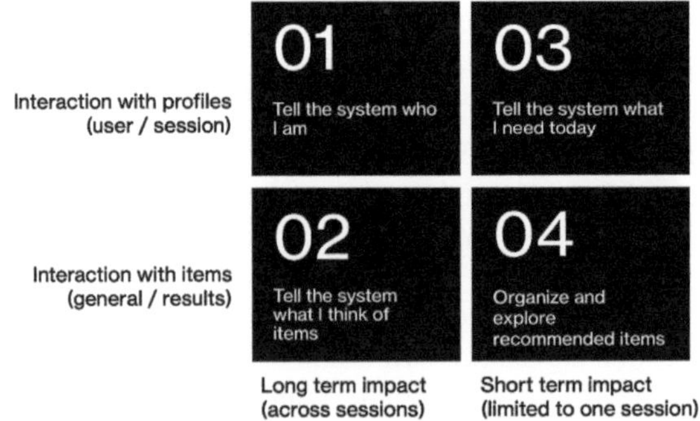

Fig. 7. User-centered classification based on the themes: interaction with profiles versus interaction with items and effect across session versus within a session

In long-term interactions with a profile, users can "tell the system who they are.: This category includes interactions where users explicitly provide information about their general interests, demographics, or other personal details that contribute to the construction of a user model. A second category allows users to "tell the system what they need today." This category pertains to short-term interactions with their current session profile. It includes interactions where users specify temporary preferences, such as while searching for a birthday gift or during the purchasing of office supplies for a one-time event. These interactions are not intended to influence future recommendations and should not carry over to subsequent sessions. What I need to today should be interpreted, therefore, as 'what I need from this search'.

The remaining two categories involve interactions with items rather than profiles. In short-term item interactions, users explore recommended content within a single session. This includes filtering, sorting, or reordering items, as well as interacting with adjustable visualizations, such as the one shown in Fig. 5. These interactions can, for instance, support users' understanding of trade-offs between different criteria. The final category involves long-term interactions with items, where users curate content, for instance, by adding items to a wish list, or providing feedback. These actions shape the user's accumulated preferences and continue – until changed – to affect recommendations in future sessions (see Fig. 1 for an example). This category will include, for instance, various feedback or critiquing interactions. While these item-level interactions technically contribute to the user model, designers perceived a distinction: interactions with a profile were seen as explicitly constructing a user model, whereas interactions with items were viewed as implicitly shaping it. As such, designers drew a clear boundary between these two types of interactions.

The four categories resulting from the two dimensions enable a relatively straightforward categorization of all examples in the set of 65 examples. However, they do not include all themes that emerged from the think-aloud protocols. Concepts such as 'level of control' (low, medium, high), or 'immediate versus delayed effect', and 'moment in the user journey' (e.g. onboarding, beginning of a search, revisitable setting) also played a large role in how participants made sense of the examples. These concepts were not treated as standalone categories in the categorization processes, but rather as features or attributes of specific examples within categories. For this reason, we refer to this classification system as filters.

In addition, designers frequently relied on UI component labels, such as slider, button, or toggle, as a means to understand what an algorithmic affordance did or how it functioned. These labels were used to form a third model, referred to as UI COMPONENTS.

All three classification models were tested in a closed card-sorting task using a set of 41 cards (15 new and 26 previously used examples). Nine designers participated, working with each of the three classification systems. For the USER INTENT and UI COMPONENTS models, they sorted cards into categories. For the filters model, they dragged relevant filters onto individual examples. After completing the sorting tasks, participants were asked which classification model they found most useful. The majority of designers indicated that the USER INTENT model offered the most insight and would likely provide the greatest source of inspiration during design. However, they also noted that the filter classification would be particularly helpful when searching for specific examples. UI COMPONENTS, despite frequently relying on the terms from this category during the open card sorting sessions, was considered least helpful.

4   Discussion and Conclusion

There is a clear need for a pattern library of algorithmic affordances in academia, in the professional practice and in education. For academics, such a library would facilitate the application of their research in real-world settings. For practitioners, it would enhance efficiency, effectiveness, and innovation, ultimately improving the quality of their work. For students, it would provide them with a quicker immersion in the field of designing human-AI interaction [62, 63].

However, the disconnect between academics and the professional field is not trivial. Logistical barriers, such as time and financial constraints, and the sheer volume of available research could be addressed with the construction of a pattern library that curates and organizes relevant research into an accessible format. More fundamentally, however, academia and industry approach algorithmic affordances from different perspectives. While algorithm-centric and user-centric viewpoints are not mutually exclusive and often overlap, they represent distinct conceptual frameworks. Bridging these perspectives requires a classification system that accommodates both approaches. Additionally, it is essential to investigate potential discrepancies in research findings. We need answers to questions such as why affordances that yield promising test results in academic research – e.g., sliders that affect the process of the algorithm – are seldomly implemented in commercial applications. Did they fail to cross the research-practice gap, or were they tested and discarded, thereby challenging the academic research paradigm and its ability to withstand scrutiny in real-world contexts?

Finally, while algorithmic affordances are often presented as tools for fostering responsible AI, preliminary research concerning the ethics of algorithmic affordances suggests that they may, in some cases, create only an illusion of control rather than actual agency [54]. Other research shows how there is a fine line between providing control and in fact causing cognitive overload: suddenly the operation of a recommender system – a tool intended to help users find and choose relevant content – becomes a whole decision process in and of itself [20, 64]. These results raise concerns about how algorithmic affordances might inadvertently make recommender systems in fact less responsible. The pattern library needs to incorporate suggestions to alert designers to this potential danger.

Acknowledgments. This study was funded by the Dutch National Organization for Practice-Oriented Research SIA (grant number RAAK.MKB20.023).

Disclosure of Interests.   The authors have no competing interests to declare that are relevant to the content of this article.

References

1. Vainio-Pekka, H., et al.: The role of explainable AI in the research field of AI ethics. ACM Trans. Interact. Intell. Syst. **13**, 1–39 (2023). https://doi.org/10.1145/3599974
2. Jobin, A., Ienca, M., Vayena, E.: The global landscape of AI ethics guidelines. Nat. Mach. Intell. **1**, 389–399 (2019). https://doi.org/10.1038/s42256-019-0088-2
3. Alfrink, K., Keller, I., Kortuem, G., Doorn, N.: Contestable AI by design: towards a framework. Minds Mach (Dordr). (2022). https://doi.org/10.1007/s11023-022-09611-z
4. Köchling, A., Wehner, M.C.: Discriminated by an algorithm: a systematic review of discrimination and fairness by algorithmic decision-making in the context of HR recruitment and HR development. Bus. Res. **13**, (2020). https://doi.org/10.1007/s40685-020-00134-w
5. Chin, J.Y., Chen, Y., Cong, G.: The datasets dilemma. In: Proceedings of the Fifteenth ACM International Conference on Web Search and Data Mining, pp. 141–149. ACM, New York, NY, USA (2022). https://doi.org/10.1145/3488560.3498519
6. Hoffmann, A.L.: Where fairness fails: data, algorithms, and the limits of antidiscrimination discourse. Inf. Commun. Soc. **22** (2019). https://doi.org/10.1080/1369118X.2019.1573912
7. Angwin, J., Larson, J., Mattu, S., Kirchner, L.: Machine Bias: There's software used across the country to predict future criminals. ProPublica, And it's biased against blacks (2016)
8. Bozdag, E.: Bias in algorithmic filtering and personalization. Ethics Inf. Technol. **15** (2013). https://doi.org/10.1007/s10676-013-9321-6
9. Mosteiro, P., Kuiper, J., Masthoff, J., Scheepers, F., Spruit, M.: Bias discovery in machine learning models for mental health. Information (Switzerland) **13** (2022). https://doi.org/10.3390/info13050237
10. Lex, E., Kowald, D., Seitlinger, P., Tran, T.N.T., Felfernig, A., Schedl, M.: Psychology-informed recommender systems (2021). https://doi.org/10.1561/1500000090
11. Smits, A., van der Zandt, L., van Turnhout, K.: Why designers must contribute to responsible AI. In: Lecture Notes in Computer Science (including subseries Lecture Notes in Artificial Intelligence and Lecture Notes in Bioinformatics), pp. 87–104. Springer Science and Business Media Deutschland GmbH (2024). https://doi.org/10.1007/978-3-031-60611-3_7
12. Terry, M., Kulkarni, C., Wattenberg, M., Dixon, L., Morris, M.R.: Interactive AI alignment: specification, process, and evaluation alignment (2023)
13. Ziegler, J.: Challenges in user-centered engineering of AI-based interactive systems (2019)
14. Raees, M., Meijerink, I., Lykourentzou, I., Khan, V.-J., Papangelis, K.: From explainable to interactive AI: a literature review on current trends in human-AI interaction. Int. J. Hum. Comput. Stud. **189**, 103301 (2024). https://doi.org/10.1016/j.ijhcs.2024.103301
15. Tintarev, N., Masthoff, J.: Beyond explaining single item recommendations. In: Recommender Systems Handbook: Third Edition (2022). https://doi.org/10.1007/978-1-0716-2197-4_19
16. Ettlinger, N.: Algorithmic affordances for productive resistance. Big Data Soc. **5** (2018). https://doi.org/10.1177/2053951718771399
17. Hekman, E., Nguyen, D., Stalenhoef, M., Van Turnhout, K.: Towards a pattern library for algorithmic affordances. Joint Proceedings of the IUI 2022 Workshops, vol. 3124, pp. 24–33 (2022)
18. Jannach, D., Jugovac, M., Nunes, I.: Explanations and user control in recommender systems: Beyond black-box personalization systems. In: Personalized Human-Computer Interaction (2023). https://doi.org/10.1515/9783110988567-006
19. He, C., Parra, D., Verbert, K.: Interactive recommender systems: a survey of the state of the art and future research challenges and opportunities. Expert Syst. Appl. **56**, 9–27 (2016). https://doi.org/10.1016/j.eswa.2016.02.013
20. Ziegler, J., Loepp, B.: User-centered recommender systems. In: Personalized Human-Computer Interaction, pp. 33–58. De Gruyter (2023). https://doi.org/10.1515/9783110988567-002

21. Ngo, T., Kunkel, J., Ziegler, J.: Exploring mental models for transparent and controllable recommender systems: a qualitative study. In: UMAP 2020 - Proceedings of the 28th ACM Conference on User Modeling, Adaptation and Personalization, pp. 183–191. Association for Computing Machinery, Inc (2020). https://doi.org/10.1145/3340631.3394841

22. Rani, N., Chu, S.L., Mei, V.R.: Investigating the effects of different levels of user control on the effectiveness of context-aware recommender systems for web-based search. In: Conference on Human Factors in Computing Systems - Proceedings. Association for Computing Machinery (2022). https://doi.org/10.1145/3491101.3519802

23. Tsai, C.H., Brusilovsky, P.: The effects of controllability and explainability in a social recommender system. User Model User-adapt Interact. **31**, 591–627 (2020). https://doi.org/10.1007/s11257-020-09281-5

24. Harper, F.M., Xu, F., Kaur, H., Condiff, K., Chang, S., Terveen, L.: Putting users in control of their recommendations. In: RecSys 2015 - Proceedings of the 9th ACM Conference on Recommender Systems (2015). https://doi.org/10.1145/2792838.2800179

25. Jin, Y., Htun, N.N., Tintarev, N., Verbert, K.: ContextPlay: Evaluating user control for context-aware music recommendation. In: Proceedings of the 27th ACM Conference on User Modeling, Adaptation and Personalization, pp. 294–302. Association for Computing Machinery, Inc, New York, NY, USA (2019). https://doi.org/10.1145/3320435.3320445

26. van Turnhout, K., Shayan, S., Smits, A.: Is AI 'just' a new technology? On integrating AI education in digital design curricula. In: Proceedings of the International Conference on Engineering and Product Design Education, EPDE 2024, pp. 61–66. The Design Society (2024). https://doi.org/10.35199/EPDE.2024.11

27. Smits, A., Van Turnhout, K.: Towards a practice-led research agenda for user interface design of recommender systems. In: Abdelnour Nocera, J., Lárusdóttir, M.K., Petrie, H., Piccinno, A., and Winckler, M. (eds.) Human-Computer Interaction – INTERACT 2023. LNCS, pp. 170–190. Springer Cham (2023). https://doi.org/10.1007/978-3-031-42286-7_10

28. Smits, A., Bartels, E., Detweiler, C., van Turnhout, K.: Results of the Workshop on Algorithmic Affordances in Recommender Interfaces. Presented at the (2024). https://doi.org/10.1007/978-3-031-61698-3_15

29. Bartels, E., et al.: Exploring categorizations of algorithmic affordances in graphical user interfaces of recommender systems. Presented at the (2024). https://doi.org/10.1007/978-3-031-61698-3_16

30. Smits, A., Bartels, E., Detweiler, C., van Turnhout, K.: Algorithmic affordances in recommender interfaces. In: Interact 2023: Design for Equality and Justice, pp. 605–609 (2023). https://doi.org/10.1007/978-3-031-42293-5_80

31. Turnhout, K., Smits, A.: Solution repertoire. In: DS 110: Proceedings of the 23rd International Conference on Engineering and Product Design Education (EPDE 2021). The Design Society (2021). https://doi.org/10.35199/EPDE.2021.41

32. Gray, C.M.: "It's more of a mindset than a method": UX practitioners' conception of design methods. In: Conference on Human Factors in Computing Systems – Proceedings, pp. 4044–4055. Association for Computing Machinery (2016). https://doi.org/10.1145/2858036.2858410

33. Boling, E., Gray, C.M.: Use of precedent as a narrative practice in design learning. In: Educational Technology and Narrative (2018). https://doi.org/10.1007/978-3-319-69914-1_21

34. van Rossen, S., et al.: Design ideas for recommender systems in flexible education: how algorithmic affordances may address ethical concerns. In: Bramwell-Dicks, A., Evans, A., Winckler, M., Petrie, H., Abdelnour-Nocera, J. (eds.) Design for Equality and Justice. INTERACT 2023. LNCS, pp. 205–213. Springer, Cham, York (2024). https://doi.org/10.1007/978-3-031-61698-3_19

35. Pott, K., Smits, A., Agotai, D.: Recognizing the algorithmic literacy of users in XAI - an example-based approach. In: Bramwell-Dicks, A., Evans, A., Winckler, M., Petrie, H., and Abdelnour-Nocera, J. (eds.) Design for Equality and Justice: INTERACT 2023. LNCS, pp. 214–222. Springer, York (2024). https://doi.org/10.1007/978-3-031-61698-3_20

36. Pott, K., Simmen, Y., Kalunder, M., Agotai, D.: Design for Learnability: challenging the State-of-the-Art in UX to foster Inclusion and Participation. In: Computer Supported Cooperative Work and Social Computing, pp. 358–361. ACM, New York, NY, USA (2023). https://doi.org/10.1145/3584931.3607490

37. Löwgren, J.: Annotated portfolios and other forms of intermediate-level knowledge. Interactions **20**, 30–34 (2013). https://doi.org/10.1145/2405716.2405725

38. Hoök, K., Lowgren, J.: Strong concepts: intermediate-level knowledge in interaction design research. ACM Trans. Comput.-Hum. Interact. **19** (2012). https://doi.org/10.1145/2362364.2362371

39. Dorst, K., Cross, N.: Creativity in the design process: co-evolution of problem-solution. Des Stud. **22** (2001). https://doi.org/10.1016/S0142-694X(01)00009-6

40. Gray, C.M.: Languaging design methods. Des Stud. **78** (2022). https://doi.org/10.1016/j.destud.2021.101076

41. Gray, C.M., Seifert, C.M., Yilmaz, S., Daly, S.R., Gonzalez, R.: What is the content of "design thinking"? Design Heuristics as conceptual repertoire. Int. J. Eng. Educ. (2016)

42. Gaver, B., Bowers, J.: Annotated portfolios. Interactions **19**, 40–49 (2012). https://doi.org/10.1145/2212877.2212889

43. Smit, A.J., Van Aken, J.: Het E2R-model voor het optimaliseren van de effectiviteit van een ontworpen interventie. In: Van Turnhout, K., Andriessen, D., Cremers, P. (eds.) Handboek ontwerpgericht wetenschappelijk onderzoek, pp. 363–373. Boom, Amsterdam (2023)

44. Van Welie, M., Veer, G.C. Van Der: pattern languages in interaction design. Academia **3** (2003)

45. Horchers, J.O.: A pattern approach to interaction design. AI Soc. **15** (2001). https://doi.org/10.1007/bf01206115

46. Dearden, A., Finlay, J.: Pattern languages in HCI: a critical review. Hum. Comput. Interact. **21**, 49–102 (2006). https://doi.org/10.1207/s15327051hci2101_3

47. Schoonderwoerd, T.A.J., Jorritsma, W., Neerincx, M.A., van den Bosch, K.: Human-centered XAI: developing design patterns for explanations of clinical decision support systems. Int. J. Hum. Comput. Stud. **154** (2021). https://doi.org/10.1016/j.ijhcs.2021.102684

48. Alexander, C., Ishikawa, S., Silverstein, M.: A pattern language: towns, buildings, construction (Cess center for environmental structure series) (1977)

49. Alexander, C.: The timeless way of building (1979)

50. Akkerman, S.F., Bakker, A.: Boundary crossing and boundary objects (2011). https://doi.org/10.3102/0034654311404435

51. Zitter, I., de Bruijn, E., Simons, R.J., ten Cate, O.: The role of professional objects in technology-enhanced learning environments in higher education. Interact. Learn. Environ. **20** (2012). https://doi.org/10.1080/10494821003790863

52. Yildirim, N., Pushkarna, M., Goyal, N., Wattenberg, M., Viégas, F.: Investigating how practitioners use human-ai guidelines: a case study on the people + AI guidebook. In: Conference on Human Factors in Computing Systems - Proceedings (2023). https://doi.org/10.1145/3544548.3580900

53. Gray, C.M., Kou, Y., Battles, B., Hoggatt, J., Toombs, A.L.: The dark (patterns) side of UX design. In: Conference on Human Factors in Computing Systems - Proceedings (2018). https://doi.org/10.1145/3173574.3174108

54. Vaccaro, K., Huang, D., Eslami, M., Sandvig, C., Hamilton, K., Karahalios, K.: The illusion of control: Placebo effects of control settings. In: Proceedings of the 2018 CHI Conference on

Human Factors in Computing Systems. Association for Computing Machinery, New York, NY, USA (2018). https://doi.org/10.1145/3173574.3173590

55. Pu, P., Chen, L., Hu, R.: A user-centric evaluation framework for recommender systems. In: RecSys'11 - Proceedings of the 5th ACM Conference on Recommender Systems (2011). https://doi.org/10.1145/2043932.2043962

56. Langacker, R.W., Lakoff, G.: Women, fire, and dangerous things: what categories reveal about the mind. Language (Baltim) **64** (1988). https://doi.org/10.2307/415440

57. Jannach, D., Jugovac, M., Nunes, I.: 5. Explanations and user control in recommender systems. In: Personalized Human-Computer Interaction (2019). https://doi.org/10.1515/9783110552485-005

58. Jannach, D., Naveed, S., Jugovac, M.: User control in recommender systems: Overview and interaction challenges. In: Lecture Notes in Business Information Processing (2017). https://doi.org/10.1007/978-3-319-53676-7_2

59. Smits, A., et al.: Assessing the utility of an interaction qualities framework in systematizing the evaluation of user control. Presented at the (2024). https://doi.org/10.1007/978-3-031-61698-3_17

60. Smits, A., Cardona, K., Berk, M., Bartels, E., Van Turnhout, K.: What do we know about interactions in recommender interfaces?: A systematic literature review of user interactions and their impact on user experience. In: IN PREPARATION (2025)

61. Millecamp, M., Conati, C., Htun, N.N., Verbert, K.: To explain or not to explain: The effects of personal characteristics when explaining music recommendations. In: Proceedings of the 24th International Conference on Intelligent User Interfaces, pp. 397–407. Association for Computing Machinery, New York, NY, USA (2019). https://doi.org/10.1145/3301275.3302313

62. Van Grondelle, J., et al.: Improving user's confidence to act when using advice algorithms through interactive use of counterfactuals. In: Resilience Through Digital Innovation: Enabling the Twin Transition, pp. 227–242. University of Maribor Press, Bled (2024)

63. Smits, A., Nguyen, D., Hekman, E., Turnhout, K.V.: Data-driven design. In: Proceedings of the 22nd International Conference on Engineering and Product Design Education, E and PDE 2020 (2020)

64. Loepp, B., Ziegler, J.: Towards interactive recommending in model-based collaborative filtering systems. In: Proceedings of the 13th ACM Conference on Recommender Systems, pp. 546–547. ACM, New York, NY, USA (2019). https://doi.org/10.1145/3298689.3346949

The Design Studio of the Future: Insights from a Practical Experiment in Remote Collaboration

Lars Erik Holmquist[1]([✉]) [iD] and Sam Nemeth[2] [iD]

[1] Nottingham Trent University, 50 Shakespeare Street, Nottingham NG1 4FQ, UK
lars.holmquist@ntu.ac.uk
[2] Poppe & Partners, Tuinstraat 118, 1015PH Amsterdam, Netherlands
sam@poppeenpartners.nl

Abstract. A *design studio* is sometimes seen as an example of an almost ideal creative workplace: a rich and dynamic environment that facilitates many different types of collaborative work. In this project, we aimed to recreate the positive features of a design studio in an educational and workplace setting using distance-spanning digital technology. We first set up a series of experimental collaboration systems to facilitate teaching and research at a university during the early days of the Covid pandemic. We quickly found that many concepts proposed in the research literature were not practically feasible. Instead, we constructed realistic solutions using off-the-shelf hardware and software that afforded nosvel and efficient ways of blending co-located and distance collaboration. This included informal interaction settings with one or multiple participants both online and in-person, as well as formal hybrid teacher/student presentations. From this we learned that although much of the required hardware already exists, it is not generally being used to its potential. We also found that the standard meeting software is not fit for this kind of creative collaboration settings. The insights from this will support the creation of better support for combining remote and in-person creative work.

Keywords: Co-design · Design Practice · Distance Working · Hybrid Working

1 Introduction

At the start of the Covid pandemic in 2020, there was uncertainty about what would happen to office work and teaching. At first, many thought that things would just go back to normal as the pandemic petered out after a few months. When it became clear that this would not be over in a long time, the dynamics of office work versus working from home changed. Distance working, for a while, became the norm, and actually turned out to be quite efficient in many respects. But at the same time, it has been acknowledged that by not having a shared, co-located workplace, creative and collaborative work becomes difficult, and informal communication suffers. Today, in the post-pandemic world, many workplaces are still in a period of calibration, where staff and management are trying to figure out the best balance between on-site and remote work.

J. Abdelnour-Nocera et al. (Eds.): ARPPID 2025, CCIS 2797, pp. 143–153, 2026.
https://doi.org/10.1007/978-3-032-15516-0_10

In this case study, we report from a project called The Design Studio of the Future, where we explored ideas around the future of creative and collaborative work and education in this emerging new world. It was proposed as an early reaction to the pandemic, and throughout 2020 and 2021 we carried out several small-scale experiments across universities in UK and the Netherlands. In these, we wanted to use technology as efficiently as possible to support creative work and learning, both online and in person. The project set out with visions of creating completely novel ways of interacting, but because it was not possible to produce bespoke hard- and software in the pandemic, we used mostly off-the-shelf technologies in new ways – something that turned out to be not a negative, but a major takeaway from the project.

2 The Design Studio

2.1 The Design Studio of the Past

Before the 1800s, the development of new products was typically done in an *atelier*, a workshop where a master worked on a product, aided by apprentices to whom they also transmitted their craft and knowledge. But the industrial revolution increased the complexity and scale of products. This called for a more collaborative process of different disciplines as well as a more advanced educational model. The name that is most immediately connected to that concept is Thomas Edison. He was aware that many inventions need infrastructural and cultural context. Still in the 19th century, in his laboratory in Menlo Park, New Jersey, a number of co-workers with very different specializations contributed to the realization of Edison's revolutionary concepts [12]. He was the multidisciplinary 'director', controlling the process where several people collaborated: "he broke the mold of the 'lone genius inventor' by creating a team-based approach to innovation" [3].

It was no coincidence that the role of the 'genius inventor' shifted towards a demystified 'designer' in the beginning of the 20th century. After the industrial revolution and the introduction of capitalism, there was a call for a more thorough, efficient development system [3]. By the end of the 19th century this modus operandi, where developing a novel application depends on a group with diverse disciplines, rather than an individual "inventor", is the operating model of the majority of design studios.

2.2 The Design Studio Now

This historical context has highly influenced the way we imagine a design studio today: a rich, creative and dynamic environment. Design studios are typically large, open plan spaces that have facilities for many different types of work. People move between different areas, taking advantage of the most relevant equipment and capabilities. The space allows for concentrated, individual work as well as fostering spontaneous communication. Residents see what their colleagues are doing; they can instantly turn to someone for help if they get stuck; they can pick up interesting ideas from each other and generate new projects.

The air is buzzing with energy and excitement, creating a positive atmosphere that inspires even better and more creative output (see Fig. 1). This is a place where both

Fig. 1. A meeting in a design studio at the turn of the 21st century

individual and group work is exponentially improved by the presence of other people as well as the physical and technical resources. But, of course, the circumstances of reality caught up with this idyll.

2.3   The Design Studio of the Future

Well before the Covid pandemic, online design collaboration tools were already in use. Most of these products, like Miro, Figma or Mural, aim at a swift workflow, today in many cases aided by AI. But this is not what we were looking for: we are interested in collaboration over distances where intuitiveness, on the spot inspiration, and exchange of ideas with co-workers who work from the studio as well as from home are part of the collaborative process.

Video communication was already used before Covid. But when it turned into a worldwide pandemic, in a matter of weeks video conferencing became the only way people could meet, when social distancing mandated working from home. This was easier said than done. When working, for instance, from a tiny home office in an annex guest room, the energy of the design studio dissolves in a mist of bad connections, rickety software and interface problems. In other words: video conferences and remote meetings impose rigid limitations and hamper spontaneous collaborations and workplace awareness. Despite many workers feeling that they are equally or even more productive when working from home, it was clear that the design studio (as well as many other workplaces) became a shadow of its former self during this time.

This discrepancy still exists. Years after the pandemic, many workers and educators are still preferring to work from home even though the management more and more insists their staff come to the office. The reason is that the social commitment, the human-human interaction in the workspace, adds not only to the quality of the product but also to the mental health of the workers.

Still, in many cases online collaboration, part-time, benefits many employees, if only to maintain a healthy relationship with the family. The term hybrid work was introduced to describe when workers partly work from home, partly at the workplace [7]. During the pandemic, home and hybrid work increased significantly in the EU, and stayed at higher levels than before [5]. In the UK, as of October 2024, 41% of workers worked remotely for at least part of their week. Of these, 28% had a hybrid work situation, while 13% were fully remote [1]. In design teaching, hybrid and distance models have also increasingly become the norm [8, 11]. The question during the pandemic as well as now is: how can we combine the advantages of flexible workplaces with the buzz and energy of a lively physical space such as a design studio?

3   What (We Thought) We Wanted to Do

Motivated by the vision that a design studio in an online context has special requirements, we provisioned a project to explore *The Design Studio of the Future*. We wanted to create a technology-supported environment that ideally would take the best of both distance work and in-person collaboration. The project was set up as a collaboration between a UK university and a university in the Netherlands. It was aimed at supporting a specific educational case, the *Interaction Design* undergraduate program at the School of Design, as well as the research and teaching staff associated with the program. We received a small budget to purchase equipment and pay for a part-time researcher.

In the original project plan, we wrote that we would create "an environment where students and teachers are able to share space both physically and virtually, in formal and informal collaboration, thus re-creating the atmosphere of a fully co-located design studio." Specifically, we wanted to implement and test a series of concepts that touch upon key activities of the design studio, including:

- *Shared Media Spaces:* Always-on, informal audio/video spaces that tie together virtual and physical locations to foster collaboration.
- *Physical-Virtual Workbenches:* An augmented reality-based setting for doing hands-on design work that can be shared by remote users as if they were in the same room.
- *Ambient Cues:* A set of simple displays and devices that sit in the background of the users' attention communicating subtle social cues, such as presence or activity.

These ideas were all heavily influenced by well-established human-computer interaction research concepts, including *media spaces* developed as early as the 1990s in the EuroPARC research center [2], the EuroPARC *RAVE* system [4], as well as MIT's Tangible Media Group's *Ambient Media* concept [8]. It is also related to other Covid-inspired collaboration and ambient awareness projects that took place in parallel, such as Royal College of Art's *Yo-Yo Machines* [6]. Our original intention was therefore to build and test several novel and bespoke interfaces that would build upon these ideas as research prototypes. We intended this as an exploration of user interface technology, going beyond existing interfaces to demonstrate novel ways of distance interacting. However, what we ended up doing was something different.

4 What We Actually Did

The project was limited by a number of real-world constraints. The first was that contrary to what we had initially believed, the Covid pandemic did not go away. This meant that we were very limited in our ability to hold in-person classes and meetings. It also meant that the collaborators could not travel between UK and the Netherlands during the duration of the project. The second limitation was that we only had a very limited budget for equipment (~1000 GBP) and no access to maker facilities and workshops, as these were all shut down during the pandemic. Finally, we had to look at the reality of our teaching and research load and use the funding to find realistic ways of supporting this, instead of developing novel – but ultimately less useful – design concepts. Taken together, this meant that if we wanted to achieve something practical, we would have to back away from the lofty intention of building entirely novel user interfaces and instead work with off-the-shelf materials that we could adapt to our needs. In this we were guided by the concept of *Conjoint Control,* a practical set of guidelines that stresses using off-the-shelf parts, user communities and soft deployment to create usable physical user interfaces in real-world settings [10].

In order to work within these limitations yet produce practical results, we carried out a number of experiments using existing and/or low-cost equipment. We stayed as close as possible to the design brief, while at the same taking advantage of readily-available resources, which allowed us to work flexible and fast, providing us with the opportunity to test out a number of different possibilities. Going by the original intention, this is what we did.

4.1 Preparation

Right at the beginning of the pandemic, we organized semi-structured interviews with current users of online collaboration tools. Some of these interviews were executed online, some were done live. From our interviews we learned that our respondents were overall happy to work at home but had problems with the hard- and software. Users said they missed physical feedback, and found the quality of the images and sound poor.

The repercussions of the pandemic at that moment were unpredictable. The immediate result was that in our own research group, most activities were done individually. In hindsight, it is clear that the pandemic also had a great impact on the cohesion of working practices and groups. Many people who stayed home did not even show up on online meetings. The pandemic also had consequences for our interviewees and respondents. For instance, we later found that one interviewee never recovered from long Covid and is still partly disabled.

4.2 Practical Experiments

Inspired by the literature on media spaces, we first created a shared hybrid space by setting up a system in a communal area, the lab kitchen. It consisted of a large-screen television connected to a computer, a high-resolution webcam, and high-quality room microphone. We designated a user in a standard telecommunication software. We then let the software run continuously, so that anyone could connect to the large screen in the kitchen and "drop in" to whoever happened to be there. In theory, this provided a media space at a much higher quality and lower cost than the original media spaces constructed in the 1990s. We expected to have our shared, informal meeting place benefit both local and distance workers.

In reality, we shut off the system after the first few hours. It turned out that for the staff and students physically present in the space, the "creepy" factor of the system was much higher than we had imagined. It was immediately obvious that nobody wanted there to be even the smallest chance of someone else remotely listening in or observing when they were interacting informally in the kitchen, or even just hanging out by themselves. Thus, despite many positive reports in research papers on "ambient awareness" and informal communication over shared media spaces [2, 4], this barrier simply was not surmountable. We did not turn the system on again.

The project plan also envisioned a shared workspace where physical and digital work was shared as if all participants were in the same room. However, due to the limitations with social distancing all Interaction Design students were working remotely from home. Staff and PhD students could come in during certain periods, as long as they were socially distanced. Some were still not able to come in due to being in risk groups or other reasons.

We decided to approach the problem very practically. Rather than trying to create an augmented reality space or a hologram representation of other users, we decided to leverage existing technologies to make it as easy as possible to collaborate. For meetings where most participants were onsite, we set up individual access through dedicated computers for those who could not come in in person (Fig. 2). That meant that they could participate in in-person meetings remotely on an equal standing to those in the room.

Fig. 2. Blended interaction with one online participant joining on a single computer (circled), getting equal standing to in-person attendants.

For blended meetings we set up a dedicated meeting place in an informal area, the kitchen (Fig. 3). This recycled the high-quality monitor, camera and microphone from the media space experiment. This inexpensive set-up worked very well: through the large screen and high-quality visual/audio connection, it almost felt like everybody was in the same room. By placing it in an informal space rather than a meeting room, it was readily accessible and less stilted than more organized meeting equipment. Throughout the pandemic the lab continued to use this set-up for all kinds of interactions. It is worth noting that this simple solution, costing less than £1000 in total, was vastly superior in quality, and was used more, than the very costly dedicated video-meeting equipment that was installed by the university's IT team.

Fig. 3. Blended interaction with multiple online and offline participants getting approximately equal standing.

For the Interaction Design undergrad program that had originally been intended as the setting for the project, we could only interact with the students remotely due to Covid restrictions. However, we adopted the above meeting system so that the tutors could attend the final presentations from the university (Fig. 4). By using personal laptops for chat and textual feedback, tutors got a back-channel to discuss and comment the student work, while watching the presentation together on a large screen. This at least gave the students an approximation of having a live audience for their presentations, and constituted a better experience for the teaching staff than attending from their own home/laptop.

Finally, in addition to these installations, we also took advantage of other technology to improve the functionality of existing software. We added a commercially available foot pedal (Fig. 5, left) to our remote meeting software to allow the user to shut down either video, audio or close the connection with one tap of the sneaker. We invested in affordable camera stands (Fig. 6, right) that made it possible to change the position of the webcam, to easily show tangible results as well as to establish a more attractive image on the webcam than the frog perspective that is inherent to using a built-in webcam on a generic laptop. These simple additions greatly improved the remote working experience at a very low cost.

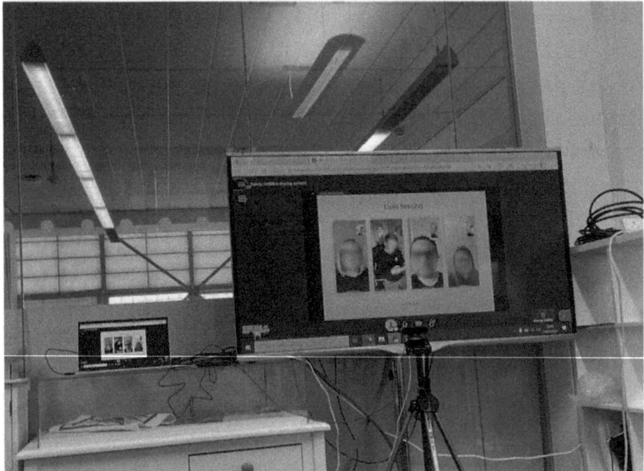

Fig. 4. Attending the final presentations of the Interaction Design undergraduate class, with tutors seated socially distanced in the university while viewing on a large screen and interacting using separate laptops.

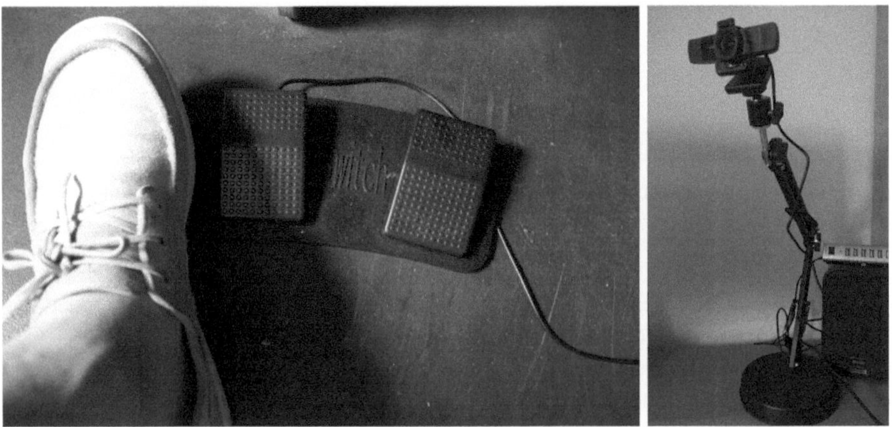

Fig. 5. Left: Commercially available pedals provided access to often used functions like closing/opening the camera or audio and opening the chat. Right: High end camera on tripod.

5 What We Learned

Despite the limitations, we learned a lot about the potential of using technology to create a vibrant "design studio of the future" from these experiments. We saw how simple and inexpensive pieces of equipment could be leveraged, but also that the current software model for distance communication is deeply flawed.

5.1 The Needed Hardware Exists but It is not Used Correctly

Technology support for distance work seems to fall into two categories. It is either a personal general-purpose machine, typically a laptop, being used for teleconferencing simply because there are no other resources. This was the typical situation that millions of workers found themselves in when suddenly confined to working from home. With many university workers (including us) denied access to their workplaces and equipment, they were limited to whatever laptop they happened to have been assigned when the pandemic struck. Most laptops unfortunately have very bad AV capabilities, including low-resolution cameras, limited-range microphones, and low-quality speakers. This severely limits the experience and makes working remotely much more difficult.

On the other hand, there is the high-end formal meeting room equipment that started to be installed by IT departments by the end of the pandemic. These expensive installations were simply not fit for purpose. They relied on only allowing one type of software (in our case Microsoft Teams) and had all kinds of built-in functionalities that were rarely used but made the system less intuitive, such as automatically focusing on movement in the camera view. By being placed on a wall at the short end of a large meeting room table, they drastically limited the types of interactions that could take place between in-person and remote viewers, as the microphone was too far away from most participants; the camera could not properly cover the whole space; and the meeting room participants were facing each other rather than the screen. Even worse, and surprisingly, the audio and video quality of these installations was significantly worse than our low-cost solution, with both cameras and microphones being sub-par quality in addition to being badly placed. All of this made the "official" meeting systems that the university invested in practically unusable, whereas our cobbled-together "budget" system continued to be used.

We do believe that there is a middle ground that this experiment demonstrated, which is to provide wide access high-quality (but inexpensive) equipment including group microphones, HD cameras, and large consumer screens, to facilitate informal as well as formal meetings. This is a grassroots, practical approach that will be cost-effective and provide a more flexible interaction with a higher audio and video quality.

5.2   The Existing Software is not Suitable, and It Needs a Drastic Re-Think

While the hardware components were fairly easy to re-combine and put into new settings, the software for remote meetings and collaborations turned out to be a much more difficult proposition. Through the experiment we used Microsoft Teams and Blackboard, as they were the university mandated software systems; however, the issues are the same with other commercial software such as Zoom, Skype, etc.

The main problem with the software has to do with the one user – one connection paradigm. Whereas we were often 3–5 people using the suite in the lab, Teams would not acknowledge this, and instead treats every user account equally. In particular, this means that the visual weight (i.e. window size) of each user account is the same, with the consequence that accounts with multiple participants are treated exactly as a single user/participant. We often found that it was hard for remote users to decipher what was going on in the group room as the faces and postures of a group of 3–5 people confined to a very small square were difficult to read. It was also hard to determine who had the "word" in a lively discussion, as co-located users tended to communicate with each other directly, something that often did not translate to the remote participants.

The other issue with this model came when we had single users join through dedicated computers. There is simply no way in Teams (or any other software we know of) to allow several screens/workstations take part in a blended meeting at the same time. The model is set up to show all users on all screens, assuming that they are not co-located. That meant that we had large difficulties to get the system to work when 2–3 people joined and were displayed on individual computers. One of the main issues had to do with audio, because if we had two or more machines joining at the same time, they would cause feedback and create a noise that made meeting impossible. In the end we only used this approach when a single user was remote (as in Fig. 2), and when there were more remote users, we used the large screen (Fig. 3) (which as noted came with its own problems).

This has led us to conclude there is a need for a drastic re-think on teleconference and collaboration software to provide a better remote and blended experience than what is currently available.

6   The Design Studio of the (Near) Future?

As the world is still recalibrating after Covid, it does seem that remote work is here to stay, perhaps especially at universities. At the site of this experiment, we initially saw only a small fraction of the staff return to the office after the pre-pandemic. Official meetings continued to be held remotely, even when all attendants were in the same building. There was no support provided for blended or informal workplace communication, and the centrally installed systems continued to be inadequate. It is not an exaggeration to say that a large part of the vibrancy and creativity of this particular school was lost after Covid, and it would take much work to gain it back.

Yet inter-personal communication is still necessary for creativity and learning. Even in remote or hybrid situations, creativity could be much better supported if existing technology was applied in more effective and flexible ways, and if meeting software would be better adapted to a more comprehensive range of different remote and in-person situations. We believe our experiment shows that there are simple, low-cost solutions to many of these problems, but there is need for a bottom-up re-think of technology for remote, blended and in-person meeting and teaching going forward. Only then will we see a remote or blended "Design studio of the future" that is as vibrant as the physically co-located design studios of today.

Acknowledgements. This work was partly supported by an NU-AUAS Pump Priming Fund Award, as a collaboration between Northumbria School of Design and Amsterdam University of Applied Sciences. Additional work was supported by Nottingham Trent University and Poppe and Partners. We also thank all participants of the practical experiments, the questionnaire and the semi-structured interviews.

References

1. Allen, E.: UK Remote & Hybrid Workforce Statistics 2025. https://www.mollearn.com/about/news/remote-hybrid-workforce-statistics/. Accessed 15 Sept 2025

2. Bly, S.A., Harrison, S.R., Irwin, S.: Media spaces: bringing people together in a video, audio, and computing environment. Commun. ACM **36**(1), 28–46 (1993)
3. Brown, T.: Design thinking. Harv. Bus. Rev. **86**, 84–92 (2008)
4. Buxton, W., Moran, T.: EuroPARC's integrated interactive intermedia facility (iiif): early experience. In: Gibbs, S., Verrijn-Stuart, A.A. (eds.). Multiuser interfaces and applications, Proceedings of the IFIP WG 8.4 Conference on Multi-user Interfaces and Applications, pp. 11–34. Elsevier Science Publishers B.V. (North-Holland), Heraklion, Crete. Amsterdam (1990)
5. Eurofound. The future of telework and hybrid work. Publications Office of the European Union, Luxembourg ((2023))
6. Gaver, W., et al.: Yo–Yo machines: self-build devices that support social connections during the pandemic. In: Proceedings of the 2022 CHI Conference on Human Factors in Computing Systems (CHI 2022), Article 458, pp. 1–17. Association for Computing Machinery, New York, NY, USA (2022)
7. Gratton, L.: How to do hybrid right. Harv. Bus. Rev. **99**(3), 65–74 (2021)
8. Ishii, H., et al.: AmbientROOM: integrating ambient media with architectural space. In: CHI 98 Conference Summary on Human Factors in Computing Systems (CHI 1998), pp. 173–174. Association for Computing Machinery, New York, NY, USA (1998)
9. Jones, D., Lotz, N., Holden, G.: A longitudinal study of virtual design studio (VDS) use in STEM distance design education. Int. J. Technol. Des. Educ. **31**(4), 839–865 (2021)
10. Nemeth, S., Holmquist, L.E.: Conjoint control: a practical approach to implementing physical interfaces in real-world settings. In: 27th International Conference on Human-Computer Interaction (HCI International 2025), Gothenburg, Sweden, 22–27 June 2025. Springer, Berlin (2025)
11. Spruce, J., Thomas, P., Moriarty, S.: From sharing screens to sharing spaces. Des. Technol. Educ.: Int. J. **26**(4), 96–111 (2021)
12. Stross, R.E.: The wizard of menlo park: how thomas alva edison invented the modern world. Crown Publishers, New York, USA (2007)

Establishing Sustained Use of Work Domain Analysis: A Collaborative Approach Between Academia and Professional Practice

Ece Üreten[1(✉)], Yeti Li[2], Selin Üreten[3], Murat Dikmen[2], and Torkil Clemmensen[4]

[1] University of Oulu, 90570 Oulu, Finland
e.uereten@tudelft.nl
[2] Independent, Kitchener, ON N2G0C3, Canada
[3] Independent, 20144 Hamburg, Germany
[4] Copenhagen Business School, 2000 Frederiksberg, Denmark

Abstract. Work Domain Analysis (WDA) supports the understanding of socio-technical work environments and demonstrates its utility across various domains. Long-lasting adoption remains still limited; challenges go beyond the theoretical complexity and pose opportunities for longer collaborations between academia and industry for its sustained use. This paper discusses current methods and practices in organizations that can be mapped to the levels of abstraction portrayed in the WDA. With this example, we want to highlight that its use can be found across various levels of organizations and thus shows links to being integrated into various work environments. The adoption of WDA in organizations can be sustained if further recommended steps are taken, as presented in this paper.

Keywords: Work Domain Analysis · Collaboration · Socio-Technical Systems

1 Introduction

In today's complex socio-technical environments such as aviation and healthcare, organizations face growing challenges in designing systems that align with operational goals, regulatory constraints, and user needs. The field of Cognitive Systems Engineering (CSE) examines how humans and technology interact within such complex socio-technical systems instead of focusing on each of them individually. Methods like Work Domain Analysis (WDA) have been taken up by various professional practices, organizations and industries (hereafter used synonymously in this paper). The purpose of using WDA in industries [1–4] is to understand the work environments to identify how the goals of the defined system underlie various levels of functions, processes, and their most granular, physical forms. Depicted as a core component of the Cognitive Work Analysis (CWA) framework, WDA has provided a base for developing an Ecological Interface Design (EID) [5] for monitoring systems and supporting decision-making across domains [6–10]. Such Ecological Interfaces shall support operators' reasoning more effectively and display the relationships of various variables of a system within its constraints.

J. Abdelnour-Nocera et al. (Eds.): ARPPID 2025, CCIS 2797, pp. 154–166, 2026.
https://doi.org/10.1007/978-3-032-15516-0_11

Academia has long contributed methods for analyzing such systems, yet the uptake of the WDA approach in the long term within industry remains limited.

Despite overarching strategic goals, many organizations operate in functional silos, with departments focusing narrowly on tasks, tools that support their 'best practice' approaches, or performance metrics that often lack continuity and are not always well connected across the organization hierarchy. Although frameworks are adopted as 'best practice' for example, through leaders of departments, they may frequently change due to reorganization or attrition. This can lead to misaligned priorities, inefficiencies, and missed opportunities for coordination. While collaboration frameworks like agile software development and lean promote effective teamwork and communication, their focus tends to be on managing tasks and workflows. These differ to CWA which rather focuses on the understanding and supporting human cognition in complex socio-technical environments, but can be seen as complementary approaches to CWA. These established methodologies provide a structured way to plan and execute tasks, whereas CWA provides a structured way to analyze and identify higher-level goals and processes that govern strategic decision-making and collaboration across multiple teams. While CWA offers a systems-oriented perspective, it can help uncover shared goals and constraints across departments, fostering communication and integrated decision-making.

Literature demonstrates the utility of WDA in various domains, however, there is limited research on how organizations and academic partners can collaboratively apply and adapt WDA to support internal learning and sustained practice. Such collaboration can help organizations not only adopt WDA effectively but also embed it into their analytical repertoire, enabling them to revisit and refine work systems over time.

We propose that such collaborations on WDA between organizations and academia provide various opportunities and are not limited to the following:

- Opportunity 1: WDA helps develop a holistic understanding and cross-functional alignment which can facilitate decision-making.
- Opportunity 2: WDA can support training of professionals by representing roles and responsibilities. These can also be beneficial for onboarding purposes to gain understanding of their work on a broader scale within the organization.
- Opportunity 3: WDA enables the understanding of work constraints and match between operations and regulatory standards.

However, there are also challenges organizations face in their long-term uptake of WDA in the continuation of their work processes:

- Challenge 1: WDA appears as a theoretical method and is often perceived as abstract and complex. The outputs of the WDA can be difficult to interpret or use for decision-making purposes. Organizations often seek implementable solutions with quick wins, while WDA proposes a rather high-level analysis and system understanding that might not immediately result in tangible outcomes. This often leads to resistance to adoption in the long-term.
- Challenge 2: Silos make it difficult to make cross-functional analyses.
   They often have differing goals, tools and metrics, and can sometimes even be conflicting. Reaching agreement on shared understanding can be fragmented. There

can be various reasons for silos, e.g., different department structures, profit centers and mindsets of individuals.

- Challenge 3: Constantly changing requirements and scopes require WDA to be adjusted. In fast-changing environments, we may face changes in regulations or stakeholder requirements which can necessitate an updated WDA model. The abstract and at the same time depth of WDA can add to the workload and time constraints.
- Challenge 4: Organizations have their own set of tools and methodologies for which they acquired familiarity and habits, which are difficult to abandon. The ease of use and perceived simplicity of already existing tools and methodologies is often preferred considering the time and effort of learning something new. WDA would require training and active work by all stakeholders. For example, hospital staff often use task-based design methods like workflow mapping; when showing a WDA, many parts of the WDA are left unused or simplified into flowcharts, which takes away the depth of the WDA that is essential for revealing the structural and functional constraints to ultimately shape behaviour.

Although many organizations reach out to academia to collaborate on conducting WDA studies, the lasting integration of WDA into everyday organizational practices remains uncertain. To constitute higher acceptance and long-lasting adoption of WDA, we propose a model that portrays opportunities for organizations on various levels for long-term uptake. In this paper, we ask:

How can collaboration between academia and professional practice support the sustained use of Work Domain Analysis within organizations?

2   Methods

The WDA portrays an environment that is controlled by the user, which requires the definition of boundaries. The starting point is to define the system of interest [11]. The aspects that are being controlled are part of the system boundaries. Table 1 presents an example of Bicycling in a city.

The top level, called the functional purpose, defines the goals, values and constraints of the work or system of interest. The priorities of the system or work are described at the abstract function level. The level of generalized functions describes the activities and processes. Physical functions can be referred to as the physical activities, processes including the equipment's capability representations. The appearance, location or configuration of equipment or objects is displayed on the physical form level. [11, 12].

Each level of abstraction is connected to the above or below abstraction level, which are referred to as means-end links (not visually presented in Table 1). These means-end links show the connection of each variable between each level and portray how or why they are related. For example, variables listed in the physical form level would be linked to the physical functions level through its means-end link, describing how its physical function is achieved [11]. An example of Table 1 would be that the pedals are needed to transmit force from the pedals to the wheels.

Table 1. Function Decomposition with an example of Bicycling in a City added to the rightmost column.

Level	Description	Example (Bicycling in a City)
Functional Purpose	Overall aim or intention of the system	Enable safe and efficient transportation in the city by bicycle
Abstract Function	General functions without specific technical details	Provide human-powered motion for urban mobility
Generalized Function	Functions described in general terms, often verbs + objects	Convert pedaling energy into forward motion
Physical Function	Functions tied to physical processes or mechanisms	Transmit force from pedals to wheels
Physical Form	Concrete structure or physical entity performing the function	Bicycle frame, pedals, chain, and wheels

3 Examples of WDA in Different Domains

The WDA can sometimes show similarities but also differences across work domains depending on the system of exploration. In the examples below, we present two previously conducted studies on power grid operations [13], as well as approaches to sustainable aviation [14].

3.1 A WDA of Voltage Management in Power Grid Operations

The example in Fig. 1 shows a focus on how electric transmission operators control voltage management, with the purpose of delivering electric power from the generation source to end-users, ensuring demand is met with minimal cost. Compliance with current quality and safety standards, as well as the maintenance of a secure, stable and reliable power transmission infrastructure are further parts of the system objectives. These are all displayed on the general purpose level of the WDA. While these elements are connected via means-end links to the abstract, general, and physical function level, the most granular, physical forms level displays dependencies and aspects related to the weather conditions, equipment status, industrial and domestic power consumers and more.

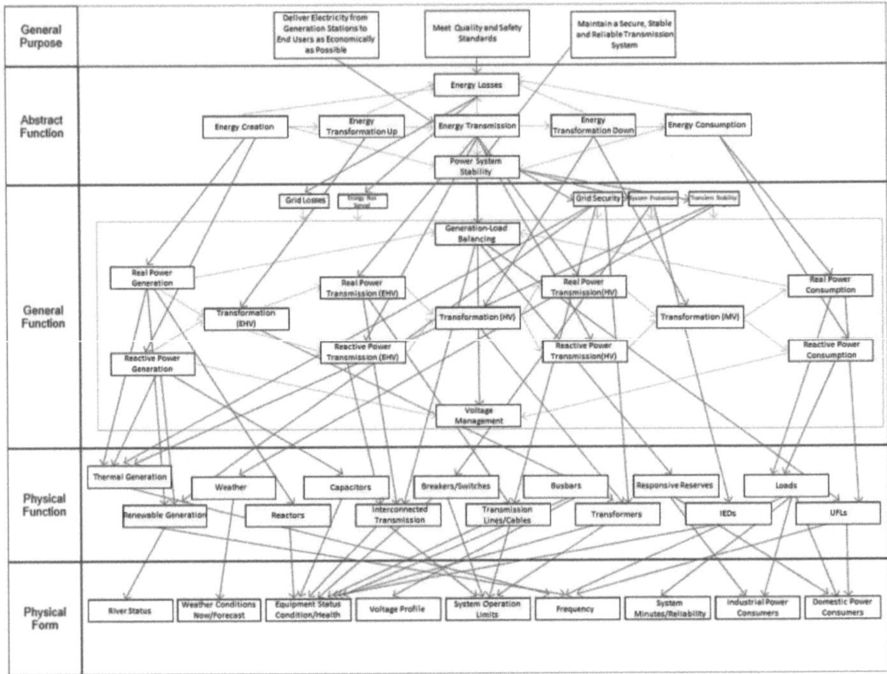

Fig. 1. A WDA of Voltage Management [13] adapted to be shown without colours.

3.2   A WDA of a Hydrogen Aircraft Powertrain Storage System (HAPSS)

A further example in the field of aviation can be viewed in Fig. 2 [14] below. While this example focused on sustainable aviation and providing an overview of how a new HAPSS could be operated by pilots, it shows that the general or functional purpose is to view the fuel and engine systems separately. The fuel system is functionally defined by its ability to supply adequate fuel to complete the mission, while the engine system is characterized by its requirement to generate sufficient thrust to achieve mission objectives. The abstract functions level portrays the balances of the system, i.e., considering the mass and energy conservation laws, connected to the power system stability. While these again are connected via means-ends links to the general and physical functions, the physical forms level portrays similarly the system health, settings, and reliability of the system to operate.

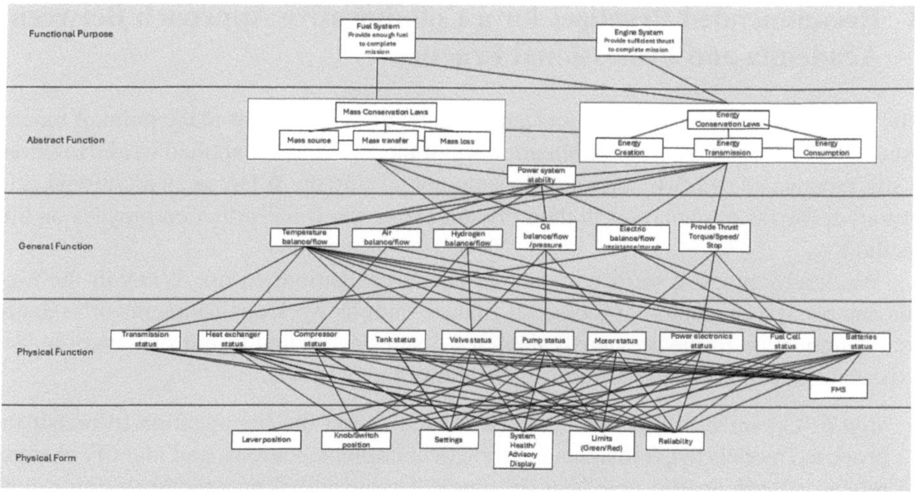

Fig. 2. The five levels of the WDA, exemplified for a Hydrogen Aircraft Powertrain Storage System (HAPSS) [14].

4   Current Practices of Academia and Organizations to Develop a WDA

Our observations and studies conducted in various work domains (e.g., healthcare, finance, aviation) show that often, when academic researchers and professionals from organizations get together to develop a WDA, they go through various steps:

- *Step 1:* Gaining in-depth insights into the system or work environment that is being analyzed (e.g., literature, previously conducted work or analyses of the organization, available resources being presented by professionals from organizations etc.).
- *Step 2:* Planning the studies, e.g., ethnographies, interviews to model the actual environment or system of analysis (often done by academic researchers).
- *Step 3:* Mapping of the WDA (prepared by academic researchers familiar with the WDA approach).
- *Step 4:* Discussing the WDA with subject matter experts and iterating the WDA if needed (conducted by academic researchers and professionals from organizations).
- *Step 5:* Publications of the WDA findings to the organization as well as in academic settings (done by academic researchers and sometimes reports prepared by professionals from the organization).

These steps often conclude the collaborative work between both academic and organizational partners. An example of this can be taken from [14] in which the researchers interviewed subject matter experts to gain understanding of the system and discuss the created WDA. The research group further proposed design ideas for an Ecological Interface but remained at an exploratory stage. Implementation approaches can be taken up by interested organizations that want to use the WDA as a systematic way of designing an interface.

5 Recommended Practices for a Collaborative Approach Between Academia and Professional Practice

The collaboration between academia and organizations often ends at the point of having established a formal report or publication about the WDA in the applied field. However, it still remains unclear why organizations do not take up the WDA as an additional skill or toolset for various analyses in their organizations and train further employees on this method.

We hereby propose steps that can support organizations to use WDA in the long run and use it as a method or toolset to analyze various work environments or systems, as a continuation to the previously depicted 5 steps according to our observations and experiences working with various organizations and domains:

- *Step 6:* Organize follow-ups between academia and the organization to revisit the proposed models to get insights into practical implementations, and identify changes related to the defined system or environment. Organizations may require training more employees on the WDA method to create awareness and constitute understanding on various levels of the organization. This would demonstrate applicability of WDA's use even in times of requirement changes.
- *Step 7:* Establish long-term adoption. Translate the WDA approach to other systems and work environments within the organization. The usefulness of WDA can thus be shown for various work contexts and connect silos with each other, creating abstract shared understanding.
- *Step 8:* Identify measures to detect its long-lasting effects in various departments within the organization. Establishing such measures can facilitate acceptance of WDA's use across various departments.
- *Step 9:* De-couple from academia having implemented WDA practices into various departments of the organization.

5.1 Measuring Sustained Use of WDA

To see whether WDA has been acquired in the long-term, we can consider various metrics. In general, the frequency of the WDA application can be analyzed. This could include the amount of application in projects, as well as the number of times updating WDA models. WDA can also provide a template or guideline for projects that require systems-understanding. The clear pointing out of using WDA as a basis for documentation about compliance, risk assessment, safety reviews, or checklists can support the use of a rigorous approach. Another measure could be the number of employees that have been trained to use WDA; an in-house expert can be selected to facilitate quick adoption across departments, groups and projects.

Less tangible success measures can include the adoption of WDA into onboarding or training of new staff, as well as the time saved for developing interface design ideas or redesigns due to better functional understanding. Also, consistency between organizational goals across departments can be viewed as a success metric and may be gathered through feedback from employees stating that WDA has helped them gain a higher-level overview of processes and goals.

In connection with design projects, WDA as a design theory (as part of ecological design) [4, 15], could be systematically assessed for design theory qualities in each design step in comparison with selected socio-technical design theories [16]. It may turn out that WDA supports different design qualities in different design steps, and this could be empirically studied as high-level design qualities (responsible design, sustainable design, explainable design) [16]. Furthermore, WDA as a design outcome could be evaluated for organizational usability in post-development contexts such as pilot-implementation, techno-change and design-in-use [17].

In the future, adjacent fields of research can be considered to evaluate transfer potentials to address the adoption of sustained use of WDA including the proposed additional steps.

Specifically, Beckmann et al. [18] provide an overview, based on literature, requirements, shortcomings of methods, as well as success factors and barriers of design method transfer. The transfer refers from academia to industry. Requirements include for example the simple use and flexibility of methods, shortcomings are e.g., that methods are too complex and are not modified to the respective user. To give an example of success factors of method transfer, it is important to incorporate the people involved by persuading them about the method and organizational embedding. Examples of barriers of the method transfer include the significant effort required to implement the method and the complexity in their presentation. [18].

These findings can be taken into account and their potential applicability in this context can be assessed with regards to the sustained use of WDA. Another thought refers to the approaches to transfer methods from academia into practice, which are described in [19] and can be taken as an inspiration for further research. In particular, the challenges in implementation, needs and stakeholders of WDA in a specific context or case can be formulated and the described approaches from literature [19] evaluated for their applicability or need to adapt, and then implemented onto WDA.

Three dimensions for testing the validity of a methodical object (e.g., model, design method, framework) in an experimental study to assess the validity can be found in Üreten et al. [20]: the applicability, usefulness and acceptance of a design method are mentioned. This notion can be applied to sustained use of WDA including the additionally proposed steps. Specifically, the common WDA approach (as described in steps 1–5) can be compared to the sustained use of WDA approach (proposed here as steps 6–9) with regards to the criteria of applicability for the user, its (perceived) usefulness and its acceptance. The goal is to gain more knowledge about WDA and the effects of a sustained use of WDA, which can ultimately lead to an improved and sustainable academia-industry collaboration. The evaluation criteria can be measured by an experimental design followed by a questionnaire for instance. The approach represented in steps 6–9 can be developed in accordance with the challenges and include solution concepts. The experimental design requires a pre-defined scenario to test if there is a difference between the WDA approach shown in steps 1–5 and the proposed WDA approach represented in steps 6–9, and if they do, to which extent do both approaches differ.

Method transfer is a crucial aspect and requires a systemic view. Formats for a collaboration between academia and industry are thus to be tested. Potential formats for academia-industry collaborations for follow-ups can be found in [21]. These include, but are not limited to, scientific projects such as scientific theses, workshop series or seminars.

6 Discussion

In this paper, we present that WDA has been used for various domain purposes to collaborate between academia and organizations. Yet, the uptake in organizations has not been long-lasting, it remains to be discussed what organizations currently use instead of WDA and what the use of WDA implies for academia and organizations. While we noticed that WDA is often perceived as theoretical or too abstract (Challenge 1), we think that this could lessen with time if it is applied and adjusted throughout multiple processes in organizations, and enable viewing measurable outcomes to organizations to accept its long-term use.

Working in silos and having varying goals, tools and metrics across different departments (Challenge 2) can be changed if WDA is applied across departments to facilitate merging silos and enhance cross-departmental understanding, while aligning cross-departmental performance metrics and making sure these metrics are not too short-sighted.

Changing requirements or scopes affect the representation of the WDA which need dynamic adjustment of the model, and is often perceived as creating workload and time-consuming (Challenge 3). The dynamics in organizations require adaptation of approaches, methods and processes which also apply to WDA; learning to use and constitute a WDA as a toolset would enable to also adjust the WDA models to new requirements. In this context, the increasing incorporation of Artificial Intelligence (AI) technologies across organizational processes introduces additional complexity and inter-dependencies that call for a re-evaluation of existing tools, methods, and workflows. As AI reshapes decision-making, task allocation, and communication patterns, understanding the evolving system constraints becomes essential. Here, WDA can serve as a valuable analytical framework to identify how AI influences work domains, to expose where adaptation is needed, and to support organizations in becoming "AI-ready" by aligning human and machine functions effectively. Adapting existing frameworks and tools to company-specific needs can increase their use and ultimately, acceptance.

Although organizations have acquired their own set of tools and methodologies which can be difficult to change (Challenge 4), WDA would not replace the current practices but show greater connectedness and a way to abstract on various levels.

6.1 Relatable Practices of Organizations Mapped to WDA

Various methods are already being implemented in organizations to strategize, organize, operate and execute work within their environment. We can see that the levels of abstraction represented on the WDA relate to organizations' methods and practices in various departments. The following examples show relations of such to the WDA and are not limited to the representation below.

- Organizations often use Balanced Scorecards to map out a strategic framework connecting to business goals and measurable objectives. The strategic level links to the *functional purpose* level in the WDA.

- Practices of lean thinking or six sigma are ways that organizations use to focus on priority management and optimizing efficiency. Agile software development and project management principles are further examples that can relate to the *abstract function* level in the WDA.
- In the operations department within organizations, designing an interface can be regarded as a process (e.g., UX design, UX research, Content Design, Accessibility). Parallels in healthcare to describe this level of the *generalized function* could be moving a patient from one unit to the other.
- Design tools like Figma [22] or other research tools can be found in organizations, relating to the *physical function* level. Further examples from healthcare would be a hemostat to stop bleeding or lathe in manufacturing.
- Their smaller components relate to both digital and physical artefacts. For example, digital artefacts would be design wireframes, programming codes or other ways of documentation. Examples of physical objects could be equipment such as stethoscopes used in healthcare settings. These relate to the *physical form* level in the WDA.

6.2 Implications for Academia and Organizations

In academic settings, theories arise from observed principles in the environment. The WDA has its roots in CSE and portrays an example of industry demands' mapping into a systematic approach. Through various applications of WDA in different socio-technical fields, it has shown applicability to a great variety of environments and real-life contexts.

It remains to be explored which metrics a WDA-based approach will likely improve in the particular organization. Through the collaboration, academics can gain insights into organizations' system constraints, regulatory expectations, and operational limits. At the same time, organizations benefit from a strong alignment between strategic, operational and technical goals, gaining a better picture of how work is done within its defined constraints. A system that highlights the shared purposes across the levels of abstraction can reduce working in silos and enable intradepartmental collaborations.

As academic expertise supports the uptake of WDA within the organization, also for complex socio-technical systems, awareness for improving decision support systems and risk management operations can be created. The systematic way of WDA can be learned and used as a toolset by professionals offering templates, visual aids or integration with familiar tools commonly used in organizations. While design tools like Figma and dedicated work functions such as UX Design are being challenged with generative AI, for example with vibe coding which quickly generates interactive prototypes and working code, CWA is also studied with AI implementations in current research environments. This would enable practical uptake and enhance long-term organizational learning as well as reduce investments on non-prioritized work in the future.

6.3 Future Research

We suggest that WDA can be understood as an example of a Human Work Interaction Design (HWID) framework or tool, and we have elaborated on that in this paper. For future research, WDA should be compared to other HWID frameworks and tools that can be used for academic-professional practice collaboration. Examples of such frameworks and tools include socio-technical approaches such as socioinformatics [23], HWID "action cards" [24], and consultants use of notions of usability and UX as core concepts in socio-technical systems development [25]. For example, HWID "action cards" are [24] concise, one-page guides designed to assist consultants throughout the socio-technical design process. A comparison with WDA should make it clear what the benefits and drawbacks of each tool in terms of bridging academia and practice are.

6.4 Limitations

We have observed common steps (1–5) that take place between academia and organizations to collaborate on WDA; however, the proposed follow-up steps (6–9) have not been evaluated yet nor put into practice. These steps remain to be discussed, tested in future cases where WDA is applied, and can benefit from further perspectives on collaborations between various stakeholders.

7 Conclusion

In this paper, we portray our common perception of academic and organizational collaboration on the use of WDA. Although practices may vary from partner to partner, we propose additional steps to keep WDA as a meaningful and useful method for organizations to keep in their skillset and make use of it in various work environments and system analyses across departments. While WDA can be taken up into the repertoire of methods within organizations, we propose that long-term uptake can be achieved through follow-ups of academic partners within the organization to detect its practical implementations and changes to the defined system or environment. The transferability of WDA can be facilitated to other departments to enhance collaboration and communication, reducing working in silos. Training professionals on this method is profitable to enable long-lasting evaluation of the effects across the organization. The de-coupling phase from academia can once be done when the knowledge and practical skills are manifested within the organization.

References

1. Read, G.J.M.: Extension and application of cognitive work analysis to improve pedestrian safety at rail level crossings, Doctoral dissertation, Monash University (2015)
2. Zúñiga, E.R., Yasue, N., Hirose, T., Nomoto, H., Sawaragi, T.: An integrated discrete-event simulation with functional resonance analysis and work domain analysis methods for industry 4.0 implementation. Dec. Anal. J. **9**, 100323 (2023)
3. Memisevic, R., Sanderson, P., Choudhury, S., Wong, B.L.: Work domain analysis and ecological interface design for hydropower system monitoring and control. In 2005 IEEE International Conference on Systems, Man and Cybernetics, vol. 4, pp. 3580–3587. IEEE (2005)
4. Uereten, E.: Models of cognitive work analysis in neurocritical care and perspectives on expertise–an ecological interface design approach (2023)

5. McIlroy, R.C., Stanton, N.A.: Ecological interface design two decades on: Whatever happened to the SRK taxonomy? IEEE Trans. Hum.-Mach. Syst. **45**(2), 145–163 (2015)
6. Ho, D., Burns, C.M.: Ecological interface design in aviation domains: Work domain analysis of automated collision detection and avoidance. In Proceedings of the Human Factors and Ergonomics Society Annual Meeting, vol. 47, no. 1, pp. 119–123. SAGE Publications, Sage CA: Los Angeles, CA (2003)
7. Jamieson, G.A., Miller, C.A., Ho, W.H., Vicente, K.J.: Integrating task-and work domain-based work analyses in ecological interface design: a process control case study. IEEE Trans. Syst. Man Cybern.-Part A: Syst. Hum. **37**(6), 887–905 (2007)
8. Shier, A.: Applying ecological interface design to improve a radiation therapy interface. University of Toronto (Canada) (2014)
9. Li, Y.: Exploring automated trading: modeling a financial system with a variable degree of automation, display design, and evaluation (2017)
10. Dikmen, M.: A cognitive work analysis approach to explainable artificial intelligence in non-expert financial decision-making (2022)
11. Burns, C.M., Hajdukiewicz, J.: Ecological interface design. CRC Press (2017)
12. Rasmussen, J., Pejtersen, A.M., Schmidt, K.: Taxonomy for cognitive work analysis. Risø National Laboratory (1990)
13. Üreten, E., Olatoye, O., Kelly, A., Burns, C.: Exploring electric transmission operation with cognitive work analysis models. In Proceedings of the Human Factors and Ergonomics Society Annual Meeting, vol. 65, no. 1, pp. 1551–1556. SAGE Publications, Sage CA: Los Angeles, CA (2021)
14. Schweitzer, M., Üreten, E., Borst, C., Stroosma, O., van Paassen, R.: Functional visualizations of a hydrogen-electric aircraft propulsion system for supporting pilot decision-making. In Proceedings of the 23rd International Symposium on Aviation Psychology, p. 66 (2025)
15. Üreten, E., McCredie, V.A., Burns, C.M.: Cognitive work analysis models of neuro-critical care. In: Proceedings of the International Symposium on Human Factors and Ergonomics in Health Care, vol. 9. no. 1. SAGE Publications, Sage CA: Los Angeles, CA (2020)
16. Clemmensen, T.: Design theory qualities: which socio-technical design theory is most sustainable, responsible, and explainable?. In: Barricelli, B.R., Valtolina, S., Bouzekri, E., Locoro, A., Mentler, T. (eds.) Human Work Interaction Design. Sustainable Workplaces by Design. HWID 2024. IFIP Advances in Information and Communication Technology, vol. 751. Springer, Cham. (2026). https://doi.org/10.1007/978-3-031-95334-7_1
17. Hertzum, M.: Three contexts for evaluating organizational usability. J. Usabil. Stud. **11**(1). (2018)
18. Beckmann, G.; Gebhardt, N.; Krause, D.: Transfer of methods for developing modular product families into practice - an interview study. In: 13th International Design Conference - Design 2014, pp. 121–130. Dubrovnik (2014)
19. Beckmann, G., Gebhardt, N.. Bahns, T., Krause, D.: Approach to transfer methods for developing modular product families into practice. In: 14th International Design Conference DESIGN 2016, pp. 1185–1194. Dubrovnik (2016)
20. Üreten, S., Eisenmann, M., Nelius, T., Cao, S., Matthiesen, S., Krause, D.: A concept map for design method experiments in product development - a guideline for method developers. In: Proceedings of the 30th Symposium Design for X (DFX 2019), pp. 147–158. Jesteburg, Germany (2019)
21. Üreten, S., Sankowski, O., Krause, D.: Aktuelle ansätze in der methodenforschung. In: Krause, D.; Hartwich, T. S.; Rennpferdt, C. (Hrsg.): Produktentwicklung und Konstruktionstechnik, Forschungsergebnisse und -projekte der Jahre 2016 bis 2020, Springer Verlag, Berlin, pp. 31–64, Heidelberg, Germany (2020)
22. Figma homepage. https://www.figma.com/. Accessed 30 May 2025

23. Wulf, V., Pipek, V., Randall, D., Rohde, M., Schmidt, K., Stevens, G. (eds.): Socio-informatics. Oxford University Press (2018)
24. Clemmensen, T.: Human work interaction design: a platform for theory and action. Springer Nature (2021)
25. Rajanen, M., Rajanen, D.: Usability as speculum mundi: a core concept in socio-technical systems development. Complex Syst. Inform. Model. Quar. **22**, 49–59 (2020)

From Cosy Games to Metaverse: Deriving Positive Interaction Qualities Through Netnography

Thi Ngoc Anh Pham$^{(\boxtimes)}$ and Lars Erik Holmquist

Nottingham Trent University, 50 Shakespeare St., Nottingham NG1 4FQ, UK
`thi.pham022024@my.ntu.ac.uk`, `lars.holmquist@ntu.ac.uk`

Abstract. *The Metaverse* has great potential to provide novel experiences that are not possible in the physical world, but there are still barriers to entry that make it less accessible for some users. To gain design guidelines for a more welcoming Metaverse, we examined *cosy games*, which offer a non-violent and relaxing experience. Using *netnography* we first observed 6 videos on how players express themselves in 5 different cosy games. We then applied thematic analysis to identify three main aspects of the positive user experience: *positive emotional experiences, anticipation experiences,* and *immersive experiences*. The findings will serve as the foundation for exploring the future potential and design frameworks for creating more inclusive Metaverse applications.

Keywords: Cosy game · Netnography · Metaverse

1 Introduction

Emerging networked immersive technologies, sometimes collectively referred to as the Metaverse, can be used to create new interactive and social experiences in gaming, performance, education, healthcare and many other sectors. Recent research also suggests that the Metaverse can promote more diverse, inclusive and equitable interactions between people [23]. However, the Metaverse currently has many barriers of entry, in particular related to user experience and usability [3].

To find design guidelines for a more inclusive Metaverse, we decided to study interaction in a popular game genre, *cosy games*. Players consider this type of games as a refuge from the strains of the real world. Cosy games have a light design, soothing sound, and low mental load when playing [8]. They can be characterised by safety, richness, and softness [24]. Therefore, we believe they could provide a set of positive qualities that can be translated to the Metaverse.

We applied *netnography* as a method to observe players experience and investigate the positive human interaction in cosy games. Our study provided data on digital footprints, focused entirely on the player experience. We believe that the results from this study can form the basis for integrating the highly social experiences from cosy games to improve the Metaverse experience. The main research questions that we aimed to investigate in this study were:

J. Abdelnour-Nocera et al. (Eds.): ARPPID 2025, CCIS 2797, pp. 167–178, 2026.
https://doi.org/10.1007/978-3-032-15516-0_12

1. What kind of experiences do players have during the entire process of playing cosy games?
2. How can the internet interaction environment, specifically cosy games, inspire the design of immersive experiences for users in the Metaverse?

2 Related Work

Since the emergence of cosy games, they have ushered in a wave of soothing gaming experiences, gradually evolving into a digital haven for a diverse range of gamers [11, 12, 21]. Cosy games have received increasing attention, and developers have created more realistic experiences, allowing players to fully immerse themselves in digital life [16, 29]. The comfortable, relaxing, and immersive experience of cosy games inspires us to shape interactive experiences that cultivate positive emotions and promote more enjoyable and meaningful user engagement [20].

However, some studies have shown that previous studies did not provide specific rules or concepts that shape players' enjoyment, interaction, and presence in games [1, 2]. Capturing diverse and unexpected emotions throughout the gaming process is a positive aspect of using psychological flow to study gaming experiences [28].

Netnography was born through how online interaction is shaping the contemporary world [4]. This new term is a combination of the term "net" (Internet) with "ethnography" [14]. The term "netnography" thus refers to a research method that involves ethnography study in the context of technology and the internet.

[10] Research has shown that when people extend their interactions to digital environments, have their avatars and customise them to their personal preferences, the higher the degree of similarity between their ideal self and their actual self, the more positively they affect their psychological well-being. Therefore, netnography is not merely about observing online interactions; instead, [15] points out that nethnographers need to consider the human connection as a transformation and need to delve into human experiences in the digital context to apply social interactions.

Psychology has shown that individuals evaluate life by making decisions about the self, social partners, and the world, which they often express through media representations of life [22]. Despite the existence of the human self in individual psychology and its limited expression in social life [5], it plays a crucial role in expressing identity.

3 Method

This study used netnography to observe digital traces through six video tutorials uploaded after 2022, with 12 people observed in the recorded videos. We selected these videos because they showed both gameplay and players' facial expressions. The researchers recorded the observed data in three main categories: illustrative quotes, the players' emotions, and the player' gaming experience. On average, each session of the players lasted from 20 min to 1 h. Three main themes emerged from the study: *positive emotional experiences, anticipation experiences,* and *immersive experiences.*

3.1 Cosy Games Used

We selected a set of cosy games (see Fig. 1) with positive, bright colours and high levels of social interaction: Potion Craft [19], Tiny Glade [26, 27], Mail Time [17], Bokura [7], and The Sims 4 [25]. This choice aimed to focus the study on the players' social interaction experiences during cosy gameplay with friends or non-player characters.

Fig. 1. Cosy games were used in the study.

Potion Craft has a unique design style. The colours of Potion Craft convey a medieval vibe – magical and cosy, though the character design contrasts with the modern designs and colors of other cozy games. The interactive interface, together with the soft sound, creates a strong sense of connection for players with the game and with each other.

Tiny Glade is a modern game, but it is popular among the cosy gaming community due to its aesthetics. Tiny Glade was developed in Sweden, with a design style inspired by the Middle Ages but incorporating elements of modern creativity. Tiny Glade draws players not through challenge or difficulty, but through the opportunity to explore creativity and interaction. Players can build castles, ruins, wooden houses, and medieval landscapes. The first-person perspective provides a sense of realism and immersion, allowing players to interact with animals in the game and receive immediate feedback.

Mail Time allows players to design and customise the appearance of a Mail Scout apprentice. It is a cosy game with an art style oriented toward female and girl players. The developer and game designer chose pastel tones combined with warm brown wood, evoking the setting of a small forest. The game also presents a storyline supported by a light, melodic soundtrack, creating a sustained immersive experience without monotony.

Bokura is a cosy game that combines adventure with puzzle challenges for two independent players. Bokura's art style is characterised by simple colour combinations and pixel graphics. The visuals and sound design provide players with a sense of familiarity. Each player's screen displays different views, allowing them to engage with their own perspective rather than sharing the same one. This design supports connectivity and ensures variety in the experience.

The Sims is a game series that aims to realistically simulate and portray human life in various contexts, depending on the player's choices. This study discusses The Sims 4, set at a university. Players can customise their characters according to their preferences and personalities. The game offers interactive features that allow users to operate and engage with objects and environments in a manner similar to real life, such as a university or dormitory. Players can also observe the lives of other characters and non-player characters in the game, enhancing socialisation in the virtual world. In addition, players can communicate and interact directly with characters following the game's standards.

3.2 Thematic Analysis Framework

We performed a thematic analysis of the data through the following steps:

Generate Initial Codes. Players can express their emotions and expectations through words, facial expressions, and actions. We manually coded and generated codes for each game, which were defined as illustrative quotes, emotions (first-order coding), and aspects of the game experience (second-order coding).

Search for Topics. We conducted a detailed reading of the players' emotional experiences and provided insights into the observed experiences of the codes. This provided data on emotional experiences and unexpected expectations that helped us understand the player's experience with cosy games.

Identify Themes. Finally, the researchers identified the following themes were identified from the analysis:

- *Curiosity:* Cosy games evoke a sense of anticipation for the next experience.
- *Surprise:* Players convey astonishment at the captivating interactions and enchanting scenery.
- *Guilt:* Players are immersed and personify the character, experiencing remorse over wrong decisions.
- *Excitement:* Interesting experiences continuously appear and await, making players eager for the following events.
- *Satisfaction:* Visual and sensory experiences give players a good impression.
- *Relaxation:* Players engage with nature and connect with characters in cosy games, which promote a deep relaxation experience.
- *Inspiration:* Every scene possesses an essence of artistry and high aesthetics, enhancing the experience for players.

The analysis of the different aspects of the seven themes in this section will be based on answering the questions in turn:

1. What actions and interactions are shown in the data?
2. What are the aims of players' interaction?
3. How do players interpret what is happening?
4. What assumptions are the players making?
5. What non-verbal actions are the players performing?
6. What do we want to learn about this?

4 Results

In contrast to action or strategy game genres that demand intense focus and challenge, cosy games focus on highly relaxing experiences for players. The cosy games investigated in this study have characteristic properties, such as a seamless connection between reality and virtuality and freedom in social interaction, creating potential themes for comfortable, interactive experiences in the Metaverse.

After identifying the themes, we grouped them in two categories, which we will discuss below:

- *Positive emotional experiences:* In contrast to other competitive and aggressive game genres, cosy games offer players affirmative emotional experiences that foster positive ties among participants.
- *Anticipation experiences:* Foreseeing subsequent encounters will be crucial in prolonging player engagement with a comfortable gaming experience.
- *Immersive experiences:* Immersion is a key factor for players to fully enjoy the experiences that cosy games bring to them.

4.1 Positive Emotional Experiences

Positive emotional experiences can be seen in the first seconds they played in all videos. This includes how players deal with excitement, surprises, relaxation, and getting a sense of satisfaction throughout the interaction. From our thematic analysis, those to emerge were:

Surprised. In the study, the first emotion that appeared in all players was the surprise at what happened in each cosy game they played. For instance, Tiny Glade affects the emotions by allowing them to explore every feature with a high level of aesthetics:

> *"This is an interesting concept. It is awesome. It creates itself like a river. If it is not a dead end and part of the castle, I like how things appear randomly."* (Tiny Glade 1)

In Tiny Glade, even if players played alone or with their friends, the new updates surprised them to customise the experience to their liking. Players expressed surprise through their conversation and facial expressions:

> *"Love that game; it is amazing. We call it Little Glade. It is beautiful in its way; it is amazing."* (P2, Tiny Glade, 3:25)

Excitement. Cosy games show players' enjoyment through simple interactions, actions and conversations, not just facial expressions, and express players' interest. Many players also expected the cosy games they participated in to spark an interest in fun, creative ideas:

> *"I just tried Summer, and I am just trying to figure it out, and it is great that the developers have made it so creative and fun."* (Tiny Glade 1, 6:42)

Empowering the player to design their character is a key element in their emotional connection to the character they will be accompanying throughout the game. Mail Time gave the player an experience of empowerment and feeling like an integral part of the story, which significantly boosted her positive emotional immersion:

> *"My favourite hair colour is fine. I am in the mood for a unique hair colour; this shade of green appeals to me. Feel free to use it."* (Mail Time, 0:40)

Unlike the other games, Bokura provides a completely different experience where two players can participate simultaneously and have two different interactive screens, but with the same goal. Therefore, when player P2 looked at player P1's screen, she was surprised by what was happening on that screen. This shows that Bokura provides the environment to interact socially and connect their experience with emotions while playing, a prerequisite that connects real players and gives them a memorable experience together during the cosy game process. Bokura indicated that cosy games are a game genre for all genders of players, not just for female players.

The Sims on the other hand has a realistic user experience design in every little detail to illustrate a human's normal life. Players meticulously focused on every detail of The Sims. Their interest in the characters shows that they paid attention to even the smallest events and elements that appear in the game.

Satisfaction. Satisfaction appears when players feel comfortable throughout the cosy game, as they reach relaxation and have a rich experience with the game. satisfaction in the interactive experience is reflected through players' confidence.

In Bokura, the rhythm and flexibility of the situation gave players the confidence to control the problem. This is drawn from the observation results that show that the smooth movement of the characters and the level of realism that Bokura conveyed have given players a highly immersive experience in the entire experience. With The Sims, players can easily enjoy themselves in a digital life because the life simulation features are realistic, and users feel they are living the game. The results empowered players to manage their experience and eliminate the need for excessive effort to build the social life they desire.

Relaxation. The relaxation element in tiny glade arises when players are given control over their interactions. on the other hand, the participants in the study also shared that the relaxation experience depends a lot on the actual space that the user is living in, the sound from the real environment, and a lot of disturbing factors that affect the user experience.

Tiny Glade 1 player described her experience of relaxing and healing the soul after a long day:

"I really feel like I'm slowing down and relaxing while playing this game, which I really appreciate. I definitely need this after a long day." (Tiny Glade 1, 14:45)

The player commented after experiencing Potion Craft as follows:

"We have so much more to go, but this was really interesting and just the chill break we needed." (P2, Potion Craft, 5:34)

The player felt the richness of the game; she quickly achieved a state of satisfaction after the experience. Furthermore, these experiences kept players for subsequent immersion in the upcoming experience. The sharing from the players showed that they have achieved satisfaction in many different aspects, from progress to relaxation.

4.2 Anticipation Experiences

We observed details of the gestures, words, and facial expressions of all the players in this study. As the game approached its finish, they all expressed appreciation for the storyline, graphics, and sound of the cosy game. The player expressed curiosity about the experience they would have in the upcoming experiences, and it was this curiosity that formed anticipation.

Curiosity. The study shows that players get used to new interactions and are navigated by that flow, which gives them creative freedom in their playstyle and allows them to explore a variety of nuanced interactions. The element of curiosity that often appears in the experience is because the player is empowered in interaction and can decide their every action.

More specifically, the Potion Craft game in this study fosters curiosity by giving them a novel, never-before-tested play experience and forcing them to learn the mechanics of play:

> *"There is a weird thing to that side, so how do we go there? I do not know what it is, but it looks fun."* (P1, Potion Craft, 4:26)

Tiny Glade is considered to be a highly aesthetic and creative game. The curiosity in Tiny Glade is not in the plot but in arousing the player imagination:

> *"You can let your imagination run wild; this is a window to see how the animation performs its function. You can make them higher."* (Tiny Glade 1, 07:18)

In most cosy games, analysing the player's monologue often reveals personal concerns and a sense of curiosity about the character or environment before they even begin to play. The Sims player speculated by understanding the context of the character's past story and deducing situations linked to the personality. This key factor connects players, characters, objects, and events in the virtual world.

Expectation. Cosy game players' observation data of tiny game showed that the players had a relaxing experience. furthermore, players were more anticipatory about upcoming features they wanted to experience next time. These expectations are aimed at more positive improvements that align with the needs of the forthcoming experiences.

Inspiration. All the aesthetic elements, storylines, and real-time feedback of the cosy game genres in this study gave players inspiration in a virtual interactive experience. Tiny Glade provides players with a unique creative experience, with high aesthetics, a calm space and giving players an endless source of creative space, immersion, and design their world:

> *"It is wonderful that the developers have made it so creative and fun. I think I will pick Autumn because it is an autumn-themed vlog, and we are going to go for the fall vibes."* (Tiny Glade 1, 6:42)

4.3 Immersive Experiences

In this study, we aimed to observe every action, gesture, and speech of all players in cosy games, in addition to focusing on documenting player experience data. A key observation in this study is the sustained experience of immersion across the gameplay. The immersion in each experience and mission is a crucial factor that helps form a positive gaming experience and connect players with games, while also increasing their expectations.

The immersion factor in this study is expressed through (1) the player's eyes always being focused on the screen, (2) the player playing the characters, and (3) the player playing the role of the situations. In particular, gaze is an element that cannot be expressed through words or actions. In contrast, the role-playing of characters or situations is inadvertently expressed by players through gestures, behaviours, and facial expressions while they play. In all six videos of players playing the cosy game, we observed them watching the computer screen intently, their heads facing the screen, and their mouths slightly open to constantly utter expressive words (Tiny Glade 2, 12:35). Facial expressions with gentle smiles (Tiny Glade 2, 17:40) are displayed simultaneously by all players when they discover a beautiful scene in the game; at the same time, in this moment, it also reminds players of experiences they have had before:

> *"It reminds me of the experience I had in California. That is just like all these different rooms."* (Tiny Glade 2, 17:45)

Notably, players sometimes do not speak, but they still interact through connection with the game's characters (Bokura, 6:19).

5 Discussion

5.1 Positive Emotional Experiences

The observation results we collected show that positive emotional experiences play a central role in shaping most of the experiences that players have in cosy games; these are also the factors that cosy game developers want to aim for. When surprise is the first and most consistent element when players start cosy games, it affirms the role of positive emotional stimulation, which affects curiosity and contributes to maintaining the player's interactive state. When excitement is significantly increased by the personalisation factor that the experience brings, players can create their own characters, which makes the experience more engaging and richer. This observation highlights the importance of personalising experiences, the relationship between players and characters in virtual interactive environments, and the strong connection between users and the system, which significantly influences the positive experience flow that players perceive.

Satisfaction and relaxation in the overall experience are two factors that go hand in hand, as they reflect the multi-layered nature that a positive emotional experience brings to the player [18]. While satisfaction was observed when the player completed the task confidently fostered by comfortable interactive environment; relaxation shaped by aesthetic and the gentle pace of interaction, which influenced by external factors arising from the player's offline environment. The two-dimensional nature of providing relaxation and comfort in this gaming experience clearly reflects the mutual influence of the player's offline and online life experiences on the cosy game experience.

Overall, the findings from the positive emotional experience aspect of this study have helped us expand our knowledge about different emotional dimensions and how they are interconnected to form a comprehensive and positive interactive experience for players [9]. The elements of positive emotional experiences are an important foundation for inspiration in the gaming experience that users can use as inspiration for various values in their real life, such as creativity, art, lifestyle, etc.

5.2 Anticipation Experiences

A key finding from our study is that gamers consistently anticipated upcoming experiences based on their gameplay. Such anticipation is not only a natural expression of players' thoughts and views on what is appropriate in the design of the user experience, but it is also a factor that affects their emotions in subsequent experiences [6]. These anticipations differ significantly because they stem from each player's unique personal context, experience, needs, and expectations.

According to our research, curiosity guides people to discover new things. Observing gestures and facial expressions helped us recognise how players bond with both character and game throughout the entire process. Players actively engage with the spiritual values of cosy game, rather than passively connecting with them. Potion Craft has sparked players' curiosity and discovery of new things through the introduction of continuous new mechanics. However, in Tiny Glade, curiosity shifts from the player's perception of the plot to fostering connections and setting expectations for future experiences. This shows that players can build their storylines and personalised experiences in the future.

In this study, various types of inspirational experiences emerged from multiple aspects, including high aesthetics, engaging storylines, soothing sounds, and comfortable environments. These inspirations not only enhance enjoyment but also encourage players to develop their perspectives on cosy games and create the immersive environment.

5.3 Immersive Experiences

Current technology is unable to provide individuals with a fully customised and immersive life tailored to their unique needs. However, people also highly appreciate the level of personalization in cosy game forms because it provides them with an empathetic, inclusive, and authentic experience that reflects the emotions they experience during the game process [13]. Such an approach is a key factor to be applied in the field of user experience design in the Metaverse and immersive environments.

We consider the immersive moments of players in cosy games to be equivalent to immersing themselves in a long-term learning or working task; every moment around the player at that moment seems to be stopping, only leaving a deep connection between players, games, and characters in the game. These non-verbal indicators suggest that the immersive value of a game does not necessarily lie in the drama alone, but also values of peace, closeness, and connection between the player's identity and the game.

6 Conclusion and Future Work

The common point of the cosy games selected in this study is their bright colours, a gentle style, and that they attract different types of players who all want to relax. Each cosy game also has its own storyline so that players can easily get immersed in the game. This study has provided a new perspective on users' emotional experiences and expectations when playing cosy games. The findings have implications for encouraging more welcoming social experiences in the Metaverse:

- *Positive emotional experiences:* By designing for surprise, excitement, satisfaction and relaxation, the Metaverse could become a refuge from the real world, where social interaction can be supported.
- *Anticipation experiences:* Curiosity, expectations and inspiration can be included in the design of the Metaverse to hold players' interest and make the experience more long-lasting and attractive over time.
- *Immersive experiences:* Providing users with an immersive experience is the way to increase connection in the Metaverse and retain users in upcoming interactions.

In addition, cosy games focusing on illustrating real-life experience, like The Sims and Mail Time, can become the direction for the Metaverse to incorporate social interaction elements.

Our research provides some aspects to inform user experience (UX) design in the Metaverse:

- *Relaxation environment in the Metaverse:* Strive for a virtual interactive environment that provides a peaceful environment for users to relax and escape from daily stress easily.
- *Stress-free interaction in the Metaverse:* Providing users with intuitive, non-competitive interactions that encourage users to connect freely in the virtual environment.
- *Customisation in the Metaverse:* The more customisation users receive, the more personalised they feel.

This study specifically investigated the player experience in cosy games, but it would also be beneficial to the construction of social identity in the Metaverse if future studies conducted research on observing the experience of social interaction in immersive experiences. More diverse social interaction experiences lead to more favourable conditions for understanding and aiming for a more satisfying Metaverse society experience.

Acknowledgments. Thanks to Derianna Thomas for the introduction to cosy games which inspired this study.

References

1. Abbasi, A.Z., Ting, D.H., Hlavacs, H.: Engagement in games: developing an instrument to measure consumer videogame engagement and its validation. Int. J. Comput. Games Technol. **1**, 7363925 (2017)

2. Abbasi, A.Z., et al.: The role of personality factors influencing consumer video game engagement in young adults: a study on generic games. IEEE Access **9**, 17392–17410 (2021)

3. Al-Kfairy, M., et al.: Unveiling the metaverse: a survey of user perceptions and the impact of usability, social influence and interoperability. Heliyon (2024)

4. Asname, F., Berrada, A.: Netnography: An innovative approach to qualitative research in the digital age. In: Qualitative Approaches to Pedagogical Engineering, pp. 1–22. IGI Global (2025)

5. Bargh, J.A., McKenna, K.A.A., Fitzsimons, G.M.: Can you see the real me? Activation and expression of the "true self" on the Internet. J. Soc. Issues **58**(1), 33–48 (2002)

6. Bhatnagar, P., Laattala, M., Dutta, S., Cole, T., Hämäläinen, P.: Beyond satisfaction: game feel design for emotionally impactful experiences. In: Proceedings of the 20th International Conference on the Foundations of Digital Games, pp. 1–17 (2025)

7. Bokura. Playing the Same Game with my GF, But We're in Two Different Worlds. Bokura (2023). https://www.youtube.com/watch?v=q63p3cZCwok

8. Boudreau, K.: Beyond aesthetics: players, player-characters and interactivity-as-demand in cozy games. Replay Polish J. Game Stud. **12**(1), 7–22 (2024)

9. Cao, Y., Sweetser, P., Zhu, X.: Exploration of player emotions, behaviours, and individual differences across game difficulty levels in a turn-based strategy game. In: Companion Proceedings of the Annual Symposium on Computer-Human Interaction in Play, pp. 143–148 (2023)

10. Chung, W.Y., Kim, D., Lee, D.: What factors affect psychological ownership when creating an avatar? Focusing on customization and the ideal self. Telemat. Inform. **88**, 102098 (2024)

11. de Gortari, A.B.O., Griffiths, M.D.: Game transfer phenomena and its associated factors: an exploratory empirical online survey study. Comput. Hum. Behav. **51**, 195–202 (2015)

12. Di Cesare, Marco, D., et al.: Setting the game agenda: reviewing the emerging literature on video gaming and psychological well-being of sexual and gender diverse youth. Games Cult. **19**(7), 933–953 (2024)

13. Karthikeyan, G., Aruna, P.: User experience optimization in immersive technologies: techniques, challenges, and opportunities. In: 2025 International Conference on Intelligent Computing and Control Systems (ICICCS), pp. 908–917. IEEE (2025)

14. Kozinets, R.V.: On netnography: initial reflections on consumer research investigations of cyberculture. Adv. Consum. Res. **25**(1), 366–371 (1998)

15. Kozinets, R.V., Scaraboto, D., Parmentier, M.-A.: Evolving netnography: how brand auto-netnography, a netnographic sensibility, and more-than-human netnography can transform your research. J. Mark. Manag. **34**(3–4), 231–242 (2018)

16. Magre, L.A.: Designing for engagement: cozy gaming for long term goals. In: Companion Proceedings of the 2024 Annual Symposium on Computer-Human Interaction in Play (2024)

17. Mail Time. Cozy cottagecore mail delivery game – Mail Time! (2023). https://www.youtube.com/watch?v=k5DCuoav1ro

18. Mella, J., Iacovides, I., Cox, A.L.: Gaming for post-work recovery: the role of immersion. In: Proceedings of the 2023 CHI Conference on Human Factors in Computing Systems, pp. 1–15 (2023)

19. Potion Craft. Potion Craft: Husband & Wife Play Cozy Potion Crafting Game (2024). https://www.youtube.com/watch?v=0lnpXcNzaYM

20. Pretty, E.J., Fayek, H.M., Zambetta, F.: A case for personalized non-player character companion design. Int. J. Hum. Comput. Interact. **40**(12), 3051–3070 (2024)

21. Prokopek, A., Waszkiewicz, A.: Avant-Garde is dead? On Arrière-Garde and digital games. Games Cult. (2024)

22. Reeves, B., et al.: Screenomics: a framework to capture and analyze personal life experiences and the ways that technology shapes them. Hum. Comput. Interact. **36**(2), 150–201 (2021)

23. Sakamoto, D., Ono, T.: Metaverse technologies can foster an inclusive society. Nat. Hum. Behav. **8**(10), 1827–1828 (2024)
24. Short, T., et al.: Group report: coziness in games: an exploration of safety, softness, and satisfied needs. In: The Twelfth Annual Game Design Think Tank Project Horseshoe (2017)
25. The Sims. Sending my Sims to University! pt. 1 (Streamed 9/14/24) (2024). https://www.you tube.com/watch?v=KAAplHBnLGo
26. Tiny Glade 1. Cozy Games for Fall – Playing Tiny Glade & ChefRPG (2024). https://www.youtube.com/watch?v=AyJndIyth14
27. Tiny Glade 2. I Made This Castle! – Tiny Glade (Gameplay Demo) (2024). https://www.you tube.com/watch?v=NUDee11j_O8
28. Zagni, L.M., Pera, R.: From immersion to invasion: a netnographic exploration of consumers' responses' to in-game advertising. In: NETNOCON 2024 Conference Proceedings (2024)
29. Zhu, L.: The psychology behind video games during COVID-19 pandemic: a case study of animal crossing: new horizons. Hum. Behav. Emerg. Technol. **3**(1), 157–159 (2021)

Design Thinking Reframed: Building a Hybrid Learning Ecosystem for Creative Disciplines

Ruben Logjes[(✉)]

Amsterdam University of Applied Sciences, Wibautstraat 2-4, 1091 GM Amsterdam,
The Netherlands
`r.p.m.logjes@hva.nl`

Abstract. This case study explores how design thinking can move beyond surface-level engagement – from sticky notes and brainstorming walls to deeply embedded, context-aware learning experiences. Drawing on 17 real-world cases developed within the DORP project, this study examines how students, educators, professionals, and starting designers can use physical and digital tools to navigate complex design processes. The cases are structured around three core principles: *'Empathise', 'Make it tangible', and 'Try it out'.*

The DORP project addressed a growing challenge in design education: toolkit fatigue – the overwhelming abundance of design methods without clear guidance or contextual relevance. By integrating metadata-driven filtering, hybrid formats, and context-led curation, a new model is proposed for facilitating design learning. Grounded in the principles of Design-Based Learning (DBL), this approach empowers creative practitioners to become critical, autonomous designers capable of selecting, adapting, and reflecting on their own methods.

Keywords: Design-Based Learning · Method Curation · Critical Design Literacy · Design Thinking · Toolkit Fatigue · Hybrid Toolkit · Creative Ownership · Process Awareness · Teacher Facilitation · Inclusive Design · Contextual Learning · Peer Learning · Metadata Filtering · Prototype Practice · Creative Education

1 Preface

Design thinking is everywhere – in classrooms, boardrooms, labs, and living rooms. Its ubiquity has led to a paradox: the more tools we have, the harder it becomes to choose the right one. This publication emerged from a desire to make design thinking more actionable, contextual, and meaningful for students and educators alike.

The DORP project brought together educators, researchers, and students to co-create a set of open, hybrid resources that go beyond templates and buzzwords. It is not a fixed toolkit, but a living collection of cases, methods, and reflections – designed to be adapted, critiqued, and expanded.

The result of the DORP research produced a collection of 17 cases, in the form of openly shared learning materials. The collection is intended for teachers, students,

© The Author(s), under exclusive license to Springer Nature Switzerland AG 2026
J. Abdelnour-Nocera et al. (Eds.): ARPPID 2025, CCIS 2797, pp. 179–194, 2026.
https://doi.org/10.1007/978-3-032-15516-0_13

and professionals who work on – often complex – issues within higher education and beyond, according to the design thinking methodology. The idea is that the examples can help them to arrive at (more) creative solutions together.

The working title of the project 'Design Open Research Platform' (DORP), refers to the Dutch word for 'village' and signifies the communal intent: approachable, local, and everyday uses of methods.

The Dutch version of the total collection including all the cases and materials can be found on Edusources in e-book format [1].

You are invited to use this publication not just as a resource, but as a starting point for conversation, experimentation, and transformation in your own design practice.

2   Introduction

In educational and applied research contexts, students and practitioners are increasingly expected to tackle complex, real-world challenges. Yet many struggle to identify where they are in the design process, which methods are appropriate, and how to reflect meaningfully on their decisions. This lack of process awareness is compounded by toolkit fatigue. Jen (2018) critiques the oversimplification of design thinking in educational settings, and at the same time an excess of available methods without sufficient filtering, contextual guidance, or pedagogical framing, causing a cognitive overload [2, 3].

Educators and facilitators face similar issues. With limited time and evolving expectations, they often rely on familiar or legacy methods, lacking support to integrate newer tools effectively. As a result, design thinking risks becoming a fragmented experience – one that fails to deliver on its promise of deep learning and innovation.

This publication responds to these challenges by reflecting on (a selection of) the 17 curated cases developed within the DORP research project, conducted across multiple universities of applied sciences and in collaboration with design professionals. These cases embed design methods within authentic, iterative learning experiences, aligned with the principles of **Design-Based Learning (DBL)** – an approach that emphasises learning through designing, reflection, and real-world engagement [4, 5].

An important motto that emerged during this process was *'design thinking beyond post-its'*. Sticking post-its can be a good start, but how do you go further? The DORP research focused on providing an answer. This case study elaborates on the efficiency and practical use of the DORP results as an ongoing process to find better ways to facilitate creative processes.

'Although it might seem as though frittering away valuable time on sketches and models and simulations will slow work down, prototyping generates results faster' (Brown 2009) [6].

3   Challenge

This case study reflects on preliminary DORP results and addresses two main questions:

(1) Is the collection of design method examples, distributed via an electronic platform (such as Edusources), useful and easily accessible for academic and professional use?

(2) Was the curation process – including filtering methods based on metadata and testing them in multiple non-online settings – beneficial for transferring this knowledge to intended users?

The first challenge has been an ongoing process of about 2 years in which 17 design methods were scouted, documented, edited multiple times, and moderated for optimal use. The second challenge involved testing the curated materials during several workshops and events.

A recurring issue is that learners are not always aware of the phase they are in, nor do they know which methods are appropriate at that moment. This lack of process awareness can lead to fragmented workflows, superficial application of tools, and limited reflection. In many cases, design activities become disconnected from the deeper learning goals they are meant to support.

In the following chapters, Sect. 4 explores the structure and categorisation of the cases; Sect. 5 describes how they were selected and applied in physical and digital practice; Sect. 6 outlines how they can be adapted and reused in diverse learning and professional contexts. The case study concludes with a broader reflection on implications for design education and facilitation (Sect. 7) and recommendations for future hybrid-toolkit development (Sect. 8).

4 Division of Methods

The DORP collection has been divided into three categories with concrete examples of application of creative methods that help you determine how, where, and when you can do design thinking. Rather than presenting a fixed or exhaustive taxonomy, a flexible framework is proposed that supports contextual selection, reflection, and adaptation.

The 17 cases developed within the DORP project are each linked to one or more design methods. These methods are grouped by function rather than by disciplinary origin. The core structure follows three overarching pillars introduced earlier:

- **Empathise** – methods that support understanding users, stakeholders, and contexts
- **Make it tangible** – methods that help visualise, prototype, and externalise ideas
- **Try it out** – methods that enable validation, feedback, and iteration

To support a meaningful selection, each method is annotated with metadata that helps educators and learners filter based on relevance. These metadata dimensions include:

- **Time investment** (quick exercises vs. multi-day formats)
- **Complexity** (low to high cognitive demand)
- **Design level** (beginner to advanced)
- **Fidelity** (from lo-fi sketches to hi-fi prototypes)
- **Materials required** (suggestion for optimal facilitation)

This metadata-driven approach allows for more intentional use of methods, tailored to the needs of learners, and the constraints of the learning environment. It also supports inclusive design by highlighting which methods are accessible to diverse users and adaptable to different contexts [7, 8].

Importantly, this structure is not static. Students and educators are encouraged to annotate, remix, and expand the method set based on their own experiences. In this way, the toolkit could become a living resource – one that grows through use, reflection, and co-creation.

The description below is copied from the DORP publication. On the next page a VENN diagram shows the relation of these three categories and 17 cases (Fig. 1):

4.1 Empathise

You usually design for others. So, it is important to be able to empathise. By putting yourself in someone else's shoes (literally or not), you understand their needs and challenges better. You gain better insight into what the problem is, for example by observing it, experiencing it yourself, or reenacting it. This also gives you a better idea of what kind of solution you can best design and what criteria it must meet. So, come out of your bubble!

4.2 Make It Tangible

A designer makes things and learns from them. That is why it is important to take the time and... come up with solutions, by making them. Making creative ideas tangible through sketches, lo-, medium-, and hi-fidelity prototypes makes it easier to develop concepts, receive feedback, and make adjustments together. It makes the abstract concrete and helps you refine your design. Go beyond post-its!

4.3 Try It Out

Trying and learning by doing are important principles in design thinking and doing. Every design you make is usually full of assumptions about what is good and about what works. So do not wait too long to test your assumptions! Because people tend to avoid mistakes – that's ingrained in us – but it's precisely by being open, honest, and curious that we discover what does or does not work in practice. That's impossible from behind your laptop. So, go outside!

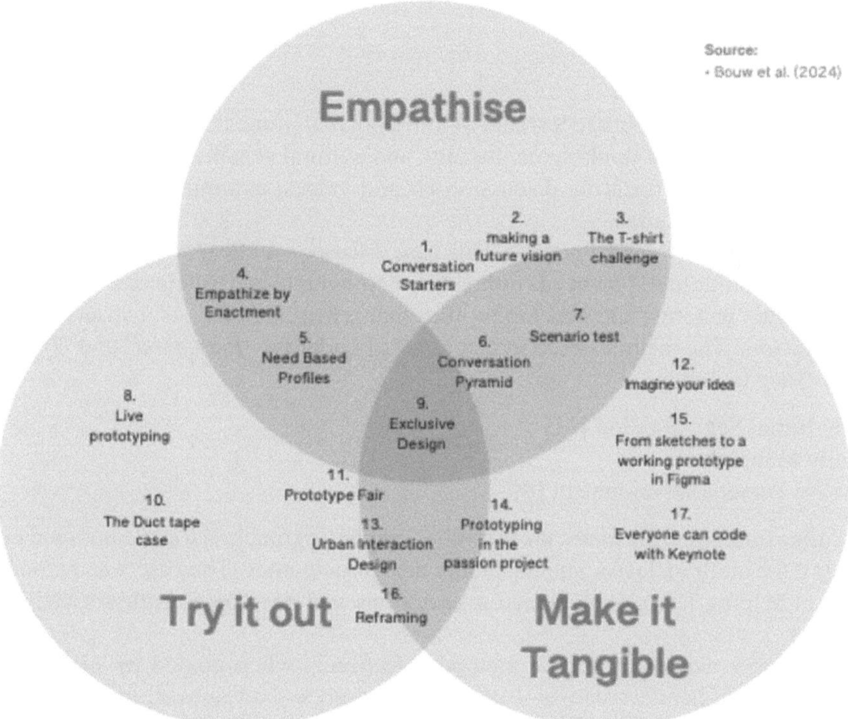

Fig. 1. Venn diagram showing the three categorisations mapping the 17 cases [1].

5   Selection of 2 Cases

Explaining all cases in detail would make this case study very lengthy, so only two are selected to show the approach of how methods were curated, processed and improved for optimal application, for instance using a step-by-step exemplary description. The two case numbers correspond with the numbers in the Venn diagram shown above.

To illustrate how the method framework introduced in Sect. 4 can be applied in practice, these two cases were chosen for their contrasting design contexts, their relevance to different phases of the design process, and their potential to foster critical reflection and ownership among learners.

Each case is linked to specific design methods and annotated with metadata to support contextual selection. The cases were tested in educational and professional settings and refined through iterative feedback from students, educators, and design practitioners.

Below you will first find a more academic approach to both cases, after which detailed content from both cases are shown to highlight details.

Case 2 – Future Vision: This case invites learners to explore speculative futures through visual storytelling and contextual mapping. Participants are asked to imagine a future scenario and develop narratives, mood boards, and visual prototypes that reflect societal shifts, user needs, and ethical dilemmas. The methods used in this case fall under the *'Empathise'* and *'Make it Tangible'* pillars. They include:

Context Mapping [9]
Design Fiction [10]
Scenario Building

These methods encourage learners to move beyond immediate problem-solving and engage with long-term thinking, ambiguity, and cultural sensitivity. The case was particularly effective in fostering discussion around values, assumptions, and the role of design in shaping futures.

Case 5 – Need-Based Profiles: This case focuses on clustering user insights into actionable profiles based on needs rather than demographics. Participants conduct interviews, extract patterns, and develop profiles that reflect motivations, barriers, and contextual factors. The methods used in this case fall under the *'Empathise'* and *'Try it out'* pillars. They include:

Needs-Based Segmentation [11]
Affinity Mapping
Inclusive Persona Development [8]

Unlike traditional personas, these profiles emphasise functional and emotional needs, allowing for more inclusive and adaptable design outcomes. The case was particularly useful in helping learners challenge assumptions and develop empathy-driven design strategies.

Both cases demonstrate how method selection – when guided by metadata and embedded in authentic contexts – can enhance process awareness, critical thinking, and creative confidence. In Sect. 6, these cases and the curation iterations are analysed to show how they can be best adapted, reused, and expanded through hybrid formats and student-led curation.

5.1 Case No. 2: Making a Future Vision

At the start of a new project or design challenge, it can be difficult to immediately identify what you really value and communicate this clearly. While rational thinking usually leads to logical and obvious solutions, it is important to also pay attention to deeper, latent desires and needs.

Challenge: You want to make a start with your team so that you understand each other and the subject better. The trick is not to go into depth right away, but to map out together what is possible. A simple discussion is an obvious starting point, but it can take a lot of time and effort to briefly and concisely explain what you mean at this stage. In addition, you may not immediately know what you really find important. Moreover, if you only think rationally, you usually come up with logical and obvious solutions, while you would rather bring out the deeper wishes and needs. This is, after all, what really affects people – their latent needs.

Solution: It is useful to start working together creatively on future scenarios. This activity can be classified as generative design – making something, arousing curiosity, looking for solutions, and telling stories. Creating visions of the future may seem difficult, but with simple tools you can get started quickly. In this case, a group of participants selected images from a set of cards spread across the table and placed them on a large sheet to tell their own story. They could write, draw, and/or narrate what their ideal future scenario entailed [12–16]. Watch the video on YouTube to understand how this works [17] (Figs. 2, 3, and 4).

- **Step 1:** Decide in advance what you want the group to think about. Present this and check during the session whether you have come up with a good direction. If necessary, adjust the focus a bit, based on an initial conversation or discussion.
- **Step 2:** Give everyone 20 min to create their own vision collage, using the cards and craft supplies spread across the table. Walk around to answer any questions or ambiguities and provide support where needed.
- **Step 3:** Let everyone present their own vision of the future, then start a conversation linking back to the previously formulated main question.

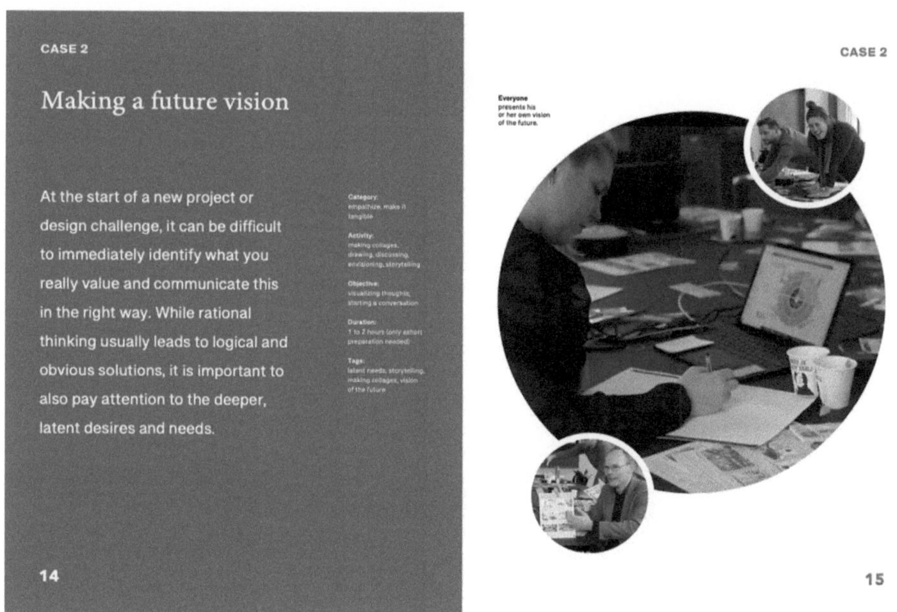

Fig. 2. Visual of participants making a future vision, with method details on the left [1].

Variation: Give the assignment a creative twist and allow participants to create their own unique card set by cutting out their favourite images from magazines.

Tips: Capture your creative moments! Take a picture of your work or collage as soon as it is finished. This creates an opportunity to reflect on it and continue exploring and iterating. Ask participants if it is okay to share the results later anonymously.

Success factor: *'By choosing a clear topic in advance and laying out all the materials, the participants can work independently and let their creativity run wild. A simple way to organise co-creation – it usually works.' – Ruben Logjes*

Fig. 3. Steps of the process: initial focus, making the collage, and discussing future visions [1].

Fig. 4. Visual of printed version (double-sided A4) and the same layout of the digital variant [1].

5.2   Case No. 5: Need-Based Profiles

Your target group probably consists of several different types of users who, on average, may seem similar, but can nevertheless differ considerably. Need-Based Profiles are a useful tool for this purpose. The most important (and difficult) task is to come up with a good name for each segment.

Challenge: The challenge is to process the insights from your user research or interviews into an easy-to-understand summary and make the profiles visually attractive so that others understand whom they concern and what those users experience.

Solution: By identifying similarities in your research, you can determine several 'profiles'. The Need-Based Profile may resemble a persona, but it differs in focus: it emphasises needs and distinctive character traits rather than demographics (age, gender, profession, income), which are often generic and less useful. These profiles help to surface unique characteristics, needs, and desires. You can display the profiles schematically next to each other to show how they relate and to indicate the relative size of each segment [18–21] (Figs. 5 and 6).

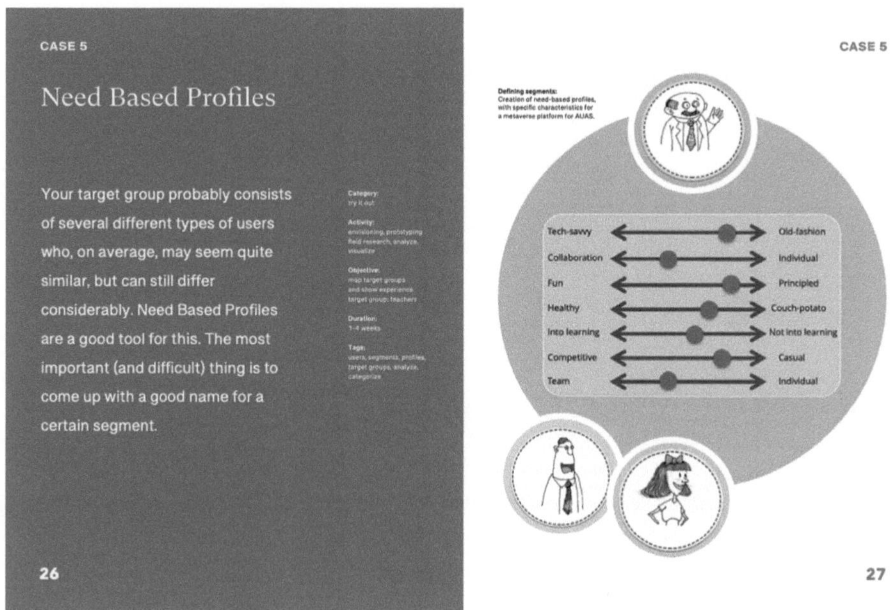

Fig. 5. Visual of Need Based Profile characteristics, with method details on the left [1].

- **Step 1:** Conduct research (observations, interviews, or existing results). Brainstorm with your team (or alone) to group the most important insights. Cluster the insights to make a realistic assessment of the types of people you are dealing with.
- **Step 2:** Choose a memorable and descriptive name for each profile (avoid using first and last names or other standard demographics).
- **Step 3:** Focus on needs and describe them clearly. You can visually show character traits or behavioural characteristics by indicating extremes on a scale. This will quickly show how profiles differ. Brainstorm about these characteristics first, and do not copy a standard list.

Success factor: 'Be critical of the elaboration of the profiles. If they are done too generally, they are of little use and take a lot of time. In addition, it can be difficult to work everything out visually, but this helps most to explain insights and conclusions to others in the form of profiles.' – Ruben Logjes.

Fig. 6. Visual of printed version (double-sided A4) and same layout of the digital variant [1].

6   Additional Ways of Using the Cases

While the cases presented in Sect. 5 were applied in structured educational and professional settings, their design allows for flexible adaptation across a wide range of learning environments. This chapter explores alternative ways of using the cases – both within and beyond formal curricula – and highlights opportunities for hybrid formats, student-led curation, and inclusive facilitation.

To support these diverse contexts, the cases were gradually improved as modular building blocks. After multiple iterations, each case included a description of a core method, a set of instructions, and examples of application. These can be used as printed versions or accessed via a digital platform. This hybrid format – combining physical materials with digital resources – enhances accessibility and engagement, especially for learners with different preferences or needs.

One of the two challenges in the DORP project was to determine which ways of interacting with methods, besides supplying an online toolbox, would be feasible and preferable for different target audiences (for example, teachers, students, researchers, and professionals). The DORP approach was to test different settings in which people could engage in a more social and interactive manner, thus activating the content in a 'practice-what-you-preach' approach that treats design thinking and doing as an iterative process. Related to physical interaction, it became clear that filtering and curating the content is needed to help people understand how cases should be applied and to provide an 'at-a-glance' overview, which was the second challenge of the DORP project.

At so-called 'DORP days', fellow teachers were invited from different universities of applied sciences in the Netherlands, alongside professionals from diverse backgrounds.

During these sessions the intention was to convey the purpose of the cases and to invite participants to respond to content curation and intended use of the materials. The first two DORP days followed a traditional 'Show and Share' format. After these gatherings it was decided to take a next step: iterate on gathered feedback and apply a more creative approach to curation.

Parallel to the DORP days, several workshops were held with small groups of design professionals who guided the DORP team toward a more creative and interactive way of presenting the curated cases and warned against merely sharing 'yet another online toolbox'. This confirmed earlier assumptions and findings from the first DORP days. Some workshop comments included: 'people are tired of receiving a lot of digital content; you need specific moments to reach your audience', 'why isn't DORP more physical?', and 'how do you filter all the content when looking for a method with a specific goal – filtering is usually the issue'. These insights led to two directions for curation: the need for practical filtering of methods, and a more physical way of presenting the cases.

The filtering iteration involved creating a hierarchy of the 17 cases and testing whether subsets of methods could be generated using variables that indicate difficulty (simple to complex), time investment (short to long), user level (beginner to advanced), and fidelity (low to high). See the image below of this process – first plotting all cases on five levels, after which the decision was made to use four variables to keep the model compact and more understandable for most users (Fig. 7).

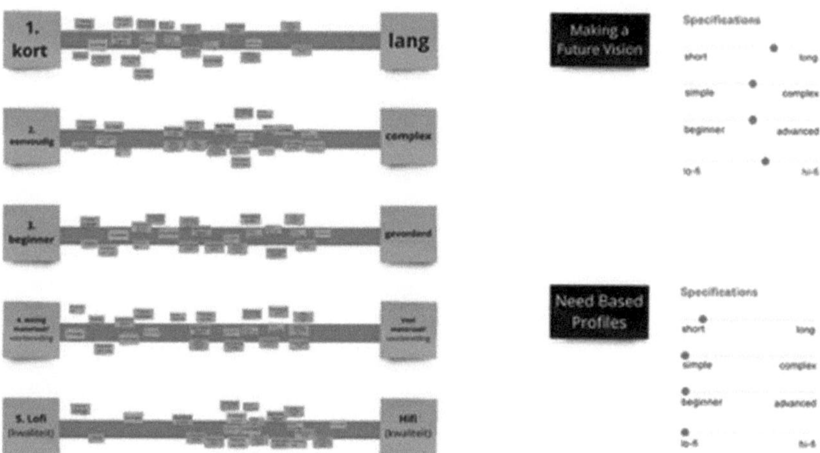

Fig. 7. Iteration of variables for the cases and filtering examples of two methods from Sect. 4, showing how this would appear in printed or online formats.

The second iteration focused on involving participants more interactively. At 'DORP day three' an exhibition of the materials invited participants to give feedback and use dot-voting to indicate whether they liked the cases themselves, and – more importantly – whether they approved of the presentation format and printed versions in different sizes. Some important feedback from the event is summarised below, collected from teachers, researchers, and design professionals (Fig. 8):

- Filtering of the variables wasn't always clear and was mentioned by several target groups.
- Participants questioned whether curating more cases at scale would be possible and how people would access all the content.
- A suggestion was to involve students to help curate the content; in that way they learn about the methods while making the digital and physical content 'ready to be used' by others.
- Some people liked the variables and visualisation style; others did not.
- The step-by-step guide was appreciated.
- *'Who is the owner of this collection, or which key stakeholders will take this a step further?'*
- *'It's a great way [the exhibition] to discuss with others, be inspired by the materials, and understand each other on deeper levels than you would normally do (this would not happen with digital content).'*
- *'It's very nice to have a moment to reflect together.'*

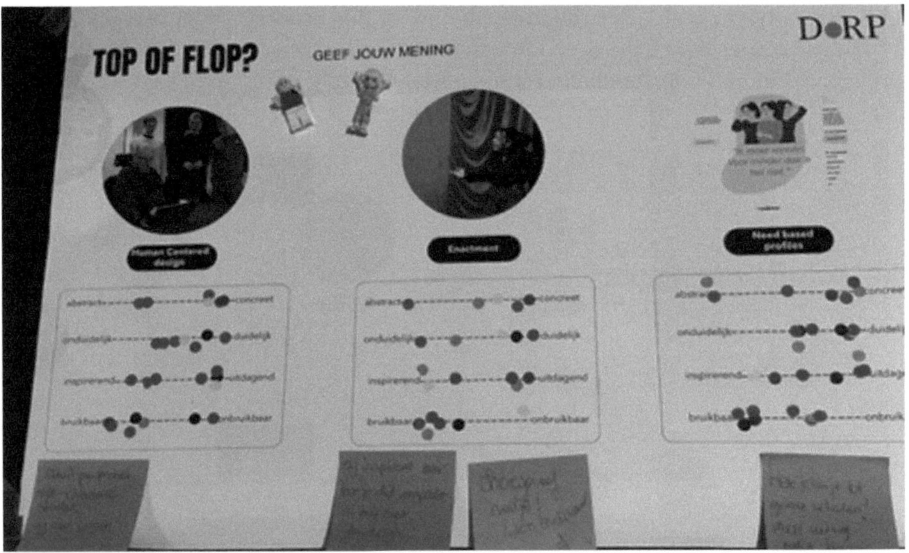

Fig. 8. One of the feedback forms, showing dot-voting and comments from DORP Day 3.

As shown in Fig. 9, several print formats of the previously displayed templates and materials were tested. All were printed on A4, some were enlarged to foamboard panels, including the actual materials used, resulting in an exhibition-style setup that included QR codes linking to additional digital content such as templates and videos.

Fig. 9. Exhibition of materials with printed versions (double-sided A4), large foamboard panels, and an introductory Welcome panel explaining the exhibition's purpose.

Beyond positive feedback and comments, the exhibition created a vibrant atmosphere where participants shared insights and proposed new ideas.

The exhibition setup was designed to fit in a single car and therefore to be transported to different locations if faculties or companies wish to host a 'show and share' event for internal or external audiences.

In the next chapter, the broader implications of the improved filtering approach and hybrid setup for optimal design facilitation are explored, including scalability and the potential to transform how design thinking is taught and learned across different contexts.

7 Discussion

The cases presented in this publication demonstrate that embedding design methods within authentic, iterative learning experiences can significantly enhance process awareness, critical thinking, and creative autonomy. By structuring methods around the pillars of *'Empathise'*, *'Make it tangible'*, and *'Try it out'* – and by supporting selection through metadata and hybrid formats – learners are better equipped to navigate the complexity of design practice.

During the DORP project the intention was to move away from traditional approaches for distributing design methods and to experiment with multiple ways of visualising, promoting, and curating collected methods and materials. This was based on the assumption that online toolkits are not always inspiring and do not always contribute to cyclical knowledge creation. As with most online toolkits – whether presented as small cards, webpages, or other formats – their creators often assume users are experienced designers who already know how to apply the methods.

Through several iterations and discussions, the final solution is a hybrid approach combining an online catalogue with printed materials for private or group use, and an exhibition format with larger poster prints and cardboard for showcasing and starting conversations. These non-digital presentations have been used in a few workshops with the target audience (designers, teachers, and researchers, but not students). Scaling the catalogue and determining whether this hybrid approach will succeed may depend on educational departments and other stakeholders being willing to curate the methods or to host these exhibitions in offices or exhibition spaces.

Summarised, the 17 DORP cases – presented here as a starting point – and the evolving hybrid toolkit can be deployed in the following contexts:

Project-based education, where students work in teams on real-world challenges
Workshops with diverse stakeholders, such as clients, community partners, or industry experts
Exhibitions and showcases, where design processes and outcomes are made visible
Peer-to-peer learning, where students exchange methods, feedback, and adaptations

At present, it cannot be concluded whether the DORP cases will function effectively as a 'living' digital database paired with physical materials for professionals, lecturers, researchers, or students – no students attended the workshops. The cases were scouted based on perceived classroom and workshop efficiency and ease of use; this initial curation drew on the knowledge of involved researchers and their 'best practices' developed over years. Experienced participants showed interest and provided many suggestions for improvement.

Finding ways to activate contributors for the database and curation process is essential. A key suggestion is student-led curation: learners maintain and expand the toolkit by documenting adaptations, adding metadata, and sharing reflections. This fosters ownership, deepens process awareness, and creates a living knowledge base that evolves over time. It aligns with Design-Based Learning (DBL), which emphasises iterative learning through authentic design practice.

Facilitators are crucial in enabling this flexibility. Instead of prescribing methods, they should guide selection, support reflection, and encourage experimentation. This shift from directive teaching to facilitative coaching empowers learners to take responsibility for their design process.

8 Conclusion

This publication set out to reframe design thinking not as a fixed set of tools, but as a dynamic learning ecosystem – one that supports students, educators, and professionals in navigating complex design challenges with clarity, ownership, and critical awareness. Through the development and application of 17 curated cases, this study shows how embedding design methods in authentic, iterative contexts can foster deeper engagement and more meaningful learning outcomes.

By structuring methods around the pillars of *'Empathise'*, *'Make it tangible'*, and *'Try it out'* – and by supporting selection through metadata, hybrid formats, and student-led curation – key challenges such as toolkit fatigue, fragmented facilitation, and lack of process awareness were addressed.

The activating approach to curating methods and materials has proven successful. Participants at the DORP days were enthusiastic: many took printed versions and scanned QR codes for later use in their professional work as teachers or designers.

Discussing and sharing information – preferably in live settings – improves and promotes the most important aspects of these methods: knowledge transfer, trying different approaches, and seeking help from others.

However, curating all content remains a frequently mentioned bottleneck; including students in this process could make curation more integrated and dynamic. Another complementary approach is to involve educational institutions (management, teachers, and researchers) to use the DORP collection in real-life projects together with professionals to tackle multi- or transdisciplinary design challenges.

In a digital age saturated with content and toolkits, people seek ways to step away from their laptops and socially engage with others. Becoming familiar with hybrid materials is key: clear, simple instructions should be sufficient to apply methods and materials. Filtering with variables clarifies each method's purpose and recommended timing. Additionally, when experienced practitioners recommend a method, others are more likely to discover and adopt it.

A final consideration is whether such an initiative can sustain engagement and keep content optimised. There is reason to believe this direction is promising, but embedding the approach into institutional practice requires further refinement.

To evaluate educational impact, Design-Based Research (DBR) is recommended as a framing methodology – it combines iterative design with empirical inquiry in real-world settings [5]. DBR supports continuous refinement of the toolkit and associated pedagogical strategies, ensuring alignment with learning outcomes and institutional goals. Opportunities for further development include:

Integration with existing digital platforms and learning-management systems
Cross-institutional sharing and peer review
Design-Based Research studies to evaluate educational impact
Inclusive design adaptations for diverse learners and contexts

Ultimately, continued development of the DORP results can contribute to a broader reimagining of design education – one that moves beyond post-its and templates toward a culture of reflective, adaptive, and socially engaged design practice.

Acknowledgments. The DORP research was funded and developed as a project of the Centre of Expertise for Creative Innovation, as part of the incentive scheme for open and online education: pillar Open learning material. All cases can be found and downloaded for free via the DORP community on Edusources.

Disclosure of Interests. The authors have no competing interests to declare that are relevant to the content of this article.
Initiators: Lectorship Design Thinking & Lectorship Creative Media for Social Change
Project leader: Inholland University of Applied Sciences
Made possible by: Esther Bouw, Pearl Fritsche, Guido Stomp, Mark Jacobs, Ruben Logjes, Maaike van Cruchten, Annika Kuijper, Roos Verleg, Tamara Witschge, Marije ten Brink, Michel Alders, Marco van Hout, Dirk Reynders, Rob Mulder, Karel Koch, Marjolijn Ruyg, Toska van der

Heiden, Suzanne Lustenhouwer, Roos Alink, Ria Jacobi, Ida Niamat, Marius van Vlijmen, Richard Visscher, Marcella Pottho, Loes van der Tuuk… and all members of the DORP community

The Dutch e-pub version of the referenced DORP research project has been published at Amsterdam, May 2024: ISBN: 9789077812624

References

1. Edusources: Design Thinking Beyond Post-its. https://edusources.nl/materials/70e11a91-f76d-454a-afa6-57c434c962cb/design-thinking-beyond-post-its?tab=0
2. Jen, N.: Design Thinking is Bullsh*t. Adobe 99U Conference (2017). https://www.designweek.co.uk/issues/5-11-march-2018/pentagrams-natasha-jen-design-monster-unleash-fix-world/
3. Liedtka, J.: Experiencing Design: The Innovator's Journey. Columbia University Press, New York (2021)
4. Biggs, J., Tang, C.: Teaching for Quality Learning at University, 4th edn. Open University Press, Maidenhead (2011)
5. McKenney, S., Reeves, T.C.: Conducting Educational Design Research, 2nd ed. Routledge, London (2019). https://doi.org/10.4324/9781315105642
6. Gonen, E., Brown, T.: Change by design: how design thinking transforms organizations and inspires innovation. Mark. Global. Dev. Rev. **4**(2) (2019). https://doi.org/10.23860/mgdr-2019-04-02-08
7. Verganti, R., Dell'Era, C., Swan, K.S.: Design thinking: critical analysis and future evolution. J. Prod. Innov. Manag. **38**(4), 603–620 (2021). https://doi.org/10.1111/jpim.12610
8. Van Gemert, V.: Exclusive Design. Master Design Thesis. Willem de Kooning Academy, Rotterdam (2020). https://exclusive-design.vasilis.nl
9. Sleeswijk Visser, F., Stappers, P.J., van der Lugt, R., Sanders, E.B.-N.: Context mapping: experiences from practice. CoDesign **1**(2), 119–149 (2005). https://doi.org/10.1080/15710880500135987
10. Dunne, A., Raby, F.: Speculative Everything: Design, Fiction, and Social Dreaming. MIT Press, Cambridge (2013)
11. Essense: Recalibrate Customer Insight with Need-Based Profiles (2020). https://essense.eu/van-personas-naar-klantbehoefte-profielen/
12. IDEO.org: Card Sorting. Design Kit. http://www.designkit.org/methods/card-sort.html
13. Positive Inquiry: Generatief onderzoek: Collectieve kracht benutten voor transformatieve verandering (2023). https://positiveinquiry.com/nl/generatiefonderzoek/
14. Service Design Tools: Tomorrow's Narratives. https://servicedesigntools.org/tools/tomorrows-narratives
15. TU Delft: Leefwereld in kaart brengen (Context Mapping). Toolkit Inclusie (2020). https://inclusie.gebruikercentraal.nl/methode/leefwereld-in-kaartbrengen-context-mapping/
16. TU Delft: Contextmapping. HCD-StudioLab. https://www.tudelft.nl/io/onderzoek/research-labs/hcdstudiolab/contextmapping
17. YouTube: Creative Media for Social Change – Co-creation: Designing the Place to be Together. https://www.youtube.com/watch?v=2YaaOBI1O8A
18. Experian Marketing: Needs-Based Segmentation. https://www.experian.com/marketing/resources/audience/needs-based-segmentation
19. Lamberts, H.: Herijk klantinzicht met klantbehoefteprofielen. Essense (2023). https://essense.eu/nl/van-personas-naar-klantbehoefteprofielen
20. Twize, B.V.: Need-Based Personas. Koos Service Design (2020). https://koosservicedesign.com/tool/servicedesign-need-based-personas/
21. Userpilot Blog: What is Needs-Based Segmentation and How to Collect Data for It? (2022). https://userpilot.com/blog/needs-based-segmentation/

Solution or Utopia? A Speculative Analysis of AI Integration in Education in the Global South

Daniel Cabezas-López[1](✉), Clara Figueiredo Amorim[2], and Jose Abdelnour-Nocera[3]

[1] Universitat Oberta de Catalunya, Rambla del Poblenou, 154-156, Sant Martí, 08018 Barcelona, Spain
dcabezasl@uoc.edu
[2] Instituto Politécnico Viana do Castelo, Praça Gen. Barbosa 44, 4900-347 Viana Do Castelo, Portugal
[3] University West of London, St Mary's Rd, London W5 5RF, UK

Abstract. Education in low- and middle-income countries (LMICs) continues to face structural challenges such as teacher shortages, linguistic diversity, and limited digital infrastructure. Drawing on case studies from Timor-Leste and field preparation in the Sahrawi refugee camps, this article critically examines the potential and limitations of integrating artificial intelligence (AI) into teacher professional development platforms like *Matenek*. While AI promises adaptive learning, real-time feedback, and personalized resources, its application in resource-constrained contexts raises issues of sustainability, algorithmic bias, and infrastructural gaps. We propose a hybrid model combining Learning Management System (LMS) and Learning Experience Platform (LXP) features with offline capabilities, situated participatory design, and strong community involvement. From an HCI4D perspective, the paper argues that AI integration can only achieve meaningful social impact if grounded in contextualized, inclusive, and ethically responsible practices. Rather than a universal solution, AI should be seen as a catalyst for locally led, sustainable educational transformation.

Keywords: HCI4D · PD · Situated Design · AI · LXP · e-learning · Speculative analysis

1 Introduction

In our professional experience working in diverse development contexts—ranging from the Asia-Pacific region to the Western Sahara—we have witnessed how the educational landscape in many developing nations is undergoing a profound transformation, shaped both by systemic challenges and by the opportunities offered through digital innovation. In Timor-Leste, one of the world's youngest nations, whose independence in 2002 followed decades of conflict and occupation, these legacies continue to weigh heavily on the education system. Despite multiple reforms aimed at improving access and quality, the country still faces persistent constraints: scarce resources, low teacher qualification levels, and structural inequalities that undermine student outcomes.

J. Abdelnour-Nocera et al. (Eds.): ARPPID 2025, CCIS 2797, pp. 195–207, 2026.
https://doi.org/10.1007/978-3-032-15516-0_14

Recognizing that teacher quality is a key determinant of educational success, initiatives such as the Matenek program have sought to empower educators through mobile technology, offering continuous professional development aligned with curricula and enriched by microlearning resources. From our field experience, we have learned that developing educational platforms in Low- and Lower-Middle-Income Countries (LMICs) creates significant opportunities to improve teaching quality and reduce learning gaps. Yet, these initiatives invariably face structural barriers: limited access to teaching materials, inconsistent connectivity, low levels of digital literacy, and linguistic diversity, as well as recurring issues of sustainability and scalability [1].

Within this context, the rise of artificial intelligence (AI) introduces new possibilities for more personalized teacher training, resource optimization, and the generation of measurable social impact. In this article, we examine the integration of AI into Matenek, a digital learning platform developed by Catalpa International in Timor-Leste in 2019, through a speculative lens grounded in HCI4D [2]. Drawing on our long-term engagement and research in resource-constrained settings, we adopt a speculative case study approach that bridges critical foresight with on-the-ground realities. This perspective allows us to explore the potential of AI-enhanced educational tools while remaining firmly anchored in the sociocultural, infrastructural, and pedagogical conditions of their implementation.

We analyze the feasibility of integrating AI into platforms like Matenek to enhance teacher learning experiences through adaptive learning and natural language processing, enabling flexible and personalized training. Nevertheless, persistent challenges remain, including the need for adequate infrastructure (given connectivity gaps in rural areas and outdated mobile technologies), the mitigation of algorithmic bias, and the necessity of teacher training for effective use of these tools.

To address these tensions, we propose a hybrid model that combines the structured approach of an LMS with the flexibility of an LXP, integrating offline functionalities and AI-driven algorithms to tailor content to individual user needs. Learning Management Systems (LMS) are digital platforms designed to organize and monitor formal teaching, fulfilling curricular and administrative requirements. In contrast, Learning Experience Platforms (LXP) allow users to explore personalized content autonomously and flexibly. Integrating both approaches in projects like Matenek fosters personalisation and accessibility in teacher training—key elements in regions with low digital literacy and cultural diversity. Finally, we put forward a framework grounded in HCI4D and AI principles, aiming not only to optimize education in Timor-Leste but also to contribute to broader debates on digital transformation in other educational systems across LMICs that face similar challenges.

2 Educational Context in Timor-Leste

Timor-Leste's education system faces multiple challenges, including a lack of qualified teachers, in 2016, only 60% of primary school teachers held a recognized degree; low learning quality, in 2009, 70% of first graders could not read a single word in Tetun, and only one-third could solve basic math problems; and high dropout rates, with curriculum accessibility and relevance contributing to school abandonment, particularly at the secondary level. One of the key barriers remains linguistic diversity [3].

As an officially bilingual country, Tetun and Portuguese are the official languages of instruction, yet Portuguese remains the dominant language in schools. This coexists with at least 16 indigenous languages [4] and several dialects, adding another layer of linguistic complexity to the educational sector.

Historical factors, such as a shortage of teachers after independence and limited resources, have contributed to gaps in teacher training and student performance. With a large segment of the population being young and underserved by traditional educational infrastructure, the government has prioritized reforms emphasizing teacher effectiveness and curriculum modernization [5]. Innovative projects like Matenek have emerged as critical interventions in this landscape.

The national education reform agenda demands a child-centered curriculum, a renewed focus on teacher training, and digital technology integration. The World Bank estimates that Timor-Leste's primary and secondary school teachers should spend 60% of their working time teaching, leaving adequate time for lesson preparation but little room for attending training programs.

Despite low internet access and digital literacy among teachers, mobile technologies offer an unprecedented opportunity to bridge these barriers. The Matenek pilot project, designed for teachers with limited digital skills, demonstrated an effort to align professional development with the realities of rural, resource-constrained classrooms. This environment sets the foundation for AI integration, promising highly personalized learning experiences and real-time feedback, ultimately empowering educators even further.

3 Matenek as a Case Study in Teacher Professional Development in Low- and Middle-Income Countries

In 2019, the Ministry of Education, Youth, and Sports (MoEJD) of Timor-Leste, in collaboration with the Australian Department of Foreign Affairs and Trade (DFAT) and the NGO Catalpa International, launched the Matenek pilot program. Its primary objective was to support the implementation of a new primary education curriculum through a mobile application. Introduced in May 2016, this curriculum included pedagogical innovations such as written lesson plans, the gradual introduction of Portuguese, and a student-centered learning approach [6]. Developed in partnership with Catalpa and ALMA/PHD, Matenek facilitated the curriculum transition through an online platform. Implemented in fourteen schools, the pilot addressed the need for integrated, in-service professional development for teachers, providing access to lesson plans, curricular resources, and microlearning videos designed to support educators with low digital literacy [7].

However, mobile learning adoption in Timor-Leste faced several structural challenges, including limited infrastructure, particularly in rural areas with scarce electricity and internet access, as well as the digital divide between urban centers and peripheral districts [8]. Additionally, teachers' lack of digital and pedagogical training led to resistance and inefficient use of technology [9]. Open-source software solutions encountered obstacles due to the shortage of trained personnel, high mobile data costs, and the need to adapt content to the local context, marked by significant linguistic diversity. Governance and management challenges, including political instability and the expectation of quick solutions without long-term planning, further complicated the implementation.

Despite these hurdles, Matenek provided access to curricular resources, promoted communication and collaboration among school leaders, mentors, and the MoEJD, and enabled data collection and monitoring related to curriculum implementation. Additionally, the platform included school management tools and had the potential to integrate with other ministry programs, such as school meals, scholarships, and national exams [7].

The adaptation to the local context through a participatory design approach was essential for the success and sustainability of Matenek as a mobile learning and management platform. Given the challenges of applying HCI4D tools, due to teachers' limited technological literacy and their literal approach to understanding, which made it difficult to grasp abstract concepts disconnected from their sociocultural reality, the project required careful linguistic and conceptual adaptation. Ensuring that the language used aligned with teachers' vocabulary was crucial. The active involvement of key stakeholders, combined with a culturally and linguistically responsive design, proved fundamental in ensuring both the effectiveness and long-term viability of these innovations in Timor-Leste.

Matenek was created based on extensive mixed-methods research, which included classroom observations and interviews with teachers, school principals, and MoEJD personnel. The iterative design process ensured that the platform met teachers' practical needs through timely notifications, a simple navigation system, and contextualized microlearning content.

Recognizing the challenges posed by bulky printed lesson plan books, the difficulty for both teachers and students in accessing them due to limited copies and restricted internet connectivity, Matenek was developed as a mobile-optimized platform. This design ensured that teachers, even in remote areas, could access up-to-date instructional materials while maintaining offline functionality.

Initial results indicated that teachers using Matenek increased their preparation time and became more effective in delivering curricular content. Improvements were observed in classroom management and pedagogical strategies, leading to greater student engagement.

Although educational policies remain a challenge, key factors such as training school principals, ensuring access to offline resources, and integrating with other initiatives were crucial in securing the long-term impact of this pilot program. Despite these positive outcomes, Matenek's initial version relied heavily on static content and predefined feedback cycles, creating an opportunity for AI to enhance the platform's adaptability to each teacher's specific needs.

4 Redesigning Matenek with Artificial Intelligence

Integrating AI into a platform like Matenek could have the potential to revolutionize professional teacher development in Timor-Leste, addressing some of the platform's current limitations, such as the need for greater digital training for teachers, static content with pre-established cycles, lack of interaction between teachers or with the platform itself, and even better adaptation of content to each user's profile.

Learning Management Systems (LMS) and Learning Experience Platforms (LXP) are two distinct yet complementary types of digital learning tools, and understanding their differences is essential to the hybrid model proposed in this paper.

LMS are traditionally used to deliver structured, curriculum-based education. They support the administration of courses, assignment submissions, assessment tracking, and instructor-led content delivery. Their focus is primarily on compliance, certification, and learning outcomes defined by institutions. For example, an LMS might guide a teacher through a linear training course that mirrors the national curriculum, with clear milestones and tests [10].

LXPs, on the other hand, shift the focus from content management to learner experience. They emphasize personalization, allowing users to access content dynamically based on their interests, prior interactions, and self-identified needs. LXPs often integrate a wide range of materials, from videos and articles to peer discussions, and use AI to recommend content that supports exploratory, self-paced learning. In corporate or lifelong learning settings, LXPs empower users to chart individualized learning paths and discover new knowledge organically [11].

In the context of Timor-Leste, neither model alone is sufficient. An LMS may provide the needed structure for curriculum delivery and formal teacher development, especially for users with limited digital experience. However, it risks being too rigid and impersonal. On the other hand, in a rural context with low connectivity and limited teacher training, adopting an LXP model could present several challenges. First, its dependence on the Internet makes implementation difficult in areas with limited connectivity, as access to multimedia materials and online social interaction may be restricted. Additionally, the self-directed approach of LXPs requires teachers to navigate the platform independently, which could be complex for those with little digital experience. Unlike LMSs, which provide a clear structure and administrative tracking, LXPs might create difficulties in evaluating teacher progress and certifying learning. Furthermore, the lack of a structured guide could result in teachers not fully utilizing the available resources.

To mitigate these limitations, a viable solution would be a hybrid LMS-LXP model, combining the flexibility and personalization of LXPs with the structure and supervision of LMSs [12]. Additionally, implementing an offline mode would allow teachers to access content without an Internet connection and synchronize their progress when they regain access. At the same time, digital skills training should be strengthened to ensure teachers can effectively operate in online learning environments.

While the use of AI in education is often associated with high-tech environments, its relevance in resource-limited settings like Timor-Leste is increasingly pragmatic rather than futuristic. Mobile phone penetration, even in rural areas, is rising steadily, and the existing Matenek platform already operates through mobile delivery. Additionally, recent advances in lightweight, offline-capable AI models, such as on-device natural language processing and predictive analytics, allow adaptive learning to occur without requiring constant internet connectivity [13]. These tools are especially valuable in contexts where human coaching and mentoring are scarce. In this light, AI is a logical next step in scaling teacher support in a context where human resources are stretched thin. Rather than replacing educators, AI can function as a scaffolding tool, augmenting their work with real-time guidance, personalized content delivery, and performance feedback tailored to each teacher's context and progression.

By collecting teacher usage data, AI-driven learning analytics can track teacher progress over time, analyzing individual usage patterns, performance data, and feedback; predicting potential learning gaps and offering more suitable learning paths for each teacher's profile [14]. By continuously monitoring teachers' interactions with the platform, the system can generate dashboards that inform both educators and administrators about areas for improvement and achievements. These insights could also guide the development of future content updates. In this way, machine learning models can determine which lesson plans and microlearning modules are most effective for each user. For instance, if a teacher repeatedly struggles with a specific pedagogical strategy, the system could automatically provide targeted content and practical exercises to address this issue.

Another useful element to enhance learning and overcome the barrier of limited technological training would be the use of a chatbot. The integration of Natural Language Processing (NLP) could create an interactive chatbot that acts as a virtual mentor for teachers [15]. The chatbot could engage in conversations to answer questions, provide instant hints, and even simulate classroom scenarios. This conversational interface would allow teachers to receive personalized and contextual guidance, adapting to each teacher rather than following a rigid learning path [16].

By integrating these AI-driven components, the redesigned Matenek platform would not only better meet the educational sector's demands in LMICs, but also provide a more personalized, data-driven learning experience that meets the specific needs of teachers in resource-constrained environments.

Empirical grounding from other contexts strengthens this argument. For example, a qualitative case study on pre-service teachers using generative AI micro-learning modules found that structured, low-cognitive-load modules improved teacher autonomy and confidence in AI tool use [17]. Another study of teachers' experiences of using AI in a South African distance-learning context highlighted substantial time-savings and enriched lesson preparation via AI tools, but also flagged infrastructure limitations and low AI self-efficacy among teachers as barriers to adoption [18]. These findings suggest that while the contexts are not identical to Timor-Leste, they do provide a foundation for the practicality of AI integration in low-resource settings, and also underline the importance of anticipating structural and pedagogical barriers.

However, these case studies also show the practical challenges of integrating AI in low-resource settings—such as limited connectivity, outdated hardware, teacher training deficits, and equity concerns around who benefits. For instance, in Pakistan [19], AI-assisted instruction in ESL contexts improved writing and vocabulary outcomes, but rural teachers reported major barriers of infrastructure and teacher preparedness.

In Timor-Leste, these issues must be confronted head-on: AI is not simply an "add-on", but requires why now (mobile penetration, existing platform base), what stage (scaffolding teacher capacity rather than full automation), and what conditions (connectivity, digital literacy, localised content) to succeed.

Therefore, our justification for selecting AI in Matenek is three-fold:

1. Why now? – Because of rising mobile usage, an existing teacher-training platform base, and the need to scale support where mentors are few.
2. What stage? – This is not a fully mature "AI everywhere" approach; rather, it is an intermediate phase in technology adoption, acting as augmentative scaffolding for teachers rather than replacing human instruction.
3. What conditions? – Implementation must include offline/low-connectivity modes, teacher training in digital & AI literacy, mechanisms for equity (ensuring rural teachers benefit), and safeguards (human-in-the-loop, localised content, participatory design).

5   Achieving Social Impact in Education Through HCI4D and AI

The fundamental purpose of educational technology in developing countries is not merely to digitize existing processes, but to create a profound social impact that transforms lives and reduces inequalities. HCI4D emerges as an approach that adapts HCI principles to resource-limited contexts, addressing the sociocultural challenges specific to the Global South, with a strong focus on equity and inclusion.

The integration of AI within the HCI4D framework for the redesign of platforms like Matenek, while not a definitive solution, has the potential to generate significant social benefits. However, its impact will depend on ensuring that technology is not implemented in isolation, but rather as part of a sustained commitment among key stakeholders, ensuring a contextualized, ethical, and socially responsible development.

In a global context, achieving equitable access to quality education remains an immense challenge. AI-enhanced platforms could equip teachers with tools tailored to their needs, language, and learning styles, ultimately positively influencing student outcomes.

Adaptive learning and AI-driven conversational agents could help bridge the gap between urban and rural education, ensuring that teachers in remote areas receive the same high-quality professional development as those in more privileged regions. This aligns with global initiatives aimed at democratizing education and reducing socioeconomic disparities.

HCI4D places a strong emphasis on participatory design and co-creation with local communities. The integration of AI in educational platforms presents an opportunity to develop culturally sensitive systems tailored to local needs [20]. However, it is crucial to maintain a clear focus on the social group being served, ensuring that HCI4D tools are genuinely useful rather than just another procedural step in these projects' methodologies.

To achieve this, incorporating ethnographic studies becomes a key tool for understanding the sociocultural context in which these technologies are implemented. It is essential to recognize that teachers, students, and local stakeholders can provide valuable feedback, helping to continuously improve the system and ensuring that the technology remains relevant and effective.

Beyond these participatory and contextual dimensions, ethical considerations form a crucial pillar in the responsible integration of AI into education. Issues of data privacy, algorithmic transparency, and the reliability of AI-generated information demand explicit attention. In low-resource settings, where digital literacy and regulatory frameworks are limited, there is a heightened risk of misuse or misinterpretation of automated outputs. Ensuring that users understand the origin and reliability of AI-generated recommendations is essential to maintaining trust and accountability. Real-world precedents such as UNESCO's AI and Education report [21] and the African Union's Continental AI Strategy [32] highlight how localized ethical frameworks—emphasizing informed consent, anonymization of user data, and community oversight—can mitigate these risks.

To address these challenges, we propose a dual-layered ethical strategy. The first layer involves privacy-by-design principles, ensuring that data collection and storage are minimal, transparent, and compliant with international best practices adapted to local contexts. The second layer focuses on capacity-building mechanisms, training educators and administrators to interpret, question, and manage AI-generated insights responsibly. Together, these measures promote a culture of critical engagement with AI rather than passive dependence, supporting a vision of education that remains equitable, human-centered, and contextually grounded.

Thus, the convergence of AI and HCI4D is not just a technological innovation but a social catalyst that can drive long-term change by building capacity, fostering inclusion, and ultimately contributing to the development of these regions.

6 Challenges and Future Directions

Despite the promise of AI to transform educational platforms like Matenek, significant inherited challenges remain that must be addressed. First, the integration of AI in resource-limited environments continues to be hindered by inadequate infrastructure, such as inconsistent internet connectivity, outdated or low-capacity mobile technology, low levels of digital literacy among teachers, and high development costs for applications intended for local implementation.

As the Prime Minister of Papua New Guinea, James Marape, stated in a 2024 address at ANU, *"If development is not locally led, it is not development."* [22] Tackling these challenges requires strategic partnerships and strong local leadership, involving institutions and private initiatives, but always backed by robust governmental support and commitment.

There is no doubt that these challenges must be addressed collectively through a context-sensitive, practical, and pragmatic approach that involves all social actors and ensures a development adapted to the local context—one that is inclusive, sustainable, and truly transformative [23].

While HCI methodologies and the implementation of LLMs have been widely studied in academic settings, their application in resource-limited contexts often reveals unforeseen challenges that require reassessment and adaptation of the tools. In environments like Timor-Leste, where connectivity is inconsistent, digital literacy is low, and technological infrastructure is inadequate, conventional HCI4D approaches cannot always be replicated without significant modifications [23]. The use of methods designed for highly digitized and globalized contexts faces major obstacles when formalizing projects in regions with distinct sociocultural dynamics. These challenges include the misalignment of technological tools, inadequate language adaptation, where the use of abstract concepts may be inaccessible, and limitations in participation during co-creation processes[24]. Factors such as social role stratification and cultural norms can create inhibitions in collaborative activities, affecting the effectiveness of focus groups and co-design workshops.

Beyond mere technical adaptation, a situated PD [25] process with educators and local stakeholders is essential to ensure that technological tools address real needs rather than becoming detached solutions from social realities. This re-evaluation and adjustment of HCI4D methodologies not only maximizes the impact of technology but also promotes its sustainability within the educational systems of LMICs [26].

Ensuring ethical use of AI in resource-constrained educational contexts requires careful attention to transparency, bias, and data governance [27, 28]. In settings like Timor-Leste, where available data may be sparse or skewed toward dominant language or social groups, poorly tuned AI systems risk reinforcing existing inequalities [29]. To mitigate this, we propose a multi-pronged situated design strategy informed by participatory HCI4D and ICT4D practices [2, 26]:

1. Localized data sourcing: AI models should be trained and tested using content that reflects the region's linguistic, cultural, and curricular realities [30].
2. Human-in-the-loop oversight: AI-generated recommendations, such as feedback or content suggestions, should always remain advisory, allowing educators and administrators to override or contextualize them.
3. Participatory dataset validation: Working from a situated iteration [25], teachers and local stakeholders should be involved in reviewing AI training data and outputs, helping to catch inaccuracies and ensure relevance [15].
4. Offline-first architecture: Where feasible, processing should occur locally on devices to reduce reliance on cloud infrastructure, limit data exposure, and maintain privacy even in low-connectivity regions.
5. Sustainable solutions: Tools should provide affordable and context-appropriate responses, aligned with local infrastructure and maintenance capacities, to ensure long-term viability and relevance.

These proposals are consistent with lessons drawn from comparable cases, such as the *Kolibri* offline learning platform developed by Learning Equality and the *Eneza Education* mobile learning initiative in Kenya [31], both of which demonstrate how ethical, context-aware design can ensure sustainability in low-resource environments.

At the same time, while real-time feedback and personalized suggestions can enhance learning, these tools should support—not replace—critical reflection and educator agency. Ensuring that AI acts as a complement, rather than a surrogate, for human judgment is crucial to preserving pedagogical depth and contextual sensitivity. Future research should explore the balance between automation and human supervision, ensuring that AI supports deep and meaningful learning, rather than fostering superficial engagement.

Finally, the sustainability of AI-powered educational platforms depends on continuous innovation and adaptation, which can become a double barrier to long-term consolidation. As technology evolves, methodologies for integrating AI into educational contexts must also evolve. This requires constant research, cross-sector collaboration, and a strong commitment to leveraging AI for long-term social impact. However, in most cases, due to the lack of trained local technicians and the finite duration of development projects, implementing these technologies remains complex in the long run. Therefore, once again, a serious commitment between governmental entities, international organizations, and local institutions is essential to sustaining these initiatives.

7 Conclusion

Our experience in development contexts, both in the Asia-Pacific region and more recently in the Western Sahara, has allowed us to confirm that education in countries such as Timor-Leste reflects common structural challenges: the shortage of qualified teachers, linguistic diversity, infrastructure limitations, and low levels of digital literacy. In this context, initiatives such as Matenek have demonstrated the potential of technology to expand access to pedagogical resources and support teacher training in low-connectivity environments. However, we have also found that having digital tools is not enough; the sustainability of these programs requires overcoming obstacles that go beyond access to devices or platforms.

The integration of artificial intelligence (AI) into projects like Matenek represents a significant opportunity to personalize teacher training, optimize resources, and provide adaptive feedback. We propose a hybrid model that combines the structure of LMS with the flexibility of LXP, complemented by offline functionalities, to ensure a more inclusive and sustainable impact. That said, our field experience shows us that transferring HCI4D methodologies or LLM applications to resource-limited environments inevitably involves tensions: the misalignment of tools with local realities, difficulties in linguistic adaptation, and cultural or hierarchical barriers that constrain co-creation.

From this perspective, we have learned that the design of technological solutions in developing countries must go far beyond the technical dimension: it requires constant attention to sociocultural factors and the active participation of local stakeholders. Moreover, we believe that the incorporation of AI must be approached with caution, ensuring transparency, ethics, and bias mitigation in order to avoid reinforcing pre-existing inequalities.

We have likewise observed that the sustainability and scalability of these initiatives remain central challenges. The lack of trained local technicians, reliance on external funding, and the short duration of many projects compromise their long-term viability. For this reason, we insist on the need for strategic alliances between governments, academic institutions, international organizations, and local communities to ensure that technology serves as a means to empower teachers and students, and not as an end in itself.

Throughout our trajectory, we have confirmed that the adaptation of situated participatory design (PD) methodologies is feasible as long as it is grounded in rigorous ethnographic analysis and the construction of trust networks through sustained presence in the field. At the same time, we have witnessed how many research projects generate expectations that later go unmet, leaving communities behind once the research stay concludes. This situation reinforces the importance of planning with contextual sensitivity and managing local expectations appropriately.

In conclusion, we are convinced that the future of AI in education in developing countries will depend on contextualized, inclusive, and sustainable approaches, capable of balancing technological innovation with cultural sensitivity and political commitment. Only then can we ensure that these tools do not become disconnected solutions, but rather authentic catalysts of educational and social transformation.

References

1. Albergaria-Almeida, P., Martinho, M.: The empowerment of education in East Timor through in-service teacher training. Procedia Soc. Behav. Sci. **191**, 2364–2368 (2015). https://doi.org/10.1016/j.sbspro.2015.04.420
2. Wyche, S.: Reimagining the mobile phone: investigating speculative approaches to design in human-computer interaction for development (HCI4D). In: Proceedings of the ACM Human Computer Interaction, vol. 6, no. CSCW2, pp. 1–27 (2022). https://doi.org/10.1145/3555648
3. No. 182 Second-chance Education in Post-conflict Timor-Leste: Youth and Adult Learners' Motives, Experiences and Circumstances – JICA Ogata Research Institute. https://www.jica.go.jp/english/jica_ri/publication/workingpaper/wp_182.html. Accedido: 9 de febrero de 2025
4. As línguas de Timor Leste: perspectivas. ResearchGate (2024). https://www.researchgate.net/publication/321830084_As_linguas_de_Timor_Leste_perspectivas. Accedido: 10 de febrero de 2025
5. Basic Education Strengthening and Transformation Project. World Bank. https://projects.worldbank.org/en/projects-operations/document-detail. Accedido: 9 de febrero de 2025
6. Ministério da Educação, Juventude e Desporto|Jornal da República. https://www.mj.gov.tl/jornal/?q=node/43. Accedido: 12 de enero de 2025
7. Matenek_-_Final_Report.pdf. https://catalpa.io/documents/3/Matenek_-_Final_Report.pdf. Accedido: 8 de enero de 2025
8. Timor-Leste – Education Since Independence From Reconstruction to Sustainable Improvement. World Bank. https://documents.worldbank.org/pt/publication/documents-reports/documentdetail/511861468761067305/Timor-Leste-Education-since-independence-from-reconstruction-to-sustainable-improvement. Accedido: 12 de enero de 2025
9. Technology in Education: A Case Study on Timor-Leste – UNESCO Digital Library. https://unesdoc.unesco.org/ark:/48223/pf0000387828. Accedido: 12 de enero de 2025
10. Kasim, N.N.M., Khalid, F.: Choosing the right learning management system (LMS) for the higher education institution context: a systematic review. Int. J. Emerg. Technol. Learn. **11**(6), Art. No. 6 (2016). https://doi.org/10.3991/ijet.v11i06.5644
11. Pavlenko, N.: LXP as a tool of the organizational learning of the personnel of IT enterprises. Form. Mark. Econ. Ukr. 48, Art. No. 48 (2023). https://doi.org/10.30970/meu.2022.48.0.4814
12. Rerhaye, L., Altun, D., Krauss, C., Müller, C.: Evaluation methods for an AI-supported learning management system: quantifying and qualifying added values for teaching and learning. In: Sottilare, R.A., Schwarz, J. (eds.) Adaptive Instructional Systems. Design and Evaluation, pp. 394–411. Springer International Publishing, Cham (2021). https://doi.org/10.1007/978-3-030-77857-6_28
13. Calderon, D.E.B.: Hybrid Edge-Cloud AI for Rural Stem Education: An Offline-Capable Mobile System Integrating Claude, Gemini, and Ollama LLMS to Optimize Assessments in Low-Connectivity Contexts, OSF (2025). https://doi.org/10.35542/osf.io/mry9k_v1
14. Wang, S., Qiu, L., Sun, C.: Adaptive education system for drama education in college education system based on human-computer. Int. J. Hum. Comput. Interact. 1–16. https://doi.org/10.1080/10447318.2022.2079169

15. Meoli, L., Nunes, F., Félix, B., Couto da Silva, J., Ntinga, X., Densmore, M.: A Not So Chatty "Chatbot": co-designing to support first-time parents in South Africa and Portugal. In: Proceedings of the 6th ACM Conference on Conversational User Interfaces, CUI 2024, pp. 1–8. Association for Computing Machinery, New York, NY, USA (2024). https://doi.org/10.1145/3640794.3665571
16. Park, J., et al.: How to Align Large Language Models for Teaching English? Designing and Developing LLM Based-Chatbot for Teaching English Conversation in EFL, Findings and Limitations (2024). https://doi.org/10.13140/RG.2.2.13490.82883
17. Kohnke, L.M.A., Zou, D., Xie, H.: Microlearning and generative AI for pre-service teacher education: a qualitative case study. Educ. Inf. Technol. (2025). https://doi.org/10.1007/s10639-025-13606-5
18. van den Berg, G.: Teachers' experiences of using artificial intelligence from an open distance learning context: successes, challenges, and strategies for success. Discov. Educ. 4(1), 192 (2025). https://doi.org/10.1007/s44217-025-00596-2
19. Saleem, T., Saleem, A., Aslam, D.M.: Integrating AI in Pakistani ESL classrooms: teachers' practices, perspectives, and impact on student performance. PLoS One 20(9), e0333352 (2025). https://doi.org/10.1371/journal.pone.0333352
20. A review of perspectives and challenges for international development in information and communication technologies. Ann. Int. Commun. Assoc. 41(3–4). https://doi.org/10.1080/23808985.2017.1392252
21. Artificial Intelligence in Education. UNESCO. https://www.unesco.org/en/digital-education/artificial-intelligence. Accedido: 20 de octubre de 2025
22. Special Address by the Honourable James Marape, Prime Minister of Papua New Guinea|Australian National University. https://www.anu.edu.au/events/special-address-by-the-honourable-james-marape-prime-minister-of-papua-new-guinea. Accedido: 10 de febrero de 2025
23. Kumar, N., Dell, N.: Towards informed practice in HCI for development. Proc. ACM Hum. Comput. Interact. 2, 1–99 (2018). https://doi.org/10.1145/3274368
24. van Biljon, J.: Theorisation as beneficiation in interaction design and international development: a global south perspective. In: Bhutkar, G., Tom, S., Roy, D., Abdelnour-Nocera, J. (eds.) Designing for Tomorrow: Innovation and Equity in Global Interaction Design, pp. 21–32. Springer Nature Switzerland, Cham (2026). https://doi.org/10.1007/978-3-032-00777-3_2
25. Simonsen, J., Svabo, C., Strandvad, S., Samson, K., Hertzum, M., Hansen, O.: Situated Methods in Design, pp. 1–21 (2014). https://doi.org/10.7551/mitpress/9936.003.0003
26. Winschiers-Theophilus, H., Chivuno-Kuria, S., Kapuire, G.K., Bidwell, N.J., Blake, E.: Being participated: a community approach. In: Proceedings of the 11th Biennial Participatory Design Conference, PDC 2010, pp. 1–10. Association for Computing Machinery, New York, NY, USA (2010). https://doi.org/10.1145/1900441.1900443
27. Georgiou, G.P.: ChatGPT exhibits bias toward developed countries over developing ones, as indicated by a sentiment analysis approach. J. Lang. Soc. Psychol. 44(1), 132–141 (2025). https://doi.org/10.1177/0261927X241298337
28. Tipping the Scales: AI's Dual Impact on Developing Nations. World Bank Blogs. https://blogs.worldbank.org/en/digital-development/tipping-the-scales--ai-s-dual-impact-on-developing-nations. Accedido: 16 de septiembre de 2025
29. Ferreira, P.: Examining the "local" in ICT4D: a postcolonial perspective on participation. In: Proceedings of the 2024 CHI Conference on Human Factors in Computing Systems, CHI 2024, pp. 1–13. Association for Computing Machinery, New York, NY, USA (2024). https://doi.org/10.1145/3613904.3642748
30. Jiang, M.: How Cultural and Linguistic Biases Embedded in AI Training Models Affect Chinese-Speaking ESL Users: A Comparative Study of ChatGPT and DeepSeek (2025)

31. Eneza Education – Financing the Digital Transformation of Education. https://www.unesco.org/en/dtc-financing-toolkit/eneza-education. Accedido: 20 de octubre de 2025
32. Continental Artificial Intelligence Strategy|African Union. https://au.int/en/documents/20240809/continental-artificial-intelligence-strategy. Accedido: 20 de octubre de 2025

Integrating Usability and UX in Public Procurement Processes Through Research-Practitioner Collaboration

Marta Larusdottir[1]([ORCID]) and Åsa Cajander[2] [ORCID]

[1] Reykjavik University, Reykjavik, Iceland
marta@ru.is
[2] Uppsala University, Uppsala, Sweden

Abstract. Public authorities face significant challenges when procuring software systems that effectively support their operations and employees. The mandatory Request for Proposal (RFP) process often prioritizes cost and technical specifications, with limited attention to the usability and user experience (UX) of the new system for users. This paper addresses this gap by exploring how usability and UX as performance factors in the RFP can be systematically integrated into the tendering process for public sector procurement. Drawing on collaboration between academic researchers and practitioners, the study examines two case studies: (1) the selection of an agile development team through RFP for developing a financial support application and (2) the selection of an already developed collaboration and information management system (CIMS) through RFP for government ministries. In the first case, team collaboration, UX focus of the team, and code quality were evaluated as performance factors in the selection criteria in parallel with the estimated cost of developing the system. In the second case, the selection factors were cost and quality, including usability metrics such as effectiveness, efficiency, and satisfaction. These cases illustrate how research-practitioner collaboration can bridge the gap between academic principles and professional practices, advancing the design and procurement of software that extends the usability and UX of the procured systems. The findings contribute actionable insights into enhancing public sector RFPs by integrating usability and UX as performance factors.

Keywords: Request for Proposals · Public Authorities · Performance factors · Usability · User Experience

1 Introduction

IT systems' usability and user experience (UX) are critical for users' efficiency, satisfaction, and overall success [1]. However, many software systems, especially workplace systems, suffer from usability flaws, leading to inefficiencies, frustration, and burnout [2–4]. Despite increasing recognition of usability, it is often deprioritized during system development, with user-centered design practices implemented inconsistently [5, 6].

When public authorities acquire or develop new software systems to support their operations, they must adhere to a complex and regulated selection process. European

J. Abdelnour-Nocera et al. (Eds.): ARPPID 2025, CCIS 2797, pp. 208–219, 2026.
https://doi.org/10.1007/978-3-032-15516-0_15

Union legislation mandates that this process be transparent and competitive, requiring public authorities to issue a Request for Proposal (RFP). These RFPs outline the requirements, selection criteria, and expectations for custom software development and the procurement of off-the-shelf solutions. Despite the pivotal role software plays in improving the efficiency and effectiveness of public services, the criteria in these processes often prioritize cost and technical specifications over usability or UX [7–9].

In practice, RFPs typically include two key sections: (1) the system requirements and needs and (2) the selection criteria [8]. Commonly, the selection process places significant emphasis on cost, often awarding contracts to the lowest bidder, even at the expense of quality [9]. For example, a study of software companies in Denmark found that developers primarily focused on what public authorities explicitly required, with little attention to quality factors such as user experience (UX) or security, unless explicitly stated in the RFP [10].

While some RFPs include methods for evaluating software development methods, such as user testing or defined performance criteria, usability considerations are rarely integrated as a core element [10]. Furthermore, selection criteria rarely evaluate the development team's competencies, such as their experience with user-centered design, which could significantly enhance the quality of the final product. Studies have shown that including usability-related requirements can positively influence the project outcome, leading to systems that are functional but also reliable, maintainable, and usable [11].

Software procurement is a crucial activity that has the potential to improve the user experience. Additionally, numerous studies have been conducted to explore the benefits of conducting usability evaluations for improving the usage of software systems. While previous research has acknowledged the importance of including usability in public sector software procurement [8, 9], only a small number of research studies have systematically integrated usability evaluation criteria into real-world procurement processes. Some usability methods, like the SUS questionnaire [24, 25], have been validated for years and have been reliable, but are rarely used in software procurement. This study builds on a collaborative effort between academic researchers and practitioners in the public sector to address this gap.

This study builds on existing work by examining two empirical case studies where user experience-focused evaluation methods were applied in public tenders. By comparing workshop-based selection with structured usability testing, we provide new insights into the effectiveness of these approaches in ensuring user-centered procurement decisions. Combining theoretical insights with real-world applications examines how usability and performance factors can be effectively integrated into RFPs to improve software procurement outcomes. The findings describe actionable ways to incorporate usability-focused evaluations into the tendering process, ensuring that public sector software systems prioritize user-centered outcomes.

Through two case studies, the paper explores (1) the selection of an agile development team for a financial support application and (2) the selection process of collaboration and information management systems (CIMS) for government ministries. In both cases, researchers and practitioners collaborated to design and implement evaluation methods, fostering a bridge between academic principles of interaction design and professional practices in the public sector.

The main research question guiding this study is:

How can usability and UX be integrated into performance factors, developed through collaboration between academic researchers and practitioners, to enhance the Request for Proposal process for public authorities?

2   Evaluating Usability and UX

In this section, we give an overview of the background literature related to UX and usability evaluations. Additionally, we briefly describe how UX and usability evaluations can be part of requests for proposals in tendering processes.

2.1   User Experience and Usability Evaluations

Over the past 20 years, the field of Human-Computer Interaction (HCI) has shifted emphasis in several key areas: from cognition to emotion, from pragmatic to hedonic, from productivity to experiential quality, and from quantitative to qualitative methods, among other developments [12, 13]. User Experience (UX) has its roots in User-Centered Design (UCD) approaches but focuses more on the experiential aspect of human-computer interactions. The concept of user experience is defined in the ISO-9241-210 standard as: "user's perceptions and responses that result from the use and/or anticipated use of a system, product or service" [15]. This definition encompasses all user perceptions and responses, including emotions, beliefs, preferences, comfort levels, behaviors, and accomplishments resulting from the use of a particular software. According to Robinson et al. [14], surveys and interviews are frequently used methods for measuring the UX of software.

Usability evaluation is a cornerstone of Human-Computer Interaction (HCI), ensuring that systems are functional, user-centered, and satisfying to use. According to the ISO 9241-210 standard [15], usability is "the extent to which a system, product, or service can be used by specified users to achieve specified goals with effectiveness, efficiency, and satisfaction in a specified context of use." Evaluating usability provides insights into user behavior and identifies design flaws, enabling systems to better align with user needs.

Early methods, such as heuristic evaluations introduced by Nielsen and Molich [16], remain foundational in HCI, offering a cost-effective way to identify usability issues. Think-aloud protocols and cognitive walkthroughs are also widely used, allowing researchers to uncover task-specific challenges and cognitive bottlenecks during interaction [17]. Additionally, usability is sometimes measured through questionnaires like the SUS questionnaire [24, 25]. More recently, advancements such as automated usability testing, remote platforms, and AI-driven analysis have enabled more scalable and precise evaluations [18].

Despite their importance, usability evaluations are often underutilized in complex socio-technical systems like public sector IT. Larusdottir et al. [19–22] highlighted that usability feedback in large projects often faces integration challenges. Poor usability can lead to inefficiencies, frustration, and resistance, making systematic evaluation essential.

2.2 Evaluations in Requests for Proposals

Integrating UX or usability evaluation into the Requests for Proposals (RFP) process is critical for ensuring that procured IT systems meet user needs and align with organizational goals, thereby improving the user experience. In public sector procurement, RFPs typically prioritize cost and technical specifications, often at the expense of usability. However, as Jokela et al. [8] argue, embedding usability considerations into RFPs can significantly enhance the quality and effectiveness of procured systems by emphasizing user-centered outcomes.

Usability evaluation in tendering can take several forms, such as defining usability criteria in the RFP, requiring vendors to demonstrate user-centered design processes, or incorporating usability testing as part of the evaluation process. For instance, Tarkkanen and Harkke [10] highlight the importance of specifying performance metrics, such as task completion rates or user satisfaction scores, to ensure that usability is objectively assessed during vendor selection. These practices help ensure that systems are evaluated not only for their functional capabilities but also for their impact on the user experience.

Despite its benefits, integrating usability evaluation into the tendering process faces several challenges. Larusdottir et al. [9] note that usability requirements are often poorly defined in RFPs, leading vendors to deprioritize usability during development. Additionally, usability evaluation may require additional time and resources, which can conflict with tight procurement timelines. However, researchers argue that the upfront investment in usability evaluation can result in long-term savings by reducing errors, inefficiencies, and user frustration [10].

Public sector organizations can ensure that procured systems are cost-effective, functional and user-centered by incorporating usability evaluation into Requests for Proposals. For HCI researchers, this represents an opportunity to explore methods for standardizing usability requirements and developing scalable evaluation frameworks that align with the unique constraints of public procurement.

3 Method

This study utilized Rapid Qualitative Analysis (RQA) to explore processes and outcomes related to the Requests for Proposals (RFP) in public procurement, focusing on integrating usability and UX considerations within case contexts. RQA was chosen because it emphasizes iterative and collaborative discussions to derive meaningful insights [23]. The RQA was well-suited for the analysis in the paper, as the two authors collaborated to analyze and discuss the findings. The analysis centered on two case studies: selecting an agile development team for a financial support application and evaluating collaboration and document management systems. The cases were analyzed in the following categories: Purpose (the purpose of using this method); Assessment focus (the focus of the assessment within the method); Strength (the strength of using the method); Challenges (challenges of using the method); and Best use case (when the method will be of best use).

Data were derived from workshop observations, case documentation, and reflective discussions among the research team. Instead of formal coding, the analysis relied on iterative discussions during the collaborative writing process. Collaborative discussions during the writing process were used to refine the analysis, ensuring that findings were grounded in the empirical data and aligned with theoretical perspectives on public procurement and system development. This comparative approach allowed the research to identify practical insights while maintaining a connection to broader academic frameworks.

4   The Cases

In this section, we will describe the two cases by describing the systems being developed or bought and the selection process.

4.1   Case 1: Selecting a Team for Developing a Financial Support Application

This case examines the selection of a development team for developing a financial support application commissioned by a public authority in Northern Europe. The selection was conducted by defining an RFP, in which development companies were able to participate. This case was initially detailed in a prior study, which focused on selecting the best agile development team to meet these objectives [26].

4.1.1   The Financial Support System

The project aimed to create a user-centered digital system that streamlined the application process for financial assistance while ensuring accessibility, operational efficiency, and regulatory compliance. The system targeted three main user groups: citizens, administrative employees, and auditors. Citizens, including individuals with intellectual disabilities, required an accessible and intuitive interface to submit applications. Administrative employees needed a reliable system to manage and process submissions efficiently, while auditors were tasked with reviewing application logs for compliance with financial regulations.

4.1.2   Evaluation Process

The development team was selected through a workshop-based evaluation process. Five teams, teams A to E, were pre-qualified based on technical requirements outlined in the RTF and invited to participate in a one-day workshop simulating real-world collaboration and development scenarios. The teams got four predefined user stories to work on during the workshop. The teams could decide whether to work on all of them or narrow their project down to one or two stories. As an example, one of the user stories was: *"As a citizen of Reykjavik city that has impaired intellectual ability, I want to be able to apply for financial assistance via web/mobile so that I can apply in a simple and easy-to-understand manner"*. The other three user stories were directed to the employees supporting the applications for financial support.

Each workshop began with a planning meeting, where teams demonstrated their ability to plan and prioritize tasks. During the development session, teams worked on the predefined user stories designed to assess their technical capabilities and focus on usability. The process concluded with a presentation from the team after the one-day workshop, showcasing their deliverables and their relevance to the identified user groups' needs.

This approach provided a practical mechanism to assess how teams balanced technical execution with user-centered practices and collaborative problem-solving.

The teams' performance and deliverables were evaluated on three primary performance indicators. First, team collaboration and user-centered focus were assessed by observing their approach during the planning meeting and their presentation at the end of the workshop. Second, the quality and completeness of predefined user stories, such as creating accessible interfaces and implementing features for audit compliance, were analyzed by two experts in those areas. Finally, code quality was evaluated based on accessibility, maintainability, and security considerations. These data points provided a comprehensive view of the teams' capabilities and suitability for the project.

The procurement process shifted towards user-centered outcomes in public sector projects by prioritizing usability and performance criteria over cost. This approach ensured that the selected team could deliver a system that met functional and usability requirements, highlighting how usability evaluation can effectively shape the Request for Proposals process. The case findings build on insights from the original study [26], emphasizing the value of integrating usability-focused practices into public procurement.

4.2   Case 2: The CFT for Buying and Developing Further a CIMS Software

In contrast to case 1, case 2 examines the selection of a developed collaboration and information management system (CIMS). The selection process aimed to acquire access to the chosen system, with the right to adjust it to meet users' needs and further develop it in collaboration with the selected software development company. The CIMS was to be used by all employees of all the ministries in a country in Northern Europe. The selection was conducted by defining an RTF, which established the criteria for selecting the right document management systems.

4.2.1   The Collaboration and Information Management System

As stated in the formal RFP, which was a part of the description of the whole selection process, the goal of the procurement was to *"implement the System as an integrated information management system solution that is user-friendly, widely in use and is actively being developed. The System should fulfill the needs and cover the procedures of Ministries, while also being economical to deploy and use. The System should enable the Customer to fulfill legal requirements [which were referred to in detail]"*.

Regarding the usability of the system, it was stated that: *"With the implementation of the System, the Customer is aiming to improve the work environment at the Ministries, with the following emphasis:*

1. *The day-to-day work of employees and other users is made easier through modern solutions for accessing information and collaborating, along with the digitization of processes for all case processing.*

2. *Modern tools will provide excellent support for work processes and document management, including documentation of case processing and fulfilling legal requirements.*
3. *Modern tools will enable automation of work processes and regulated case processing."*

The estimated number of direct users was 850 persons at 10 ministries, and the number of external users in various committees and consuls was estimated to be 3.300 persons. The yearly number of cases was estimated to be 30.000, and the yearly number of new documents was estimated to be 350.000.

The requirements of the system were defined in several categories: General requirements, requirements for records management, requirements for workflow management, requirements for statistics, requirements for the user interface, requirements for collaboration, other requirements, and technical requirements. The requirements were grouped as Must (A) (total number = 85), Should (B) (total number = 3), and Could (C) (total number none). One example of a general requirement was: "***Processes, projects and cases** – The System shall support the users in managing processes, executing projects handling cases and required approvals*".

4.2.2   The Selection Process

The selection of the system was done through a five-step process, which is illustrated in Fig. 1.

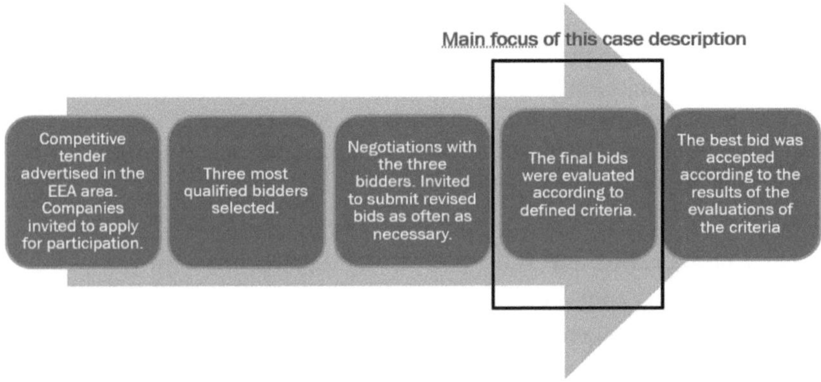

Fig. 1. Illustration of the whole selection process

As can be seen in the figure, the tendering process was in five steps. First, the competitive tender was advertised in the EEA area. Six companies applied for participation, four from Iceland and two from Denmark. In the second step, the bids were compared according to how well they fulfilled the baseline requirements. In that step, three companies were selected to be evaluated in more detail. In step three, negotiations were conducted with the three bidders, that were invited to submit revised bids as often as necessary.

When the final version of the bids had been handed in, the three bids were evaluated according to several criteria in step four. The selection criteria factors, along with their weights, are shown in Table 1.

Table 1. Selection factors and their weight.

Selection criteria factor	Weight
Cost – estimation for implementation and operation for 10 years	25%
Quality	75%
Usability of the software: 20% Strength of the software: 15%	
Quality of the implementation team: 10%	
Quality of the project management process: 20%	
Special adaptations: 10%	

We describe in more detail the process of evaluating the usability of the software in the selection process; see Sect. 4.2.3.

In step five of the selection process, the best bid was accepted based on the evaluation results.

4.2.3   The Usability Evaluation Process

The system's usability was measured in user testing by observing how easily users could solve specific tasks. The measured factors included effectiveness, as evidenced by task completion, efficiency, as measured by task completion time, and satisfaction, assessed through the SUS questionnaire.

The users were grouped into three groups: Managers, Document managers, and General users. Eighteen users took part in the usability evaluation, six from each user group. During the user testing, each participant used the three systems selected for 30 min each. Typically, the evaluation sessions lasted for 2 h, with breaks in between.

Three conductors guided the participants in the usability evaluation, one from each user group. The conductors first introduced the evaluation process and then asked the participants to fill in a background questionnaire. Then the conductor handed the user's tasks to the participant to solve by using the particular system. During that session, the conductor noted the information on the effectiveness and efficiency. The conductor noted the question and how much help the user needed if the user wanted to ask questions. After each task-solving session, the conductor handed out the SUS satisfaction questionnaire for each system.

The tasks were based on the traditional handling of cases, traditional document types, and simple classification systems. Each task consisted of one example of the usage and was defined to be realistic in the context of use for the users. Experts in documentation management were responsible for defining the tasks.

A pilot test was conducted as a rehearsal for the usability evaluation. The systems needed to be set up correctly at that point. One pilot user, who was not among the expected participants, was asked to take part in the pilot test. The pilot user completed the entire user testing process for all three systems, and bidders were allowed to observe the pilot testing online. The contact persons observed how the user testing process was conducted during the pilot user testing. The contact persons were responsible for ensuring their systems worked correctly during both the pilot and actual testing phases. Through the pilot testing, they could ensure their system was set up and functioned correctly. The contact persons were not allowed to be present during the actual user testing. After the pilot testing, the bidders were allowed to make one A4 document as support material for their system for the usability evaluation.

4.3   Synthesis of Case Study Findings

The two case studies demonstrate different approaches to incorporating usability and UX evaluations into public procurement. Case 1 focused on evaluating development teams through a workshop-based selection process, assessing their collaboration, UX focus, and code quality. Case 2 involved structured usability testing of existing software, measuring effectiveness, efficiency, and user satisfaction. Each approach provided insights into usability integration in RFPs, highlighting differences in evaluation criteria and selection processes. These findings set the stage for further discussion on the implications of usability-focused procurement strategies.

5   Discussion

This study analyzed two approaches to integrating UX and usability considerations into the Request for Proposals (RFP) process. In this section, we will discuss and compare the two cases and discuss the limitations of the study.

5.1   Discussions of the Two Cases

The two case studies illustrate different approaches to integrating UX and usability factors into public procurement: workshop-based team selection and structured usability testing of existing systems. While both methods effectively introduced user-centered criteria into the RFP process, they differ in scope, application, and suitability for different procurement contexts.

The first case focused on selecting an agile development team for developing a financial support application, using a workshop-based methodology to evaluate team performance, collaboration, and adaptability. The second case examined procuring a collaboration and information management system (CIMS), relying on structured usability evaluation to assess the usability of three possible systems across diverse user groups.

In the first case, the workshop allowed evaluators to observe team interactions and their ability to align with user needs and the user experiences in real time. This approach was particularly beneficial for assessing the team's flexibility and capacity to adapt to the unique challenges presented by the project. However, the workshop methodology

Table 2. Key Differences Between the Two Methods

Aspect	Case 1: Workshop-Based Selection	Case 2: Structured Usability Testing
Purpose	Evaluating development teams' focus on UX while developing new software	Assessing existing systems for usability and fitness for the expected users
Assessment focus	Collaboration, UX focus, and code quality	Effectiveness, efficiency, and satisfaction based on user testing
Strength	Captures real-time collaboration, adaptability, and UX focus	Provides quantifiable usability metrics with real users in a realistic environment for decision-making
Challenges	Resource-intensive, requires significant preparation and expert observation	Does not assess vendor adaptability or future usability improvements. It is also resource-intensive
Best use case	When selecting a development team for a new system	When evaluating existing software solutions in procurement

required significant preparation and participation, which could limit its scalability in large-scale procurement processes (Table 2).

In contrast, the structured usability testing in the second case provided clear, measurable insights into how easy it was to use the preselected systems for the various user groups. The evaluation captured valuable measurements on the systems' usability, effectiveness, efficiency, and satisfaction by involving representative users. The evaluations were conducted while running the actual systems and in as realistic an environment as possible. However, this approach focused primarily on the usability of the systems. It did not evaluate the vendors' ability to adapt to the users' needs or collaborate effectively on making the systems more user-centered, which might be critical in specific contexts.

The findings of this study align with prior research that emphasizes the advantages of evaluations as a part of public procurement. The workshop-based approach in the first case resonates with studies highlighting the importance of assessing collaboration and adaptability during vendor selection. For example, Tarkkanen and Harkke [10] stress that interactive evaluation methods, such as workshops, provide valuable insights into how teams work together and respond to user needs in real time. Similarly, Jokela et al. [8] argue that collaborative approaches allow procurement processes to focus on vendor flexibility and user-centered design, making them well-suited for custom development projects. However, this study also corroborates critiques regarding the resource-intensive nature of workshops, which limits their scalability in extensive or time-constrained procurement processes [26].

In the second case, structured usability evaluations support prior findings that this method generates precise and actionable data, particularly regarding effectiveness, efficiency, and user satisfaction [27]. Such testing is especially effective in evaluating preselected systems where measurable metrics are needed to guide decision-making [9].

However, usability evaluations alone are not sufficient for procurement decisions. Specifically, structured evaluations do not address vendor adaptability or the ability to respond to broader organizational requirements, often critical in public sector contexts. This underscores the need for hybrid approaches that combine the strengths of collaborative and structured methods to achieve more comprehensive procurement outcomes.

5.2 Limitations

This study focuses on two case studies, aiming to provide insights that can be applied in similar contexts. While the detailed descriptions support transferability, the reliance on collaborative discussions rather than formal qualitative coding may limit methodological rigor. Furthermore, the study emphasizes procurement processes and does not explore the long-term impact of these decisions on the users. Future research could address these aspects to provide a more comprehensive understanding. Despite these limitations, the findings contribute to perspectives on improving procurement practices to advance the quality of software systems.

Acknowledgments. This research was partly supported by Afa Försäkringar, Sweden [grant number 220244]. Additionally, we thank the participating researchers, practitioners, and organizations who contributed valuable insights and support throughout this work. Their collaboration has been instrumental in the successful completion of this research.

References

1. Roto, V., Law, E.C., Vermeeren, A.P., Hoonhout, J.: User experience white paper: Bringing clarity to the concept of user experience (2011)
2. Cajander, Å., Larusdottir, M., Hedström, G.: The effects of automation of a patient-centric service in primary care on the work engagement and exhaustion of nurses. Qual. User Exper. **5**(1), 1–13 (2020)
3. Golay, D., Salminen-Karlsson, M., Cajander, Å.: Negative emotions induced by work-related information technology use in hospital nursing. Comput. Inform. Nurs. (2021)
4. Tarafdar, M., Tu, Q., Ragu-Nathan, T.S., Ragu-Nathan, B.S.: Crossing to the dark side: examining creators, outcomes, and inhibitors of technostress. Commun. ACM **54**(9), 113–120 (2011)
5. Cajander, Å.: Usability – Who Cares? The Introduction of User-Centred Systems Design in Organisations. PhD Thesis at Uppsala University (2010)
6. Inal, Y., Clemmensen, T., Rajanen, D., Iivari, N., Rizvanoglu, K., Sivaji, A.: Positive developments but challenges still ahead: a survey study on UX professionals' work practices. J. Usabil. Stud. **15**(4) (2020)
7. Jokela, T.: Determining usability requirements into a call-for-tenders: a case study on the development of a healthcare system. In: Proceedings of the NordiCHI Conference, pp. 256–265 (2010)
8. Jokela, T., Laine, J., Nieminen, M.: Usability in RFP's: the current practice and outline for the future. In: Kurosu, M. (ed.) Human-Computer Interaction Applications and Services, pp. 101–106 (2013)

9. Billestrup, J., Stage, J., Larusdottir, M.: A case study of four IT companies developing usable public digital self-service solutions. In: Proceedings of the International Conference on Advances in Computer-Human Interactions (2016)

10. Tarkkanen, K., Harkke, V.: Evaluation for evaluation: usability work during tendering process. In: Proceedings of the 33rd Annual ACM Conference Extended Abstracts on Human Factors in Computing Systems, pp. 2289–2294 (2015)

11. Solomou, T., et al.: Bridging language barriers in healthcare: a patient-centric mobile app for multilingual health record access and sharing. Front. Digit. Health **7**, 1542485 (2025)

12. Bargas-Avila, J.A., Hornbæk, K.: Old wine in new bottles or novel challenges: a critical analysis of empirical studies of user experience. In: Proceedings of the SIGCHI Conference on Human Factors in Computing Systems, pp. 2689–2698 (2011)

13. Vermeeren, A.P., Law, E.L.C., Roto, V., Obrist, M., Hoonhout, J., Väänänen-Vainio-Mattila, K.: User experience evaluation methods: current state and development needs. In: Proceedings of the NordiCHI Conference, pp. 521–530 (2010)

14. Robinson, J., Lanius, C., Weber, R.: The past, present, and future of UX empirical research. Commun. Des. Q. Rev. **5**(3), 10–23 (2018)

15. International Organisation for Standardisation: ISO 9241-210:2019. Ergonomics of Human-System Interaction – Part 210: Human-Centred Design Process for Interactive Systems (2019)

16. Nielsen, J., Molich, R.: Heuristic evaluation of user interfaces. In: Proceedings of the SIGCHI Conference on Human Factors in Computing Systems, pp. 249–256 (1990)

17. Boren, T., Ramey, J.: Thinking aloud: reconciling theory and practice. In: IEEE Transactions on Professional Communication, pp. 261–278 (2000)

18. Ha, S., et al.: Digital health equity and tailored health care service for people with disability: user-centered design and usability study. J. Med. Internet Res. **25**, e50029 (2023)

19. Larusdottir, M.K.: Usability evaluation in software development practice. In: IFIP Conference on Human-Computer Interaction, pp. 430–433 (2011)

20. Larusdottir, M.K.: User Centred Evaluation in Experimental and Practical Settings. PhD Thesis at KTH, Media Technology and Interaction Design (2012)

21. Larusdottir, M.K., Cajander, Å., Gulliksen, J.: Informal feedback rather than performance measurements: user-centred evaluation in Scrum projects. Behav. Inf. Technol. **33**(11), 1118–1135 (2014)

22. Larusdottir, M.K., Gulliksen, J., Hallberg, N.: RAMES–Framework supporting user centred evaluation in research and practice. Behav. Inf. Technol. **38**(2), 132–149 (2019)

23. Vindrola-Padros, C., Johnson, G.A.: Rapid Techniques in Qualitative Research: A Critical Review of the Literature. Qual. Health Res. **30**(10), 1596–1604 (2020)

24. Sauro, J., Lewis, J.R.: When designing usability questionnaires, does it hurt to be positive? In: Proceedings of the SIGCHI Conference on Human Factors in Computing Systems, pp. 2215–2224 (2011)

25. Brooke, J.: SUS-A quick and dirty usability scale. Usabil. Eval. Ind. **189**(194), 4–7 (1996)

26. Larusdottir, M.K., Kyas, M.: Selecting the best agile team for developing a web service. In: Human Computer Interaction and Emerging Technologies: Adjunct Proceedings from the INTERACT 2019 Workshops, pp. 289–302 (2020)

27. Jaspers, M.W., Steen, T., Van Den Bos, C., Geenen, M.: The think aloud method: a guide to user interface design. Int. J. Med. Inform. **73**(11–12), 781–795 (2004)

Viva Slough's #Artscape: Applying ID Principles to Redesign the Perceptions of a Town

Tarcila Broder^(✉)

Viva Slough, Slough, UK
tarcila@vivaslough.org

Abstract. This paper reflects on how principles of interaction design (IxD) can inform the redesign of urban spaces through public art. Using the Viva Slough #Artscape project as a case study, it describes the process of transforming Mackenzie Street, a neglected passage at the gateway to Slough's town centre. Through workshops, prototyping, and iteration with residents, artists, and local groups, we developed design ideas that transformed both the appearance and the use of the street. A large-scale Welcome installation and music-themed murals encouraged people to cross, pause, and interact within the space. The outcomes were assessed through observation, informal feedback, and social media, which indicated increased pedestrian use, positive local responses, and online sharing of the artworks. At the same time, tensions around aesthetics, funding, and maintenance revealed the limits of design alone. The case demonstrates that participatory interventions can shift perceptions of place and highlights the importance of sustained engagement for lasting impact. It offers insight into how interaction design principles can extend beyond digital systems to shape more inclusive and engaging urban environments.

Keywords: Urban Design · Interaction Design · User-Centred Design · Public Art · Placemaking · Community Participation

1 Introduction

Slough, in Berkshire, is often ranked as one of the less desirable places to live in the UK. Representations in poetry and television, most famously John Betjeman's *Slough* and the sitcom *The Office*, along with negative press, have reinforced this perception, shaping both how residents experience the town and how it is viewed by the wider public.

Despite ongoing social and economic challenges, including higher-than- average crime rates, Slough is changing. There are plans to redevelop the town centre with new housing, retail spaces, and public areas. Viva Slough #Artscape is part of that shift, bringing together artists, designers, community members, and investors to co-create public art that makes the town feel alive and welcoming.

In this case study, I reflect on my role as lead designer for the project, focusing on Mackenzie Street, a neglected pathway leading into the town centre. Based on principles explored during my master's degree, I translated interaction design (IxD) concepts into practice to structure collaboration with residents and artists.

J. Abdelnour-Nocera et al. (Eds.): ARPPID 2025, CCIS 2797, pp. 220–230, 2026.
https://doi.org/10.1007/978-3-032-15516-0_16

In doing so, I grounded the design process in real experience by considering how everyday users engaged with the space, developing personas that represented daily journeys along Mackenzie Street. These personas helped define the challenge: how to transform it into a place that felt safe, relevant, and worth pausing in, rather than bypassed.

The reflection centres on a core design question: How can principles from interaction design (IxD) and participatory practice be applied to transform neglected urban spaces into places that feel safe, relevant, and engaging? The following section outlines the theoretical background informing this question before turning to the Mackenzie Street case.

2 Background Literature

Urban spaces are dynamic environments that influence how people interact, experience emotions, and develop a sense of identity. Public art plays a central role in this process by enhancing cultural life and strengthening local economies.

Artistic interventions such as murals and installations help residents identify with, navigate, and emotionally connect to their environment. This connection is reinforced by Januchta-Szostak [1] who argues that public art can act as a community integration factor and a means of building the identity of the public domain. Larger- scale interventions, such as monuments, buildings, and gardens, as well as community- led projects, have been shown to revitalise neighbourhoods while encouraging belonging, cultural identity, and civic involvement. In addition, Zhou et al. [2] suggest that public art can contribute to a city's economic viability, linking creative activity to the broader goals of urban sustainable development.

Principles from interaction design (IxD) provide a useful lens for public art and spatial interventions. Norman [3] emphasises that human-centred design places people's needs and experiences at the core of the process, ensuring that outcomes are understandable, usable, and enjoyable. Although his work primarily addresses products, he also notes that everything is designed, from clothes to the layout of cities, and that design shapes how people behave and interact. This perspective supports the idea that concepts from IxD can extend beyond digital systems to inform physical, social, and urban environments. Scholars have expanded on this view by suggesting that the city itself can be understood as an interface. Farkas [4] argues that this perspective helps uncover overlooked design opportunities, while Heikkilä [5] sees it as a way for urban planning and interaction design to inform one another.

Iteration and prototyping lie at the core of design practice. Brynskov et al. [6] describe prototyping as an effective means of addressing urban challenges, enabling designers to test solutions within real contexts and generate insights that guide further development. Similarly, Pozzi and Bagnara [7] highlight the value of engaging directly with users and environments to refine interventions through observation and adaptation. In parallel, Tidwell et al. [8] demonstrate how interaction design patterns, collections of established interface solutions, allow designers to apply familiar structures across different contexts, helping users feel oriented and confident. Together, these perspectives underline that iterative, context-responsive methods and transferable design knowledge are central to shaping both digital and physical environments.

Participatory and co-creative approaches are widely recognised as essential for sustainable change. Wacnik et al. [9] emphasise that participatory design is most effective when communities are involved throughout the process, allowing outcomes to reflect lived experience rather than external assumptions. Such engagement helps ensure that regeneration efforts and design interventions are grounded in the realities of those who inhabit and use the spaces, rather than being shaped solely by top-down visions.

Beyond participation, a further crucial dimension concerns urban safety. Piroozfar et al. [10], in their study of Brixton, examined the use of Crime Prevention Through Environmental Design (CPTED), a method that seeks to reduce crime through spatial design features such as visibility, access control, and maintenance. They found that these strategies often fail when implemented without attention to local conditions, and that lack of upkeep and limited community engagement can further undermine their effectiveness. This suggests that urban safety depends not only on physical design but also on ongoing social participation and care.

Together, this body of work highlights the value of integrating public art, interaction design (IxD), and participatory practice in shaping urban spaces, while reminding practitioners that lasting outcomes depend on continued engagement and sustained community involvement. These insights provided the conceptual foundation for the Mackenzie Street case study that follows.

3 The Challenge

3.1 Mackenzie Street

Building on these theoretical insights, this section turns to the specific case of Mackenzie Street, one of the main approaches into Slough's town centre. Previously, it was grey, dull, and often avoided. The design challenge was to transform it into a space that felt inviting, recognisable, and worth engaging with, rather than one to be avoided. My goal was to turn it into a place people would not only pass through but also choose to spend time in. I focused on three objectives: showcasing Slough's multicultural identity, making the pathway more inviting, and encouraging cultural events such as artistic performances.

To frame the challenge, I developed two personas. The first, the resident commuter, represented those crossing the street daily but often with unease. The second, the event visitor, came to town for cultural activities yet found the place lifeless and neglected. These perspectives reinforced the need for a transformation that addressed both appearance and perception (Fig. 1).

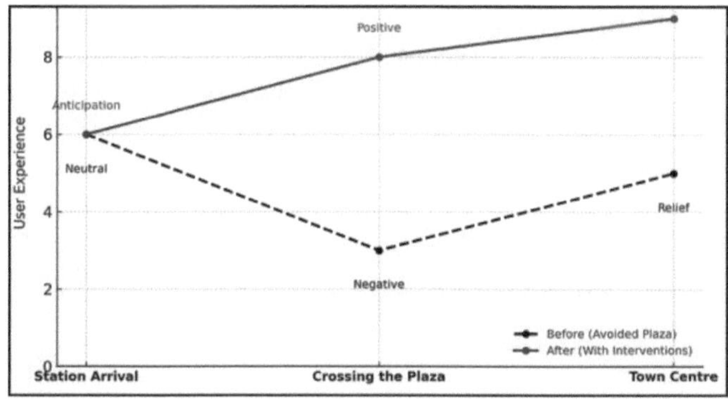

Fig. 1. User journey map for commuter and event visitor personas.

3.2 Interventions

In response to this challenge, I developed interventions through an iterative design process guided by community needs. Artists played a central role in shaping the visual identity of the place and ensuring that the installations resonated with residents.

The Duke's House, an office building at the entrance of Mackenzie Street and facing the railway station, became the most prominent site. Its 45 windows each displayed the portrait of a resident alongside the word Welcome in their native language, representing one of more than one hundred spoken in Slough. Together, these images symbolised the diverse communities that make up the town (Fig. 2).

Fig. 2. Duke's House installation with portraits and languages.

Other interventions reinforced this welcoming identity. Inspired by a local saxophonist, artist Maralin Cotteham created a music-themed mural that celebrated Slough's cultural vibrancy. Located in the central part of Mackenzie Street, opposite the entrance to The Curve cultural venue, the mural was designed to encourage performances and bring activity into the area (Fig. 3).

Fig. 3. Music-themed mural by Maralin Cotteham.

The process followed an iterative design cycle in which workshops generated ideas, prototypes made these tangible, feedback sessions enabled refinement, and selected designs were implemented. Mock-ups were especially valuable, as they allowed participants to test concepts directly and suggest adjustments before anything became final (Fig. 4). This step made the design process visible and collaborative, reinforcing trust and showing that contributions were actively shaping the outcome.

Fig. 4. Prototyping with community input.

To connect these interventions back to theory, Fig. 5 maps the interaction design principles guiding the project to the specific features implemented in Mackenzie Street. It shows how abstract IxD concepts were turned into concrete spatial and visual elements.

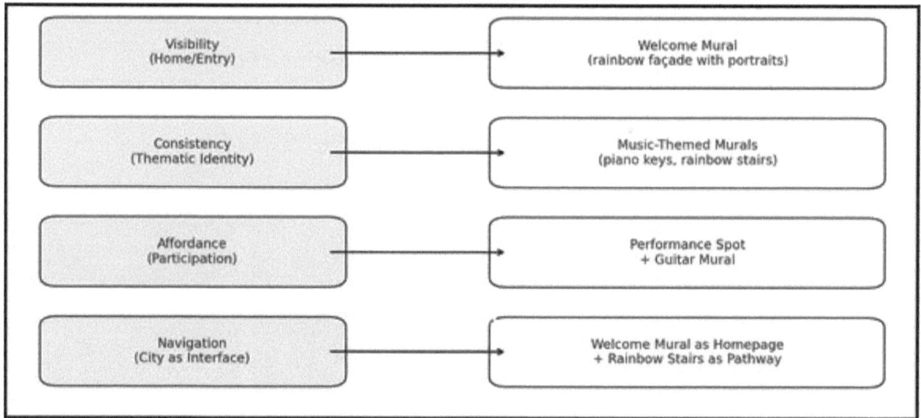

Fig. 5. Mapping (IxD) principles to interventions

3.3 Volunteers and Workshops

Several aspects of the project were developed through community workshops and volunteer efforts. Photographer Mike Swift facilitated the Welcome installation by coordinating with residents and teaching them photography skills. This meant the artwork was not only about residents but also produced with them, reinforcing the project's participatory ethos.

Claire Giacobbe led a storytelling course, helping mural participants compose short texts for the project website that explained their personal connection to Slough.

Other interventions were implemented with the support of volunteers, under the coordination of artists Gozan John and Jho Plazas. They organised community painting sessions that invited residents to take part in creating the murals, making the process a shared experience. These efforts reduced costs but, more importantly, helped participants feel directly connected to the finished space.

The variety of contributions, from professional artists to volunteers, illustrated the co-creative ecology of the project (Fig. 6). A further example is provided in Fig. 7, which shows residents learning photography skills, writing techniques, and painting murals, making visible the hands-on involvement that shaped the outcome. These activities deepened community ownership, turning the project from a design intervention into a collective creative act.

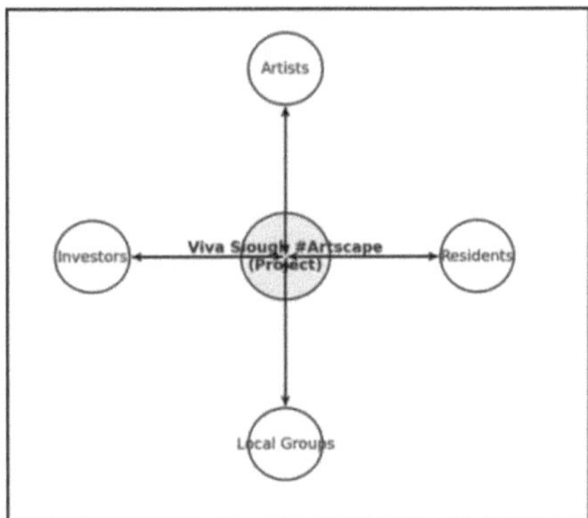

Fig. 6. Diagram of community participation.

Fig. 7. Workshops and volunteer activities.

3.4 Validation

Validation combined direct observation, informal feedback, and social media analysis to assess how the interventions changed Mackenzie Street. After the installation of murals and performance areas, pedestrians were noticeably more willing to walk through, pause, and take photographs, indicating that the street had shifted from a place to hurry past into one worth pausing in (Figs. 8 and 9).

Fig. 8. Before intervention.

Fig. 9. After intervention

Movement through Mackenzie Street also changed: while many had previously avoided it in favour of other routes, more people later began crossing directly through the area, suggesting that the street had become part of everyday circulation rather than bypassed (Fig. 10).

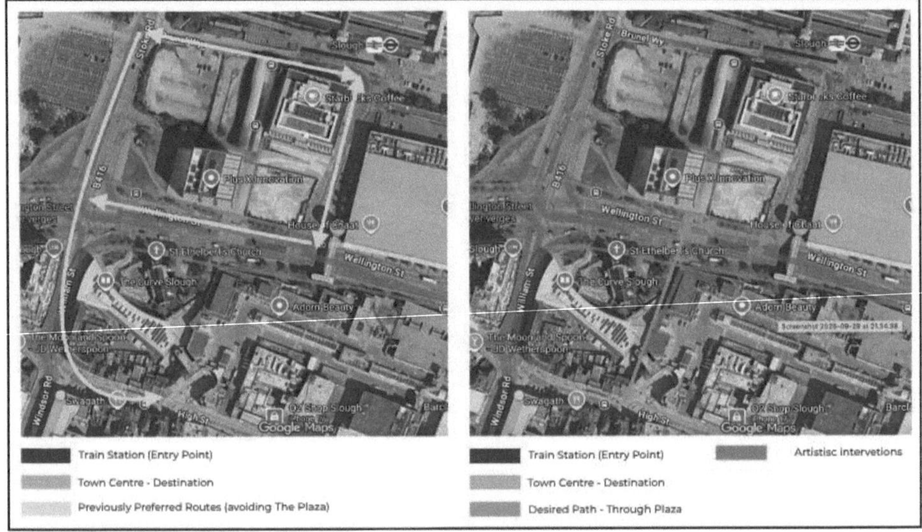

Fig. 10. Shift in pedestrian movement

On social media, images of the murals circulated widely, often accompanied by enthusiastic comments, extending the project's reach beyond those physically present. These reactions reinforced the perception that the intervention reshaped both how the town was represented and how it was experienced.

Not all responses were positive. Some conservative groups criticised the colour palette as too bold or linked it to "woke" initiatives. More significantly, there was a common misconception that public money had been used to fund the project. In fact, it was sponsored by Slough BID, a business-led, not-for-profit organisation representing around 400 businesses in the town centre, together with contributions from partners, artists, and volunteers. This misunderstanding highlighted that beyond aesthetics, transparency about funding sources and processes was critical in shaping how communities judge public art projects.

At the time of observation, the artworks were well maintained and largely free from vandalism, indicating sustained community care and respect for the project, even as some antisocial behaviour re-emerged nearby.

These findings suggested that community-driven interventions could influence both movement patterns and emotional connections to a space, while also demonstrating that engagement was never uniform. These reflections raised broader questions about the role and limits of design in shaping urban experience, which are explored in the following discussion.

4   Discussion

The Mackenzie Street initiative demonstrates the potential of applying interaction design (IxD) principles to urban contexts, but it also raises questions that extend beyond this single project. If public art and participatory processes can reframe how a place is perceived, how lasting are those effects, and under what conditions do they persist? Does the temporary impact generated by the artworks translate into longer-term shifts in how people identify with their town, or does it require reinforcement through policy and maintenance?

Another question concerns the role of participation. Involving the community helped align the interventions with local values and gave the work visibility, but can this kind of involvement guarantee a stronger sense of belonging, or can it also reveal differences in how people expect public space to be used? How should designers navigate their own expertise alongside community input, and what does that mean for the way such projects are understood?

A further point to consider is how well methods from digital design translate to non-digital settings. Concepts such as visibility, consistency, and affordance proved useful in guiding decisions for Mackenzie Street, but how well do they translate when the "interface" is not interactive in a digital sense, but physical, social, and cultural? Are these ideas enough to capture the complexity of public space, or do they risk oversimplifying the layered realities of urban life?

These questions point to the complexity of extending design approaches into public space. They suggest that while such perspectives can open new ways of thinking about urban environments, they also need to be considered critically, acknowledging the social, cultural, and political conditions that shape outcomes. Rather than offering definitive answers, the Mackenzie Street project highlights areas where further exploration is needed, including the durability of participatory processes and the challenges of translating design concepts from digital to urban settings.

5   Conclusion

The Viva Slough #Artscape project demonstrated that user-centred, participatory, and iterative approaches can reshape public space. Involving residents and artists directly ensured that the work remained relevant and connected to community values. The "city as interface" perspective also proved useful in practice: the Welcome installation worked as an entry point, orienting and reassuring, while other features encouraged interaction and expression.

While the outcomes were validated through observation, informal feedback, and social media responses, these methods provided only a partial view of impact. Even so, they suggested progress toward the original challenge, making daily journeys more welcoming for commuters and more enjoyable for cultural visitors. Nearly two years on, the artworks remain largely intact, suggesting a degree of community pride and identification.

Looking across the project, several lessons stand out. Extending methods from IxD into a non-digital context helped create an environment that felt more intuitive and engaging. Community participation gave the work relevance, while the durability of the artworks reflected longer-term respect from residents.

The project demonstrated its capacity to influence both everyday use and cultural visibility. At the same time, the return of antisocial behaviour highlights the continuing need for support beyond design interventions. The Mackenzie Street initiative illustrates how participatory design and user-centred thinking can foster pride, belonging, and identity in urban contexts, though sustaining such change ultimately relies on ongoing community engagement and care.

References

1. Januchta-Szostak, A.: The role of public visual art in urban space recognition. In: Perusich, K. (ed.) Cognitive Maps. IntechOpen, Rijeka (2010). https://doi.org/10.5772/7120
2. Zhou, Y., Sanz-Hernández, A., Hernández-Muñoz, S.M.: Artistic interventions in urban renewal: exploring the social impact and contribution of public art to sustainable urban development goals. Societies **14**, 1–19 (2024)
3. Norman, D.A.: The Design of Everyday Things. The MIT Press, Cambridge, MA
4. Farkas, P.: Defining HCI/UX principles for urban environment. In: Marcus, A. (ed.) Design, User Experience, and Usability: Interactive Experience Design, pp. 346–356. Springer International Publishing, Cham (2015)
5. Heikkilä, H.: The Lost Connection Between Urban Planning and Interface Design: Ideas Towards a Re-enactment. https://www.labopen.fi/en/lab-rdi-journal/the-lost-connection-bet ween-urban-planning-and-interface-design-ideas-towards-a-re-enactment/
6. Brynskov, M., et al.: Urban interaction design: towards city making. Urban IxD Booksprint (2014)
7. Pozzi, S., Bagnara, S.: Designing the future cities: trends and issues from the interaction design perspective. City, Territory Architect. **2**, 5 (2015). https://doi.org/10.1186/s40410-014-0018-x
8. Tidwell, J., Brewer, C., Valencia, A.: Designing Interfaces: Patterns for Effective Interaction Design. O'Reilly, Sebastopol, California (2020)
9. Wacnik, P., Daly, S., Verma, A.: Participatory design: a systematic review and insights for future practice (2024). https://doi.org/10.48550/arXiv.2409.17952
10. Piroozfar, P., Farr, E.R.P., Aboagye-Nimo, E., Osei-Berchie, J.: Crime prevention in urban spaces through environmental design: a critical UK perspective. Cities **95**, 102411 (2019). https://doi.org/10.1016/j.cities.2019.102411

Bridging Academia and Industry: A Catalyst for Digital Transformation and AI Strategy

Teresa Macchia[1]([✉]) and Jose Abdelnour-Nocera[2]

[1] Rolls-Royce plc, London, UK
`teresa.macchia@rolls-royce.com`
[2] University of West London, London, UK
`jose.abdelnour-nocera@uwl.ac.uk`

Abstract. This case study investigates how hybrid forms of academic and industry collaboration, combining formal teaching roles with informal engagements, can contribute to corporate digital transformation and the development of effective AI strategies. Drawing on a case study of a practitioner serving as a visiting lecturer, the study highlights how structured teaching and open dialogue created a dynamic channel for reflection, knowledge transfer, and strategic foresight. The findings show that informal collaboration provides early visibility of emerging technologies, supports responsible and ethical adoption of AI, and fosters protected spaces for strategic reflection that are often absent in operational corporate settings. By embedding academic perspectives into day-to-day industrial practice, organisations can strengthen their innovation capacity and maintain competitiveness in an AI-driven economy. The paper introduces a collaboration framework that illustrates how continuous, flexible engagement between academia and industry enhances adaptability, resilience, and long-term strategic renewal, offering practical insights for organisations seeking to leverage academic expertise without the overhead of formal partnership agreements.

Keywords: Human-Computer Interaction · Academic–Industry Collaboration · Knowledge Transfer · Innovation Ecosystem

1 Introduction

The digitalisation of services has become a critical strategic priority for corporations across multiple sectors, driven by shifting customer expectations and continuous technological advancements. Moreover, the rapid acceleration of advances driven by Artificial Intelligence (AI) has further amplified both the potential for transformative innovation and the pressure on organisations to respond at a speed [3]. However, the immediate demands of day-to-day business operations frequently constrain the capacity of corporate environments to prioritise innovation, experimentation, and long-term strategic thinking. These dimensions, often more systematically cultivated within academic contexts [2], require intentional spaces for reflection, knowledge exchange, and critical engagement beyond operational requests. For industries to fully capitalise on emerging

J. Abdelnour-Nocera et al. (Eds.): ARPPID 2025, CCIS 2797, pp. 231–239, 2026.
https://doi.org/10.1007/978-3-032-15516-0_17

technologies, it is therefore essential to create dedicated occasions, such as structured collaborations with universities, practitioner–academic exchanges, and cross-sector dialogues, that allow leaders and practitioners to both keep pace with technological changes and critically assess their challenges and opportunities. In this respect, visiting lecturers and similar roles play a valuable bridging function, bringing academic perspectives into corporate settings and helping to sustain reflective practices that might otherwise be overlooked.

This case study highlights the positive impact that a hybrid model of academic–industry collaboration, combining formal teaching with informal engagement, can have on the shaping of effective corporate digital transformation practices with a specific focus on the development of a digital service roadmap. Central to this model is the role of visiting lecturer, which serves a dual purpose. Formally, it delivers lectures and classes, in this case on Human–Computer Interaction (HCI), embedding rigorous academic frameworks within professional practice. Informally, it fosters a two-way exchange of knowledge, bringing industry insights into academic contexts while transferring emerging academic perspectives back into corporate environments. Crucially, this dual engagement does more than create opportunities for reflection and dialogue: it directly informed the design of digital service roadmaps, ensuring that corporate strategies remain aligned with cutting-edge research and forward-looking innovation. In the absence of such collaboration and opportunities for knowledge transfer, organisations are likely to remain absorbed by the immediate pressures of daily operations, neglecting the continuous innovation and strategic renewal needed to remain competitive in an AI-driven economy.

The experience explored in this paper moves from the traditional view that academia and industry collaboration must be highly structured and formalised. Instead, we unpack how ongoing engagement with academic perspectives through structured teaching and informal interactions can enrich corporate practices to maintain a long-term strategic focus through operational pressures. At the same time, organisations provide invaluable empirical ground for validating academic research insights, accelerating the application of theoretical frameworks in real-world business environments.

By documenting the benefits of informal collaboration, this study introduces a *collaboration framework* describing the key organisational aspects most influenced by sustained informal academic-industry interactions. This framework highlights aspects and mechanisms through which informal engagements inform digital transformation efforts, offering practical insights for companies seeking to leverage academic expertise without the overhead of formal partnership agreements.

2   The Case of the Digital Service Roadmap

Traditional models of corporate-academic collaboration often emphasise formal partnerships, structured research projects, and defined deliverables. Although these arrangements provide immeasurable value, they can also create barriers to rapid knowledge exchange and practical implementation, particularly in projects that are not research-centric [1, 4]. In contrast, developing an effective digital service roadmap requires agility and a nuanced understanding of both theory and practice. Such roadmaps are designed to articulate vision, milestones, and implementation strategies for digital services, aligning user needs, business goals, and technological advances to guide an impactful digital transformation. Achieving this balance calls for a continuous dialogue between academic and industrial practitioners, one that not only challenges existing practices, but also translates theory into actionable use cases.

Our experience suggests that maintaining continuous dialogue with academic communities can provide several distinct advantages:

Knowledge Accessibility: Informal engagement allows organisations to access current academic thinking without the overhead of formal partnership agreements. This includes staying current with emerging research, understanding theoretical frameworks, and gaining exposure to innovative methodologies.

Flexible Application: Without the constraints of formal collaboration structures, organisations can adopt and adapt academic insights based on specific needs and contexts. This flexibility enables rapid experimentation and learning while focusing on business objectives.

Cultural Enhancement: Regular interactions with academic communities help foster a culture of inquiry and innovation within corporate settings. This cultural change facilitates a focus on long-term strategic planning by addressing immediate operational demands. Although an inquisitive and curiosity-driven culture may be the norm in certain corporate areas like R&D and strategic divisions, it is relatively rare in more operational departments, as they often have restricted connections with academic circles and limited time for strategic thinking.

2.1 Collaboration Framework: Synthesis of Formal and Informal Approaches

Based on our observations, we propose a collaboration framework that illustrates how informal approaches to academic–industry collaboration can complement and extend organisational strategies. Although formal partnerships often establish the boundaries of projects and define outputs, informal engagements create a parallel layer of interaction that is more flexible, iterative, and context sensitive. These engagements are not intended to replace structured research collaborations, but rather to augment them by addressing areas where agility, reflection, and rapid knowledge transfer are most critical. Table 1 summarises this framework by mapping key organisational aspects against the contribution of informal engagement and the resulting impact. It provides a structured way to understand how informal exchanges, through dialogue, continuous interaction, and low-cost integration, can support adaptability, innovation, and long-term strategic renewal in corporate environments. The framework thus acts as both an analytical lens and a practical guide for organisations seeking to systematise the benefits of ongoing, less formalised collaboration with academic communities.

Beyond the individual aspects listed, the framework can also be understood as a looping process. Knowledge exchange initiates a flow of ideas that feed into experimentation and innovation. As these practices unfold, they generate results that reinforce and enhance adaptability and resilience, feeding back into the ability of organisations to engage in further knowledge exchange and experimentation. In this direction, this framework is not representing a static checklist to build a stronger and more effective academic-industry interaction, but a continuous loop of learning, reflection, and renewal, where informal collaboration acts as a dynamic bridge between academia and industry.

Table 1. Collaboration Framework: Informal Academic-Industry Collaboration

Aspect	Informal Engagement	Organisational Impact
Knowledge Exchange	Regular dialogue, ongoing conversations	Enhanced organisational learning capability
Timeline	Continuous, fluid interaction	Improved adaptability to change
Resource Commitment	Minimal additional resources, integrated with existing activities	Optimised resource utilization
Innovation Process	Rapid experimentation and adaptation	Accelerated innovation capability
Risk Management	Flexible adaptation and quick course correction	Enhanced risk resilience
Outcome Measurement	Qualitative assessment and practical validation	More nuanced performance understanding
Cultural Impact	Broad organisational influence	Sustained organisational transformation
Knowledge Retention	Informal networks and shared understanding	Improved organisational memory

This experience demonstrates that informal collaboration goes beyond complementing formal academic-industry partnerships. Informal collaboration can act as a catalyst for enhanced organisational learning and innovation. Furthermore, the framework provides a model that companies can replicate to incorporate reflective practices, facilitate knowledge exchange, and accelerate digital transformation. By embedding informal interactions within formal frameworks, organisations can more effectively align strategic goals with technological advancements, promoting resilience and competitiveness in an AI-driven economy.

2.2 Collaboration Framework: Roadmapping as an Example of Integration

In the process of building a digital roadmap for people services, the *visiting* experience provided a supportive environment to craft a consistent, robust, yet flexible and innovative approach to roadmapping. Specifically, the dual engagement between academia and industry enabled a dynamic exchange of ideas and methodologies, enriching the roadmap development process able to combine theoretical and practical insights.

Roadmapping is an intriguing task due to its complex nature, which requires a balance between prioritisation, focus, and perspective. It is a structured way to bring the future into the present and the present into the future. It aligns future changes and organisational decisions and actions, via strong method and flexibility, required to generate consensus and strength. The dual role of rapidly synthesising and gathering knowledge in the roadmap development process, which aims to navigate future uncertainties and identify, as well as reduce, risks of failure, has become a successful strategic instrument [5].

Due to the multilayered nature of the roadmapping tool, informal academic collaboration has been extremely valuable, especially in relation to the three core dimensions of roadmapping.

Strategic alignment: Developing a digital services roadmap requires a careful balance between short-term operational needs and long-term strategic objectives. The academic way of working encourages broader thinking, helping to maintain focus on the medium-term and long-term objectives while effectively addressing business operations requirements. In an operations-focused division, the task of roadmapping requires frequent focus adjustments and close collaboration with other departments to ensure that strategic alignment incorporates all operational solutions. Hence, effectively and successfully managing the skill of zooming in and out proves to be challenging.

Referring to the Collaboration Framework described above (see Table 1), Strategic Alignment benefits significantly from the interplay of three key aspects:

Knowledge Exchange: Continuous dialogue and collaboration between academia and industry introduce new perspectives, enhancing understanding of emerging trends and strategic implications.

Innovation Process: Engaging with innovative methodologies and academic insights fosters creative approaches to solving complex challenges, ensuring that the roadmap is both forward-thinking and practical.

Cultural Impact: Incorporating academic practices into the organisational mindset cultivates a culture of curiosity, adaptability, and long-term thinking, which is essential to maintain alignment across varying priorities.

Stakeholder engagement: A successful roadmap must integrate input from multiple stakeholders across the organisation. The informal academic engagement provides access to frameworks and methodologies that support the management of this complexity, ensuring that stakeholder contributions are effectively integrated while maintaining a clear and practical focus. The stakeholder engagement involves gathering input and actively leveraging two critical components of the Collaboration Framework described in Table 1: commitment to resources and knowledge retention.

Resource commitment: A well-defined engagement process ensures that stakeholders are not just contributors but active participants, committing the necessary time, effort, and resources to the success of the roadmap. Informal academic interactions serve as a reminder of a work approach that cultivated a spirit of cooperation and collective ownership.

Knowledge Retention: Engaging stakeholders efficiently promotes the preservation and integration of knowledge. By incorporating multiple viewpoints early and consistently, the roadmap benefits from a collective repository of expertise.

Innovation opportunity: Regular exposure to academic thought facilitates the identification and evaluation of innovative and effective approaches to service development and technology adoption. This ongoing dialogue fosters creative problem solving, helping to anticipate future challenges and opportunities while ensuring that solutions remain grounded in business relevance. Innovation Opportunity stands out as the dimension that most effectively benefits from informal collaboration with the academic world. This is because informal engagements uniquely leverage key aspects described in Table 1:

Timeline: Implies the ability to adapt to changes, allowing the organisation to address new opportunities and incorporate them into the roadmap
Innovation Process: As mentioned above, this involves the promotion of experimentation and adaptation.
Risk Management: Academic input provides a neutral ground for validating ideas, refining concepts, and anticipating challenges.
Outcome Measurement: Consistent with Risk Management, an unbiased collaboration with academia assesses the potential impact and metrics of the digital service roadmap beyond traditional quantitative methodology.

This experience and the integrated approach to the roadmapping exercise highlight how continuous academic engagement enhances the development of strategic and practical thinking, which is valuable for the development of digital roadmaps, providing a unique perspective that supports both strategic and operational goals.

2.3 Collaboration Framework: Enriching Practice Through Academic Engagement

The visit experience has highlighted how multiple academic engagement collaboration channels can enrich corporate practices in developing a digital service. These channels and their impacts, teaching interactions, thesis supervision, and ongoing dialogue with academic practitioners unfold as follows.

Teaching interactions are an essential channel for knowledge exchange and innovation. Through this type of engagement, student questions challenge established assumptions, bringing fresh perspectives to corporate practices. The corporate benefits are substantial: teams gain deeper reflection on their established practices and exposure to emerging thinking patterns.
Thesis supervision facilitates a structured deep dive into specific challenges, allowing methodologically rigorous research on practical problems. Industries often miss such opportunities, thus benefiting from evidence-based solutions and targeted explorations, whereas academic institutions receive real-world cases and validation of theoretical frameworks. This collaboration fosters a robust environment for the creation of joint knowledge.
Academic dialogue facilitates the continuous exchange of ideas and the integration between theory and practice. Corporate teams gain strategic perspective and innovation inspiration, while academic practitioners can benefit from direct insight into implementation challenges and practical research validation. This ongoing dialogue creates a sustained learning ecosystem that benefits both communities.

The synergy between these channels creates a rich environment for knowledge exchange and innovation. Although each channel has distinct characteristics and benefits, their combination provides a comprehensive framework for academic-industry collaboration that enhances both theoretical understanding and practical application specifically in digital service development.

2.4 The Power of Reflection: The Academic Time as a Knowledge Transfer Mechanism

A critical aspect of this experience is that the academic environment and specifically the lectures serve as the main knowledge-sharing mechanism. Unlike the constant delivery pressure of operational industry settings, the time and space needed for teaching and academic engagement created an unforeseen opportunity for deep reflection, moreover, triggered by an external and neutral point of view.

The space for reflection manifested itself in three key moments. The pre-class preparation forced the articulation of tacit corporate knowledge and transform implicit knowledge into explicit, transferable insights by using practical examples. During class interactions, student questions and discussions triggered real-time reflections on established practices, often revealing assumptions and biases embedded in existing approaches. The post-class review session invited reflection on classroom insights, enabling rapid identification of concepts applicable within the corporate context. Furthermore, the intervals between classes offered a precious space for processing and connecting academic theories with operational challenges, a cognitive luxury rarely available to intertwine into day-to-day corporate operations focused on constant delivery. This form of reflection-based mechanism addressed a fundamental challenge in knowledge transfer: the lack of cognitive space in operational environments. Although many standard collaboration programmes may need immediate action over reflection, this model embedded reflections within the academic role itself, creating a whole new format of practice.

3 Building Effective Collaboration Between Industry and Academia in a Fast Shaping AI-Driven Economy

It is increasingly evident that AI is evolving at a very rapid pace [6], making it difficult for industries to keep up with these changes on their own. Our experience with academic–industry engagement provides key insights into how collaboration can strengthen the development of digital services. Organisations must cultivate a culture that values academic perspectives and continuous learning, supported by regular knowledge-sharing activities such as lunch-and-learn sessions or short seminars. Dedicating time to educational initiatives and academic exchanges helps establish consistent dialogue forums that expand professional networks and generate reciprocal value through guest lectures, case studies, and access to current research. Moreover, as businesses operate within an AI-driven economy, the ability to purposefully embrace AI and accelerate the development of effective strategies for this rapidly evolving technology has become essential to long-term competitiveness. The speed of AI innovation requires organisations not only to experiment with new tools but also to integrate them into coherent digital transformation strategies. Academic partnerships can play a pivotal role in this process in several ways:

Providing early visibility of emerging technologies by giving organisations access to frontier knowledge, including methodologies and tools not yet available on the market but likely to become critical within a few years.

Supporting responsible and ethical adoption by helping organisations address issues such as bias, transparency, and accountability in AI, ensuring compliance with ethical standards and regulatory frameworks.

Contributing to the development of human–AI capabilities. Through teaching and co-designed training programmes, academia supports practitioners in acquiring the skills needed to integrate AI into daily operations, enhancing human–machine collaboration rather than replacing human expertise.

Facilitating strategic reflection by creating protected spaces for questioning assumptions, evaluating risks, and evaluating long-term opportunities. These practices are essential for developing AI strategies that extend beyond short-term efficiency gains.

Enhancing innovation by accelerating cross-sector learning and fostering resilience in rapidly evolving technological landscapes.

In this context, collaboration between academia and industry serves not only as a source of knowledge for digital innovation but also as a strategic partner in shaping responsible and future-orientated AI strategies. The case of the visiting lecturer illustrates how these principles can work in practice. By combining structured teaching with informal exchanges, the role provided a continuous channel for reflection, knowledge transfer, and strategic foresight. This created a unique space where the demands of daily operations could be balanced with long-term planning, allowing the organisation to explore opportunities for AI adoption and digital service innovation that might otherwise have been overlooked.

4 Conclusion

This case study demonstrates that ongoing dialogue between academia and industry can significantly enhance corporate digital transformation initiatives, even without formal and extended collaborative structures. Regular engagement with academic perspectives creates a unique reflective space in which the constant pressures of operational delivery are temporarily suspended, allowing organisations to question assumptions, explore alternatives, and strengthen their strategic focus. The visiting lecturer role exemplified this by bridging academic and industry environments, providing a channel for bidirectional knowledge transfer, and fostering a culture of inquiry that enriched both academic learning and industrial practice.

Crucially, this ongoing engagement supported not only immediate innovation and digital service development, but also longer-term strategic thinking. By creating protected occasions for reflection, organisations were able to consider emerging technologies, particularly AI, beyond their immediate operational utility. This dialogue enabled early identification of opportunities and challenges, informed discussion of responsible and ethical adoption, and laid the groundwork for building robust AI strategies aligned with business objectives and expectations.

The success of this model highlights the value of integrating academic perspectives into corporate contexts, not as peripheral or occasional contributions, but as a sustained and embedded practice. Academic environments provide the legitimacy and depth required for critical reflection, while also providing early visibility of technological advances and methodological innovations. When coupled with the practical focus of industry, this creates a powerful mechanism for strategic renewal that supports competitiveness in the fast changing AI-driven economy.

Future research will extend this exploration by examining alternative models of academia–industry collaboration that can accommodate the operational realities of businesses while maximising the benefits of academic engagement. Such work will seek to identify the conditions under which knowledge exchange, reflective practice, and strategic foresight can be institutionalised, enabling organisations to move beyond short-term gains and establish long-term resilience in the face of rapid technological change.

Acknowledgements. Thanks to University of West London and Rolls-Royce, Dr. Macchia and Prof. Bdelnour-Nocera had the opportunity to explore new bridges and forms of collaboration.

References

1. Ankrah, S., Al-Tabbaa, O.: Universities–industry collaboration: A systematic review. Scand. J. Manage. **31**(3), 387–408 (2015)
2. Buck, C., Clarke, J., Torres de Oliveira, R., Desouza, K.C., Maroufkhani, P.: Digital transformation in asset-intensive organisations: the light and the dark side. J. Innov. Knowl. **8**, 100335 (2023). https://doi.org/10.1016/j.jik.2023.100335
3. McAfee, A., Rock, D., Brynjolfsson, E.: How to capitalize on generative AI. Harvard Bus. Rev. (2023). https://hbr.org/2023/11/how-to-capitalize-on-generative-ai
4. Perkmann, M., Walsh, K.: University–industry relationships and open innovation: towards a research agenda. Int. J. Manag. Rev. **9**(4), 259–280 (2007)
5. Phaal, R.: Technology roadmapping – a planning framework for evolution and revolution. Technol. Forecast. Soc. Change **71** (2004). https://doi.org/10.1016/S0040-1625(03)00072-6
6. Thomas, R., Zikopoulos, P., Soule, K.: AI Value Creators: Beyond the Generative AI User Mindset. O'Reilly Media (2025). ISBN: 978-1-098-16835-3

Author Index

J. Abdelnour-Nocera et al. (Eds.): ARPPID 2025, CCIS 2797, p. 241, 2026.
https://doi.org/10.1007/978-3-032-15516-0